Jay Fagan, DSW
Alan J. Hawkins, PhD
Editors

Clinical and Educational Interventions with Fathers

Clinical and Educational Interventions with Fathers

HAWORTH Marriage and the Family
Terry S. Trepper, PhD
Executive Editor

Parents Whose Parents Were Divorced by R. Thomas Berner

Multigenerational Family Therapy by David S. Freeman

Therapy with Treatment Resistant Families: A Consultation-Crisis Intervention Model by William George McCown, Judith Johnson, and Associates

Developing Healthy Stepfamilies: Twenty Families Tell Their Stories by Patricia Kelley

Propagations: Thirty Years of Influence from the Mental Research Institute edited by John H. Weakland and Wendel A. Ray

Structured Exercises for Promoting Family and Group Strengths: A Handbook for Group Leaders, Trainers, Educators, Counselors, and Therapists edited by Ron McManus and Glen Jennings

Making Families Work and What to Do When They Don't: Thirty Guides for Imperfect Parents of Imperfect Children by Bill Borcherdt

Family Therapy of Neurobehavioral Disorders: Integrating Neuropsychology and Family Therapy by Judith Johnson and William McCown

Parents, Children, and Adolescents: Interactive Relationships and Development in Context by Anne-Marie Ambert

Women Survivors of Childhood Sexual Abuse: Healing Through Group Work: Beyond Survival by Judy Chew

Tales from Family Therapy: Life-Changing Clinical Experiences edited by Frank N. Thomas and Thorana S. Nelson

The Therapist's Notebook: Homework, Handouts, and Activities for Use in Psychotherapy edited by Lorna L. Hecker and Sharon A. Deacon

The Web of Poverty: Psychosocial Perspectives by Anne-Marie Ambert

Stepfamilies: A Multi-Dimensional Perspective by Roni Berger

Clinical Applications of Bowen Family Systems Theory by Peter Titelman

Treating Children in Out-of-Home Placements by Marvin Rosen

Your Family, Inc.: Practical Tips for Building a Healthy Family Business by Ellen Frankenberg

Therapeutic Intervention with Poor, Unorganized Families: From Distress to Hope by Shlomo A. Sharlin and Michal Shamai

The Residential Youth Care Worker in Action: A Collaborative, Competency-Based Approach by Robert Bertolino and Kevin Thompson

Chinese Americans and Their Immigrant Parents: Conflict, Identity, and Values by May Paomay Tung

Together Through Thick and Thin: A Multinational Picture of Long-Term Marriages by Shlomo A. Sharlin, Florence W. Kaslow, and Helga Hammerschmidt

Clinical and Educational Interventions with Fathers by Jay Fagan and Alan J. Hawkins

Developmental-Systemic Family Therapy with Adolescents by Ronald Jay Werner-Wilson

The Effect of Children on Parents, Second Edition by Anne-Marie Ambert

Couples Therapy, Second Edition by Linda Berg-Cross

Family Therapy and Mental Health: Innovations in Theory and Practice by Malcolm M. McFarlane

How to Work with Sex Offenders: A Handbook for Criminal Justice, Human Service, and Mental Health Professionals by Rudy Flora

Clinical and Educational Interventions with Fathers

Jay Fagan, DSW
Alan J. Hawkins, PhD
Editors

The Haworth Clinical Practice Press
An Imprint of The Haworth Press, Inc.
New York • London • Oxford

Published by

The Haworth Clinical Practice Press, an imprint of The Haworth Press, Inc., 10 Alice Street, Binghamton, NY 13904-1580

Client identities and circumstances have been changed to protect confidentiality.

Cover design by Jennifer M. Gaska.

Library of Congress Cataloging-in-Publication Data

Fagan, Jay.
  Clinical and educational interventions with fathers / Jay Fagan, Alan J. Hawkins.
    p.   cm.
  Includes bibliographical references and index.
  ISBN 0-7890-0645-6 (hardcover : alk. paper)—ISBN 0-7890-1238-3 (pbk. : alk. paper)
  1. Father and child. 2. Fathers—Psychology. 3. Family psychotherapy. I. Hawkins, Alan J. II. Title.
BF723.F35 C55 2000
306.874'2—dc21   00-040775

CONTENTS

ABOUT THE EDITORS

Jay Fagan, DSW, is Associate Professor of Social Work in the School of Social Administration at Temple University. His research and clinical interests have been in low-income fathers and fathers involved in Head Start. His work has been published in the *Early Childhood Research Quarterly, Families in Society, The Journal of Family Issues,* and *Early Education and Development.*

Alan J. Hawkins, PhD, is Associate Professor of Marriage, Family, and Human Development and Associate Director of the School of Family Life at Brigham Young University in Provo, Utah. His work includes a volume co-edited with David Dollahite, *Generative Fathering: Beyond Deficit Perspectives.* His current work focuses on marriage as a developmental foundation for responsible fathering.

CONTRIBUTORS

Tommy Davis III, PhD, is Assistant Professor of Clinical Psychology, Institute of Graduate Clinical Psychology, Widener University, Chester, Pennsylvania.

David C. Dollahite, PhD, is Associate Professor of Marriage, Family, and Human Development in the School of Family Life at Brigham Young University, Provo, Utah. His scholarship and teaching interests focus on fathering, faith, and families.

Anderson J. Franklin, PhD, is Professor of Clinical and Health Psychology at the Graduate Center and City College of the University of New York.

James L. Furrow, PhD, is Associate Professor of Marriage and Family Therapy, Graduate School of Psychology, Fuller Theological Seminary, Pasadena, California.

Vivian L. Gadsden, PhD, is Associate Professor and Director of the National Center on Fathers and Families, School of Education, University of Pennsylvania, Philadelphia, Pennsylvania.

Travis R. Grant, MS, is a doctoral student in Marriage, Family, and Human Development in the School of Family Life at Brigham Young University, Provo, Utah. He is the father of three children and actively involved in father education on the World Wide Web.

Geoffery L. Greif, DSW, is Associate Dean and Professor in the University of Maryland School of Social Work, Baltimore, Maryland. He has written extensively on the family, with a focus on single-parent arrangements.

Wade F. Horn, PhD, is President of the National Fatherhood Initiative, Gaithersburg, Maryland, and an adjunct faculty member at the Georgetown University Policy Institute.

Charles C. Humphrey, PhD, is Scoring Director, National Computer Systems-Performance Scoring Center, Brooklyn Center, Minnesota.

Tracey Y. Lewis is a doctoral student in the Department of Child and Family Studies, Syracuse University, Syracuse, New York. She is currently conducting research on sexual risk-taking behavior among African-American teenagers.

Brent A. McBride, PhD, is Associate Professor of Human Development, Department of Human and Community Development, University of Illinois, Urbana, Illinois.

Anne P. Mitchell, Esq., is a fathers' rights attorney in Santa Clara, California. She is the author of several publications on legal issues for the single father, and teaches Community Property Law at Lincoln Law School, San Jose, California.

Glen Palm, PhD, is Professor of Child and Family Studies at St. Cloud University, St. Cloud, Minnesota, and Coordinator of the Dad's Project, a parent education initiative of the St. Cloud Early Childhood Family Education Program.

Edward W. Pitt, MSW, is Senior Research Assistant and Co-director of the Fatherhood Project at Families and Work Institute, New York, New York.

Thomas R. Rane, PhD, is Assistant Professor, Department of Human Development, Washington State University, Pullman, Washington.

Jaipaul L. Roopnarine, PhD, is Professor of Early Childhood Education, Brooklyn College, City University of New York. He has conducted research on fathers in different cultures.

Meera Shin is a doctoral student in the Department of Child and Family Studies, Syracuse University, Syracuse, New York. She is currently conducting research on Korean mothers' beliefs about child rearing.

Neil Tift, MA, is Director of Professional Advancement, National Practitioners Network for Fathers and Families, Washington, DC.

Mark Toogood, MSW, is Assistant Manager for Children's Services, Department of Human Services for the State of Minnesota, St. Paul, Minnesota.

Foreword

In his epic biography of Paul Revere, David Hackett Fischer cautions the prudent historian to reconsider Revere's message as he awakened the countryside to approaching troops. Hackett refutes the long-held assumption that Paul Revere said, "The British are coming! The British are Coming!" In Revere's day, the majority of New England still thought of themselves as British. His words to the Clarke household were: "The Regulars are coming out" (Fischer, 1994, p. 109).

With this eminent warning, Revere's proclamation emphasized the need for action. In a matter of hours the King's men and the American militia were battling in Lexington. Their movement signaled the beginning of a revolution. The time was ripe for a declaration of independence and the birth of a nation.

There is a parallel here for those of us who seek to encourage and equip fathers to be more engaged in the lives of their children. Although it is sometimes helpful to describe the extent of fatherlessness in our nation and the imminent dangers that are looming over our communities, we must also call men out to the noble and rewarding duties of fatherhood. Yes, "the effects of fatherlessness are coming," but the fathers of this generation are ready to respond.

For more than a decade I have been closely observing fathers and the communities supporting them in my role as President of the National Center for Fathering in Kansas City. Increasingly, fathers are already answering the call. These courageous and bold leaders believe posterity is a better measure of success than prosperity. Recognizing that children deserve so much more than just the leftovers, these millennial men are not allowing their past, or their current pursuits and aspirations, to keep them from developing a deep, abiding bond with their children. By taking action—one dad at a time—a fathering movement is born.

Today we are experiencing a whirlwind of activity. I cannot recall a time when fathering has been so evident in the public eye. I've often asked myself, "Why all this hullabaloo? What is behind this desire in men's hearts and the culture's soul that screams for responsible fathering?" I think it is obvious. Menahem Herman, Program Specialist at the U.S. Department of Education summarizes it succinctly: *"Fathers matter!"* I know, in my household, good fathering rocks!

More and more people are realizing that fathers make a significant difference in children's lives; that having a dad who loves and believes in you is more important than inheriting stocks and bonds; that the solution to fatherlessness is fatherfullness—doing all you can to be a better dad to your own children and then reaching out to the fatherless.

The real litmus test of this hypothesis, however, is the hearts of children. A sixth grade boy summed it up succinctly: "If I had a dad I would feel like the luckiest kid in the whole wide world. A dad could help you build a model airplane or help you make a doghouse. If you're lucky, he will give you help on your homework. It's just too bad that I don't have a dad" (National Center for Fathering, 2000).

Current public opinion supports the call for responsible fathers. A 1992 national opinion poll completed by the Gallup organization noted that the American public is very interested in fathers and fathering issues. The poll revealed that 70 percent of Americans agreed with the statement, "The most significant family problem in America is the physical absence of the father from the home" (Gallup, 1992). In 1996, a second random sample was commissioned using a number of the same items from the 1992 survey, and this time 79 percent agreed with the same statement (Gallup, 1996). Not only is there a consensus, but it is growing. In 1999, a third poll was commissioned and focused on father involvement in children's learning. The need for more father involvement in their child's education was obvious as less than half (40.9 percent) of fathers between the ages of twenty-five and forty-four knew the name of their child's teacher and 32.4 percent of fathers never attended a child's class event or school meeting (MarketFacts, 1999). America increasingly needs its fathers to become aware and more involved in the lives of children.

David Blakenhorn, President of the Institute of American Values, and Vivian Gadsden, Director of the National Center on Fathers and Families, have concluded independently that the debate about the importance of fathers in the lives of children is over. Few leaders will disagree with the premise that "responsible fatherhood is a critically positive contributor to child well-being." The larger and more difficult question we must now wrestle with, according to Blank-enhorn and Gadsden (1998), is, *What are we going to do about it?* This book and its contributors offer some guidance about what we should do. Jay Fagan and Alan Hawkins have labored diligently to bring a diverse collection of ideas to the table for our feasting.

I am thoroughly convinced, after laboring over a decade as a quasi-researcher and practitioner, that education is the great equalizer in this country. When applied to fatherhood, as it is throughout this volume, it can be the single most helpful strategy in strengthening fathers. Al-though there are several effective ways we can educate fathers, I want to focus here on the importance of intervention based on small group work.

I believe small groups have the greatest potential to create lasting positive change in fathers' behavior. Over the years I have had the privilege of speaking to some 50,000 men during our two-day training events designed to inspire and equip men to be more committed fa-thers. At each event, I spend about eight hours describing the best practices of effective fathers. I can "blow in" on a Friday afternoon, "blow up" with facts, ideas, and illustrations to motivate the attendees, and then "blow out" on Saturday afternoon to get back to fathering my own family. The sequence is all too familiar. Yet, for all my efforts, I realize that the real goal of the events is to stimulate what I believe is the long-term solution, small group interaction. If we can provide local organizations with small-group curricula and a framework for getting men into the groups, and then provide a large event to help stir men's hearts to action, those small groups have the most potential for life change. At the National Center for Fathering, we have invested re-sources in developing curricula using small groups to enhance fathers' acquisition and application of fathering skills. Several chapters in this volume provide excellent information for using small groups to work with a diversity of fathers.

I am bullish that, more than anything else, this will help the father-ing movement take deep roots. I offer with my colleague, Bill Beahm, these evidences of the importance of groups:

1. *Most social behavior occurs in groups.* We live with families, travel in car pools, work as teams, worship in congregations, are entertained as audiences, learn in classes, and socialize with friends.

Therefore, having fathers meet together in a small group to learn fathering skills is a natural experience.

2. *Research for over a century has revealed the importance of groups.* Over 700 studies were conducted concerning groups in the past century. In fact, the earliest studies in social psychology concerned performance in groups (Triplett, 1898; Ringelmann, 1913; Allport, 1920). Although early work on small groups tended to focus on basic social psychological processes in an attempt to generate general theories (Asch, 1956; Lewin, 1951; Sherif, 1936), the more recent work on small groups has tended to focus on practical issues. Much of this research follows trends in the use of groups in such domains as industry, education, and community relations (Tindale et al., 1998).

Research has repeatedly shown that groups are important and exert powerful influences on the lives of individuals. Applied to father training, we have the opportunity to help another father who may face challenging economic or personal issues. This was the idea Al Gore had in mind when he called for a Father-to-Father initiative. Fathers would meet together for mutual support and extend that outreach to specific fathers in need. In his words, "I'm asking you to join me in launching a nationwide Father-to-Father movement. We must mobilize a national movement of fathers meeting together to mutually support and reach out to one another" (Gore, 1994).

3. *Small groups can have a powerful impact on how individuals learn.* In fact, one of the great success stories in the development of leaning theory is the widespread use of what has come to be called "cooperative learning." I have listened to hundreds of fathers give testimony over the years about how the small group experience helped them prepare and execute new actions in their fathering. These men almost always attributed their learning to the shared experience with other fathers.

Social psychologists have also confirmed that members of a group experience higher achievement and greater cooperation than individuals' efforts in learning (Tindale et al., 1998). In addition, social psychologists have discovered that group members have more:

- willingness to take on difficult tasks and persist, despite difficulties, in working toward accomplishing goals;
- long-term retention of what is learned;
- higher-level reasoning and critical thinking;

- creative thinking;
- transfer of learning from one situation to another (group to individual transfer); and
- positive attitudes.

4. *Small groups create positive interdependence among group members.* Small groups also foster "promotive interaction," as when individuals encourage and facilitate one anothers' efforts to reach the group's goals (i.e., maximize each member's learning). I have seen this work in urban fathering groups. Members of the Urban Fathering Initiative discovered that fathers in challenging economic and complex family situations helped one another by:

- giving and receiving financial help and assistance;
- exchanging resources and information;
- giving and receiving feedback on task work;
- challenging one another's reasoning;
- advocating increased efforts to achieve;
- mutually influencing one another's reasoning and behavior; and
- engaging in the interpersonal and small group skills needed for effective teamwork (Williams, 2000).

One of the most effective places to employ small group strategies is within faith communities. Many of the small groups that we have initiated have formed in faith communities, which seems to be a natural place to help men with family issues. Wade Horn provides an overview of the work that faith communities are doing with fathers in this volume.

David Popenoe (1999) sees faith communities playing a role in transforming our culture:

> Renewing fatherhood is ultimately about infusing into our culture a stronger sense of moral obligation for the well-being of others, especially children, and thus counterbalancing the radical strains of individualism. It may be that a fully restored sense of moral obligation can be accomplished entirely through secular means, but I doubt it. Religion has always been the main cultural repository of morality, and it is not likely that we can have permanent moral renewal without a society-wide religious reawakening.

What form that reawakening might take, and should take, is an open question. (p. 23)

Finally, a father and mother form perhaps the best small group team. I believe that nonmarried men can be fantastic fathers, and I encourage a broad and redemptive view of fatherhood that can address the needs of all dads—married, divorced, or single—and help them make the best of their situations. Still, the ideal situation for children involves a father and mother laboring together as a team in the home. Marriage is an important, potentially divisive issue, but it plays a significant role in our quest to promote responsible fatherhood. Although some social commentators have concluded that the most prudent way to promote fatherhood is to restore marriage, our discussions will be more successful if we include nonmarried fathers and describe marriage as a great asset to a father's efforts to stay connected to his children. In that context, it would be wise to consider new strategies that seek to reverse the tide of divorce and strengthen the marriage bond. This fathering movement can be broad enough to encourage all men to be responsible father figures, and redemptive enough to admit that there are no perfect fathers.

One exception to the importance of small groups in working with fathers, however, is the rapidly increasing use of Web-based information and education. My colleague Marty Erickson of the University of Minnesota long ago saw the wisdom in investing in the Internet, so she set up FatherNet as an information and networking system to assist dads in a variety of situations, using a list of programs and experts to promote responsible fathering. At the same time, however, she recognized that the Internet is not available to all fathers: "Fathers from all walks of life, not just those well-off economically and educationally, must have access to equipment, know-how to navigate the system, and literacy skills to make effective use of the vast array of material found therein" (Erickson, 1999, p. 162). In the spring of 1999 the National Center for Fathering was pleased to partner and build upon her leadership by incorporating much of the helpful material from FatherNet into its ongoing database at www.fathers.com.

Still, the Internet is fast becoming a dominant source of information for most Americans—including fathers. It also provides us with an efficient means of delivering fathering tips, resources, interactive programs, profiles, and training to dads and is available twenty-four hours a day, seven days a week, from anywhere in the world. The e-mails I have read remind me that this is a growing medium for learning. In this book, Travis Grant, Alan Hawkins, and David Dollahite give a detailed description of their Web site, called FatherWork. Their chapter provides some of the first evaluation data about the effectiveness of Web-based education for fathers. Looking at the growth of activity on our own Web site—and the explosion of the Internet as a whole—the possibilities seem unlimited to expand the world of fathering education to dads across the globe. It is also possible that Web-based education, with its continuing supply of good ides, will function best as a way to supplement small group interventions.

America loves to celebrate and venerate its heroes. George Washington is pictured on our currency, Martin Luther King has a holiday. Michael Jordan, Joe Montana, and Wayne Gretsky have earned places in their respective halls of fame. Sports stars, clergymen, civic, corporate, political, and military leaders are all important role models to the coming generation.

But I see a new group of heroes emerging. Ron Clark, the energetic leader of the Virginia Fatherhood Campaign, found that the most compelling models to present to fathers were the ordinary, everyday dads who were doing their part day by day, community by community, family by family. The real heroes are everyday dads who have quietly and faithfully foregone power, prestige, position, and their own desires to become successful with their kids.

These heroes know that the true test of greatness is service. They rise early and labor diligently to provide for their families. They help with homework, become taxi drivers for their children, and write notes of encouragement. Even in difficult circumstances, they are faithful in paying child support and in visitation. They respect women. They know that true manhood is based on commitment to children, and give their all for the next generation. They came from every ethnic heritage, economic situation, and age group, but they are united by their shared purpose—becoming better dads. Their very lives become their message—they walk their talk, they keep their promises, and their hearts are connected to their children.

I do not have a horse, but I still want to proclaim in the street like Paul Revere, "The real heroes are coming out!" If you are a dad or father figure, do not underestimate your opportunity to change the world by reaching out to your children and the fatherless. If you are a supporter of responsible fathering, as many of you who are reading this book are, stay on course: you are vitally important to the future of this country. This book and its writers are committed to supporting and raising a generation of involved, caring, and committed fathers. The information and ideas in this book will help you to better serve fathers and their families.

Ken R. Canfield, PhD
President, National Center for Fathering
Kansas City, Kansas

REFERENCES

Allport, F.H. (1920). The influence of the group upon association and thought. *Journal of Experimental Psychology, 3,* 159-182.

Asch, S.E. (1956). Studies in independence and conformity: A minority of one against a majority. *Psychological Monographs, 70*(9, No. 416). <http://fathers.com/html/articles/March6,1998fathersweekly>.

Blankenhorn, D. and Gadsden, V. (1998). <http://fathers.com/htmlarticles/march6, 1998fathersweekly.html>.

Erickson, M.F. (1999). A few ideas: Voices for fatherhood. In W.F. Horn, D. Blankenhorn, and M.B. Pearlstein (Eds.), *The fatherhood movement: A call to action* (pp. 161-168). Lanham, MD: Lexington.

Fischer, D. (1994). *Paul Revere's ride.* New York: Oxford.

Gallup. (1992). <http://fathers.com/research/gallup/index.html>.

Gallup. (1996). <http://fathers.com/research/gallup/index.html>.

Gore, A. (1994). Speech given at the Family Reunion IV, Nashville, Tennessee July 11.

Lewin, K. (1951). *Field theory in social science.* New York: Harper.

MarketFacts (1999). <http://fathers.com/research/involvement.html>.

National Center for Fathering (2000). <http://fathers.com/research/essays.html>.

Popenoe, D. (1999). Challenging the culture of fatherlessness. In W.F. Horn, D. Blankenhorn, and M.B. Pearlstein (Eds.), *The fatherhood movement: A call to action* (pp. 17-24). Lanham, MD: Lexington.

Ringelmann, M. (1913). Recherches sur les moteurs animes: Travail de l'homme [Research on animate sources of power: The work of man]. *Annales de l'Institut National Agronomique, 12,* 1-40.

Sherif, M. (1936). *The psychology of social norms.* New York: Harper.

Tindale, R.S., Heath, L., Edwards, J., Posavac, E., Bryant, F., Suarez-Balcazar, Y., Henderson-King, E., and Myers, J. (1998). *Theory and research on small groups.* New York: Plenum Press.

Triplett, N. (1898). The dynamic factors in peacemaking and competition. *American Journal of Psychology, 9,* 507-533.

Williams, G. (2000). <http://fathers.com/urban/index.html>.

Acknowledgments

We are extremely indebted to Vivian Gadsden, Director of the National Center on Fathers and Families, for her support and encouragement. Dr. Gadsden donated the services of Dianne Eyer, a highly competent editor, to work on the final draft of this volume. We value Diane's patience and skill.

We owe special thanks to our families. Without the constant love and support of Anna, Lisa, and Jo Fagan, and of Brian, Caitlin, and Lisa Hawkins, this book would not have been possible.

We are also appreciative of the help provided by the staff at The Haworth Press.

Introduction

Jay Fagan

Alan J. Hawkins

In 1981, Jessie Bernard, a family sociologist, wrote that a "subtle revolution" was taking place in America. She was referring to the changes that were occurring in family structure and family life. The revolution that started in the 1960s has been anything but subtle. Indeed, the dramatic changes in family structure and family life that started four decades ago continued to occur throughout the 1990s.

There are many facets to this revolution in family life. Divorce and remarriage rates have remained high. A significant proportion of children are being raised in single-parent households, and many of these children have little or no contact with their fathers. An unprecedented number of children are born to unmarried teenagers, and many of these parents never marry. Women with children have entered and stayed in the labor force, and their wages have increased steadily relative to those of men. Young children who are not yet old enough for school are likely to spend much of their time in the care of adults other than their parents. Fathers are now one of the primary sources of care to their young children when the mother is working outside of the home (O'Connell, 1993).

These changes in family structure and family life have caused an explosion of interest in fathers. Professional journals in sociology, psychology, and family studies have published a wide range of research related to fatherhood. There have been studies on the changing roles of fathers; the determinants of father involvement and behavior; the influence that fathers have on various aspects of their children's behavior; the effects of divorce and separation on fathers and their children; the differences in parenting styles between mothers and fathers; and the association between father involvement, marital relationships, and children's well-being.

The growing awareness of the importance of fatherhood has stimulated practitioners and scholars in some quarters to ask what is being done to support fathers at this time of rapid change. These professionals have begun to ponder questions such as:

1. What are the major psychological, social, and economic issues faced by fathers?
2. What are the "best practices" for working with fathers?
3. What kinds of outcomes can be expected from intervening with fathers?
4. What are the major barriers to involving fathers in interventions?
5. What kinds of outreach methods are needed to recruit fathers?

A review of the literature reveals that very little has been written about interventions to increase father involvement and enhance fathering skills (e.g., Dienhart and Dollahite, 1997; Fagan and Stevenson, 1995; Johnson and Palm, 1992; Kiselica, Stroud, and Rotzien, 1992; Levine and Pitt, 1995; Palm, 1997; Shecket, 1995). Well-articulated theoretical approaches to working with fathers are absent from many of the writings on fatherhood interventions. Furthermore, only a handful of intervention approaches have been subjected to evaluation or rigorous outcome studies. Given the paucity of literature on working with fathers, it should come as no surprise that many practitioners ponder how to intervene with fathers.

While the clinical and research literature on fathering interventions is sparse, a growing number of practitioners in various types of programs have been working with fathers. These programs range from grass-roots efforts to mobilize fathers to address the problems of families in their communities, to well-established programs such as the Fathers' Resource Center in Minneapolis, Minnesota, which offers a variety of ongoing support programs for fathers, to the broad-based international religious movements that call forth greater commitment to responsible fathering (see Levine and Pitt, 1995).

It is not the intention of this book to present a specific, detailed model of practice that can help guide practitioners working with different fathers in diverse situations. We think the serious study of fathering interventions is still too young for that. Instead, this book brings together the ideas and experiences of experts in the field of fathering interventions. We hope that by bringing these ideas together and then summarizing and synthesizing the ideas (see Chapter 12), we will be able to contribute to the emerging knowledge base of this field.

ORGANIZATION OF THE BOOK

All the interventions described in this volume share the value of working with men to strengthen their positive desires to be "generative" fathers and improve their skills in caring for the next generation.

The first four chapters of the book describe therapeutic interventions for fathers. James L. Furrow's chapter on clinical work with fathers in family therapy recommends using narrative therapeutic strategies that focus on the father's paternal images as a way to offer new options for responding to the challenges of being a father. Anderson J. Franklin and Tommy Davis III discuss the use of therapeutic support groups for addressing issues of fatherhood with African-American men. These authors suggest using an integrative approach to conducting support groups, with an emphasis on addressing the numerous societal struggles experienced by the participants, while at the same time being mindful not to overlook the strengths, diversity, and presence of responsible and committed fathers. Geoffrey L. Greif has contributed a chapter about therapeutic approaches for helping one of the most difficult populations facing mental health professionals—fathers who are out of touch with their children following divorce. Greif recommends using a Structural Family Therapy approach for its emphasis on clearly defined boundaries and hierarchy. Charles C. Humphrey and Mark Toogood have written a chapter about teaching anger management skills to fathers; their approach is based on a psychoeducational, multicomponent program that follows a cognitive-behavioral model.

The next six chapters focus on educational interventions. Glen Palm describes a twelve-session parent education program for incarcerated fathers; some of the salient issues that are unique to working with this population are described in this chapter. Travis R. Grant, Alan J. Hawkins, and David C. Dollahite discuss the potential of an Internet-based educational intervention for fathers called FatherWork. These authors suggest that the overwhelming number of fathers searching for information on the Web, and the good fit between Web-based education and men's learning styles suggest promise for this type of remote parent education. Brent A. McBride and Thomas R. Rane have contributed a chapter about training staff members to work with fathers in early childhood programs. The results of their carefully designed evaluation reveal that staff training has the potential to increase father involvement in early childhood programs for high-risk children.

Wade F. Horn has written a chapter about the approaches of faith-based organizations to educate fathers and promote responsible fathering. Horn gives a detailed analysis of the religious foundations of these fatherhood organizations. He also describes in some detail many of the different faith-based fatherhood organizations that currently exist in the United States. Anne P. Mitchell's chapter describes legal interventions for one of the most undersupported groups in America today—fathers who are separated from their children. This chapter provides a wealth of information about the father advocate's role in helping these fathers navigate the family law system, and helping them to find their way back home to their children. Jaipaul L. Roopnarine, Meera Shin, and Tracey Y. Lewis have written a chapter about working with Caribbean fathers in the United States and the challenges these fathers face. This chapter provides extensive background information on these fathers and their families in both the United States and the Caribbean, as well as the authors' recommended strategies for increasing their paternal involvement with young children.

Vivian L. Gadsden, Edward W. Pitt, and Neil Tift have examined the nexus between practice, research, and policy in the field of fathering and how these three domains have the potential to work more collaboratively with one another. The editors of this volume conclude the book with a summary and synthesis of the ideas about fathering interventions discussed by the contributors. It is hoped that this chapter, as well as those written by the contributors, will add to the emerging knowledge base of this field.

OBJECTIVES OF THE BOOK

The book's objectives are fourfold. First, because this volume brings together a wide range of authors who are conducting significant interventions with fathers, it will provide a rich knowledge base for practitioners. Second, the book describes and critically analyzes various interventions that are being used with different groups of fathers. Each author was asked to apply a specific analytical framework in writing about their intervention approach; this framework is described in greater detail later in this chapter.

Third, the book is intended to stimulate the development of new knowledge that will help practitioners to tailor approaches that have worked with other populations (e.g., mothers) to the different characteristics of fathers. While many practitioners would agree that fathers should participate in programs intended to enhance the role of fathers in the context of the family, experience has shown that few fathers actually participate in such programs. Traditional intervention approaches that have been used with women frequently do not work with men (Brooks, 1998). Brooks has suggested that a new perspective is emerging that shifts the focus from changing men to fit the current technologies of psychotherapy—to changing the ways therapists work within men's culture. Several articles and curricula have been published recently describing content areas, such as the meaning and value of being a father, that are unique to working with fathers (Dienhart and Dollahite, 1997; Fagan and Stevenson, 1995; Wilson and Johnson, 1995). Indeed, professionals in the field are beginning to understand that specialized areas of knowledge are needed to work successfully with fathers (Levine and Pitt, 1995; Palm, 1997).

A fourth objective of this book is to suggest theoretical perspectives that we believe are critical for fatherhood interventions. This volume builds on the work of scholars such as John Snarey (1993), and Alan Hawkins and David Dollahite (1997), who apply Eriksonian developmental theory to an understanding of fathering. In Erikson's theory, the mature individual is one who has a social-psychological need to nurture the next generation (Erikson, 1950). These authors conceptualize fathering as this sort of "generative" work (Dollahite, Hawkins, and Brotherson, 1997; Dollahite, Morris, and Hawkins, 1997). Generative fathering is seen as a developmental process that demands continuous efforts to move toward mastery of parenting. This perspective is particularly appropriate for conceptualizing interventions with fathers because it (1) deemphasizes thinking about fathers as deficient and emphasizes fathers' strengths and potential for growth; (2) allows for diversity in parenting styles among fathers from various ethnic, racial, and class backgrounds; and (3) does not set a minimum standard that excludes fathers who may be struggling but are nonetheless striving to become good fathers.

THE NEED FOR FATHERING INTERVENTIONS

There are many reasons why intervention programs for fathers are needed. But the reasons can generally be sorted into two categories: those that suggest that fathers' deficiencies contribute to other social problems, such as children's poverty and social-emotional problems (e.g., Blankenhorn, 1995), and those that suggest that fathers benefit from support in parenting because parenting is challenging work. It is beyond the scope of this book to make a case for the appropriateness of one approach versus the other, or to fully examine the evidence regarding the "social problem" versus the "challenging work" hypotheses. Our position is that there is probably validity to both perspectives, although we are inclined to think that fathers are more likely to avoid deficiency-focused programs.

Fatherwork Is Challenging

Many people regard parenting as one of the most challenging endeavors in which adults engage. Dollahite, Hawkins, and Brotherson (1997) use the term "fatherwork" to describe the conduct of generative fathering. They have observed that paid employment is limited by time and place, whereas fatherwork, like motherwork, is less so. The amount of knowledge and skill that is needed to rear children today also makes parenting highly challenging. To illustrate this point, consider the number of popular books and magazines that have been written during the past fifty years that provide parents with information and guidance on almost every facet of parenting. Parenting is also complicated by the degree of emotional investment that parents have in their children. Osherson (1995) has aptly stated that, over the course of a lifetime, the emotions that parents experience toward their children are probably more intense than the emotions they feel toward any other people. Furthermore, fatherwork frequently takes place within the context of scarce resources, including material resources, human resources (e.g., energy), and time (Dollahite, Hawkins, and Brotherson, 1997).

A number of factors have made the challenge of fatherwork an even greater one. First, more fathers are sharing the responsibilities of direct child care with mothers than they have in the past (Pleck,

1997). Yet fathers, like mothers, receive little formal training for the challenging work of parenting. Children in America are seldom exposed to parenting education or information about child development in their secondary-school experiences. Older school-age children and adolescents may receive informal training about parenting when they care for younger siblings or work as babysitters, yet boys seldom participate in these activities. Studies have shown that parents, even dual-earner parents, assign household tasks to their adolescents based on traditional gender roles (Benin and Edwards, 1990).

Other facets of early male gender-role socialization also may contribute to the challenges that adult men experience as fathers. From an early age, boys are socialized to be autonomous and independent, and girls are socialized to be connected to others. Chodorow (1978) observed that this differential process of socialization is reflected in the ways that mothers relate to their daughters and sons. According to Ehrensaft (1995) "the mother identifies with the daughter, on the basis of their shared gender, and keeps her close to her heart and close to the hearth" (p. 50). The daughter takes note of the identification and remains connected to her mother. In contrast, mothers do not identify with their sons, but instead encourage their strivings for autonomy and independence. Ehrensaft further suggests that this socialization process prepares females for the responsibilities and relationships of mothering, but leaves males less prepared for the primary identification, empathy, and connectedness that are basic requirements of parenting.

The dislocation of jobs is yet another factor that contributes to the challenge of fathering. Many fathers continue to view income generation as their primary responsibility to the family (Coltrane, 1996). As one young father said, "You can be a provider without being a parent, but you can't be a parent without being a provider" (Fagan and Stevenson, 1995). These attitudes have created a quandary for the large number of men who have not been able to find employment or who are underemployed. Research studies have shown that unemployment has a greater negative impact on fathers than it does on mothers (Elder, Liker, and Cross, 1984; McLoyd, 1989). Minority fathers have been hit the hardest by the changing economy and are consequently more likely to be debilitated by the economic expectations of their fathering role (Staples and Johnson, 1993).

Starrels (1992) has suggested that men cannot be fully blamed for their reluctance to become involved in parenting responsibilities since institutions have also been slow to support father participation in the family. A society that pressures employed women to take primary responsibility for child care can anticipate that fathers will view the parenting role as secondary to the work role. Numerous examples of institutional practices that discourage father involvement can be cited. Employers are often reluctant to allow male workers to take advantage of family-supportive policies, such as paternity leave and flextime (Hochschild, 1997; Peterson and Gerson, 1992; Pleck, 1983). Catalyst (1986) reported that 41 percent of employers of companies that permit paternity leave do not believe that fathers should take any time off when children are born. Workplace practices such as these are likely to cause parents to experience considerable conflict between the demands of work and family. In a national study of dual-earner families (mothers and fathers work full time), the Families and Work Institute found that 20 percent of the men reported a lot of conflict and 40 percent of the men reported some conflict between work and family life (Galinsky, Bond, and Friedman, 1993).

Raising children today is challenging to both mothers and fathers. While many forces work against mothers and fathers, fathering may be even more sensitive to interpersonal and environmental factors than mothering, possibly because cultural norms are "stricter on the centrality and endurance of the mother-child dyad" (Doherty, Kouneski, and Erickson, 1998, p. 287). Considering the increasing desires of many men to be good fathers (Pleck, 1983), society needs to develop strategies that have the potential to support fathers in achieving their goals.

Poor Fathering As the Cause of Other Social Problems

This perspective suggests that intervention programs for fathers are needed because there is a great cost to society when fathers do not fulfill their parenting responsibilities. Of particular concern to practitioners and policymakers is the involvement of divorced, separated, and never-married fathers. The *1994 Green Book,* prepared by the House Ways and Means Committee (1994), indicated that divorce and separation are the main reasons that families go on welfare. Poverty is associated with many negative psychosocial outcomes for children, including school dropout, lower school achievement, teenage pregnancy, poor child health, and delinquent behavior. Yet noncustodial fathers often do not provide the financial support to their children that could reduce the risk of living in poverty. Using nationally representative data, Sorenson (1997) found that nonresident fathers spend about 7 percent of their income on child support. The cost of raising two children in a two-parent family has been estimated to be between 19 percent and 39 percent of family income (Bassi and Barnow, 1993). Sorenson (1997) concluded that nonresident fathers could devote much more of their income to child support than they currently provide.

Divorced and never-married fathers also see their children less frequently as time passes (Greif, 1997; Maccoby and Mnookin, 1992; Seltzer, 1991; Seltzer and Bianchi, 1988). In fact, reduced contact with fathers may be one of the most pronounced effects of divorce on children (Amato and Keith, 1991). In a study of children born to teenaged mothers in Baltimore, Maryland, Furstenberg (1995) reported that the "intentions of fathers far outstrip their ability to make good on their goal of becoming involved caretakers" (p. 144). The negative effects on children of reduced contact with nonresidential fathers have been extensively investigated (Popenoe, 1996). For example, Amato and Rezac (1994) found that children's problem behaviors are negatively related to the amount of involvement by nonresidential fathers in the presence of low interparental conflict.

An increasing number of studies have shown that children's serious emotional and behavioral problems are affected by paternal involvement and behavior (for review, see Phares, 1997). Delinquent behavior in children and adolescents has been shown to be associated with fathers' antisocial behavior (Goetting, 1994; Loeber and Dishion, 1987). Hawkins, Catalano, and Miller (1992) found that paternal alcohol abuse was associated with alcohol problems in adolescents. A meta-analysis of thirty-two studies of alcoholic adults showed that both male and female alcoholics were more likely to have fathers who abused alcohol (Pollock et al., 1987). In a review of seventeen studies of paternal depression and child adjustment, Phares (1997) concluded that strong evidence supports the theory that fathers' depression is a risk factor for the development of psychopathology in children.

Male violence against women and children in the family may be the "darkest feature" of masculinity (Brooks and Silverstein, 1995). The majority of men who batter their wives also abuse their children or abduct them as a way of terrorizing their wives (Finkelhor, Hotaling, and Yllo, 1988). Research has shown that children who witness violence between adults or who experience abuse perpetrated by family members are at greater risk for displaying behavior problems (Sternberg, 1997; Sternberg et al., 1993).

Of course, the problem with this perspective for intervention is that it assumes a deficit or role-inadequacy perspective of fathers. Thus, intervention is likely to meet resistance without external forces (e.g., court orders) to motivate fathers' positive participation. Brooks and Silverstein (1995) have argued that focusing exclusively on the deviancy of these men misses the opportunity for more creative interventions. They advocate for interventions that help men to become aware of the cultural context that celebrates behaviors such as violence, while at the same time holding men fully accountable for their behavior.

WHAT PRACTITIONERS NEED TO KNOW TO WORK WITH FATHERS

As our contributors present their knowledge about working with fathers, we have asked them to address seven general questions.

What are the major psychological, social, and economic issues faced by fathers targeted by the intervention?

All practice approaches rely upon some body of knowledge about these issues. For example, Levant and Kelly's (1989) psychoeducational program for teaching emotional empathy to men relies heavily on findings showing that many men restrict the expression of emotions, particularly those related to vulnerability and caring, and that they are unaware of those emotions (Levant, 1995). Some interventions are based on findings suggesting that structural conditions in society promote attitudes that discourage father involvement with children (Fagan and Iglesias, 1999). For example, Levine and Pittinsky (1997) reveal the social and economic obstacles to father involvement created by employment and work policies.

What are the basic assumptions and values that inform this approach to working with fathers?

All practice builds on sets of assumptions about human behavior, the social environment, and the process of change. These assumptions can exert a powerful force on the ways that practitioners process information, construct interpretations, and determine actions (Miley, O'Melia, and DuBois, 1998). For example, psychodynamic practitioners often assume that the best way to facilitate an individual's behavior change is to help that person resolve internalized conflicts from childhood.

Several studies on fathering interventions have identified the assumptions underlying the program intervention. In Dail and Thieman's (1996) study of the Renewing Parental Partnerships Project, it was assumed that noncustodial parents need to improve their communication and reduce their conflict with each other, and that such improvements would lead to better quality and more frequent visitations by the noncustodial parent (usually the father). Increased child contact was also believed to lead the father toward greater provision of child support.

Values are beliefs about what is desirable or undesirable. All practice approaches are based on some set of values about the delivery of services. For example, feminist practice theory has clearly espoused an ideology that values women's perspectives and experiences and an end to all systems of subordination and privilege (Bricker-Jenkins and Hooyman, 1986). The 1990s saw the development of programs designed to promote "responsible" fathering (Knitzer and Bernard, 1997). These programs seem to be based on the value that fathers should meet their family obligations and strive to become "good family men" (Palm, 1998).

What are the explicit approaches and "best practices" that work with fathers?

Practice is ultimately defined by what one does in the case situation. For example, structural family therapists often use techniques such as boundary making, unbalancing, and challenging the family's assumptions (Nichols and Schwartz, 1995). The identification of explicit practice approaches and "best practices" is just beginning to appear in the literature on working with fathers (e.g., see Hawkins and Dollahite, 1997; Palm, 1997). Several authors have emphasized the importance of using a strengths- or competency-based approach with fathers (Dienhart and Dollahite, 1997; Palm, 1997); interventions that focus on fathers' deficiencies may discourage fathers from participating in the intervention. Palm (1997) cautions against using representations of the "good mother" as the measure of fathers' competencies, because fathers may have some very unique strengths that are quite different from those of mothers. For example, Snarey (1993) found that a unique paternal child-rearing strength is the "work-hard-at-playing" quality used by fathers when they interact with their children. Dienhart and Dollahite (1997) espouse the use of narrative techniques for helping fathers to change. Narratives can be used to explore the father's experiences of being fathered, fathering competencies, parenting experiences, and experiences with children.

What kinds of outcomes can be expected from the intervention?

Some practice approaches aim for cures or resolution of problems, other approaches work for adaptation or maintenance, while others strive to modify situations that contribute to the persistence of problems. The potential outcomes from working with fathers have received some attention in the professional literature. Dail and Thieman (1996) hypothesized that the Renewing Parental Partnerships Program would result in increased child support compliance and social support from the noncustodial parent (usually the father). Levant (1995) has emphasized the importance of improving fathers' parenting skills, the lack of which he believes is one of the major reasons men do not participate more in child care. Other interventions have emphasized increasing father involvement (Fagan and Iglesias, 1999; Hawkins et al., 1994; McBride, 1990).

What are the major barriers to involving fathers in the intervention?

Considering the challenges of fathering and the potential effects of father involvement on children, practitioners have frequently pondered why fathers don't participate in programs for parents. The lack of male involvement in such programs can be attributed to a number of factors; some are institutional in nature, while others can be attributed to fathers themselves. Many agencies approach parents in a way that is more compatible with female than male socialization practices. Social service agencies generally expect their clients to seek help, express weakness, and openly display emotions (Brooks, 1998; Davis and Proctor, 1989), actions which are more often associated with women (Levant, 1995). Men who are socialized to appear strong and inexpressive often avoid such programs.

Brooks (1998) has pointed out an interesting irony about working with men in psychotherapy that may have relevance to working with fathers. Therapists have frequently noticed the tendency of men to fight for control over therapy and to compete with the therapist. Professional helpers often view such behavior as a manifestation of resistance to the therapy process. Yet men are raised to think hierarchically—therefore competition for control is a common element of their relationships with others. The irony is that practitioners who view the man's struggle for dominance as nothing more than dysfunctional are likely to encourage the male client to compete even harder to avoid being viewed as such. In a sense, the practitioner is inadvertently exacerbating the man's struggle for control.

Agency staff or other professionals who lead interventions for fathers may have a counterproductive set of criteria for defining responsible parenting (Palm, 1997), criteria which are often associated with highly nurturing primary caretakers. When fathers do not meet these typically maternal criteria they are often viewed as disinterested and uninvolved when in fact they may be highly involved in more traditional forms of fathering, such as providing moral guidance or breadwinning. They also may be viewed as the primary source of their family's problems when in fact it is the whole family system that is problematic. Program staff may therefore discourage the participation of these fathers by viewing them as the "source of the problem" (Ballard, 1995).

Levine and Pitt (1995) have also found that some agency staff members falsely assume that fathers do not want help with fathering, and therefore fathers are routinely neglected in the planning and implementation of programs. Staff with traditional attitudes toward parental involvement may expect mothers, rather than fathers to take responsibility for the child (Fagan, 1996). In the case of "absent" fathers, agency personnel often assume that being absent from the home is the same as being uninvolved and uncaring (Levine and Pitt, 1995), while the reality is that nonresident fathers are often very involved with their children. As a result of staff attitudes, programs may discourage male involvement.

Men's attitudes may influence their participation in programs for parents. According to Brooks (1998), men tend to see themselves as problem solvers, as people who fix things when they are broken. For many men, the suggestion that help is needed evokes feelings of failure and a sense of shame about their abilities to be competent problem solvers.

What kinds of outreach methods are needed to recruit fathers?

Researchers and practitioners have given increasing attention to the importance of doing outreach with fathers. Palm (1997) has suggested that the value of parent education is best conveyed to fathers on an individual basis. Direct invitations to the father may be particularly important when the mother has reservations about the man's involvement in programs for fathers. Levine and Pitt (1995) have described the importance of going to the father's home or meeting the father in the community before encouraging him to come to a formal program. Morris, Dollahite, and Hawkins (1999) suggest that the combination of "cool" technology, privacy, and control offered by the Internet may be an effective way to offer family-life education to fathers.

What are the results of evaluations of the intervention?

Practitioners have the responsibility to evaluate the effectiveness of their services as well as the efficacy of particular actions and interventions (Garvin and Seabury, 1997; Toseland and Rivas, 1998). The scholarly literature contains very few evaluations of fathering interventions or services. The field needs to promote evaluations so that practitioners and policymakers can make informed choices about programs and activities that should be replicated.

For example, McBride (1989, 1990, 1991) evaluated the effects of two ten-week parent education programs for new fathers. Compared to control-group fathers, treatment-group fathers became more comfortable with their parental roles, increased their sense of competence as fathers, and interacted more and were more accessible to their children on nonworkdays. Long-term follow-up evaluations were not conducted, therefore the efficacy of these positive program effects was uncertain.

Hawkins and colleagues (1994) evaluated the effects of a six-week psychoeducational program for dual-earner couples designed to increase fathers' involvement in child care and housework. Program fathers increased somewhat their daily involvement in both child care and housework, and this increase was still evident six months after the program ended. Wives' satisfaction with the allocation of housework and child care also increased substantially, and remained high six months later.

Such evaluations, however, are scarce. Indeed, the need to promote the evaluation of fatherhood interventions is one of the motives of this book.

CONCLUSION

We believe that the time is right to produce this book. Changing patterns of family life, the desire of many fathers to be more involved with their children, and the struggles that many groups of fathers have gone through to maintain contact with their children all call for improved clinical and educational strategies to better support and promote fatherhood. To the best of our knowledge, no single volume has yet brought together such a wide array of experience in fatherhood interventions. We hope that this volume contributes to the growth and sustainability of this field.

We also think that the time is right to encourage collaborative relationships between practitioners, researchers, and policymakers on behalf of fathers and families. The field of working with fathers is still in its infancy. It is not too late to avoid the mistakes of earlier social programs that have done little to bring together the interests of these three groups to enhance the lives of the people being served.

REFERENCES

Amato, P. R. and Keith, B. (1991). Parental divorce and the well-being of children: A meta-analysis. *Psychological Bulletin, 110,* 26-46.

Amato, P. R. and Rezac, S. J. (1994). Contact with nonresident parents, interparental conflict, and children's behavior. *Journal of Family Issues, 15,* 191-207.

Ballard, C. A. (1995). Teaching responsible fathering. In J. L. Shapiro, M. J. Diamond, and M. Greenberg (Eds.), *Becoming a father* (pp. 155-164). New York: Springer Publishing.

Bassi, L. J. and Barnow, B. S. (1993). Expenditures on children and child support guidelines. *Journal of Policy Analysis and Management, 12,* 478-497.

Benin, M. H. and Edwards, D. A. (1990). Adolescent chores: The difference between dual- and single-earner families. *Journal of Marriage and the Family, 52,* 361-373.

Bernard, J. (1981). Facing the future. *Society, 18,* 53-59.

Blankenhorn, D. (1995). *Fatherless America: Confronting our most urgent social problem.* New York: Basic Books.

Bricker-Jenkins, M. and Hooyman, N. (1986). Not for women only: Social work practice for the feminist future. Silver Spring, MD: National Association of Social Workers.

Brooks, G. R. (1998). *A new psychotherapy for traditional men.* San Francisco: Jossey-Bass.

Brooks, G. R. and Silverstein, L. B. (1995). Understanding the dark side of masculinity: An integrative systems model. In R. F. Levant and W. S. Pollack (Eds.), *A new psychology of men* (pp. 280-333). New York: Basic Books.

Catalyst (1986). *Report on a national study of parental leaves.* New York: Author.

Chodorow, N. (1978). *The reproduction of mothering.* Berkeley, CA: University of California Press.

Coltrane, S. (1996). *Family man: Fatherhood, housework, and gender equity.* New York: Oxford University Press.

Dail, P. W. and Thieman, A. A. (1996). Improving parental partnerships in low-income families as a means for increasing noncustodial parental compliance with child support orders. *Journal of Family Issues, 17,* 688-703.

Davis, L. E. and Proctor, E. K. (1989). *Race, gender, and class: Guidelines for practice with individuals, families, and groups.* Englewood Cliffs, NJ: Prentice Hall.

Dienhart, A. and Dollahite, D. C. (1997). A generative, narrative approach to clinical work with fathers. In A. J. Hawkins and D. C. Dollahite (Eds.), *Generative fathering: Beyond deficit perspectives* (pp. 183-199). Thousand Oaks, CA: Sage Publications.

Doherty, W. J., Kouneski, E. F., and Erickson, M. F. (1998). Responsible fathering: An overview and conceptual framework. *Journal of Marriage and the Family, 60,* 277-292.

Dollahite, D. C., Hawkins, A. J., and Brotherson, S. E. (1997). Fatherwork: A conceptual ethic of fathering as generative work. In A. J. Hawkins and D. C. Dollahite (Eds.), *Generative fathering: Beyond deficit perspectives* (pp. 17-35). Thousand Oaks, CA: Sage Publications.

Dollahite, D. C., Morris, S. N., and Hawkins, A. J. (1997). Questions and activities for teaching about generative fathering in university courses. In A. J. Hawkins and D. C. Dollahite (Eds.), *Generative fathering: Beyond deficit perspectives* (pp. 228-241). Thousand Oaks, CA: Sage Publications.

Ehrensaft, D. (1995). Bringing in fathers: The reconstruction of mothering. In J. L. Shapiro, M. J. Diamond, and M. Greenberg (Eds.), *Becoming a father* (pp. 155-164). New York: Springer Publishing.

Elder, G., Liker, J., and Cross, C. (1984). Parent-child behavior in the Great Depression: Life course and intergenerational influences. In P. Baltes and O. Brim (Eds.), *Life span development and behavior* (Volume 6) (pp. 109-159). Orlando, FL: Academic Press.

Erikson, E. H. (1950). *Childhood and society.* New York: Norton.

Fagan, J. (1996). Principles for developing male involvement programs in early childhood settings: A personal experience. *Young Children, 51*(4), 64-71.

Fagan, J. and Iglesias, A. (1999). Father involvement program effects on fathers, father figures, and their Head Start children: A quasi-experimental study. *Early Childhood Research Quarterly, 14*(2), 243-269.

Fagan, J. and Stevenson, H. C. (1995). Men as teachers: A self-help program on parenting for African-American men. *Social Work with Groups, 17*(4), 29-42.

Finkelhor, D., Hotaling, G. T., and Yllo, K. (1988). *Stopping family violence: Research priorities for the coming decade.* Newbury Park, CA: Sage Publications.

Furstenberg, F. F. (1995). Fathering in the inner city: Paternal participation and public policy. In W. Marsiglio (Ed.), *Fatherhood: Contemporary theory, research, and social policy* (pp. 119-147). Thousand Oaks, CA: Sage Publications.

Galinsky, E., Bond, J. T., and Friedman, D. (1993). *National study of the changing workforce.* New York: Families and Work Institute.

Garvin, C. D. and Seabury, B. A. (1997). *Interpersonal practice in social work* (Second edition). Boston: Allyn & Bacon.

Goetting, A. (1994). The parenting-crime connection. *Journal of Primary Prevention, 14,* 169-186.

Greif, G. L. (1997). *Out of touch: When parents and children lose contact after divorce.* New York: Oxford University Press.

Hawkins, A. J. and Dollahite, D. C. (Eds.) (1997). *Generative fathering: Beyond deficit perspectives.* Thousand Oaks, CA: Sage Publications.

Hawkins, A. J., Roberts, T. A., Christiansen, S. L., and Marshall, C. M. (1994). An evaluation of a program to help dual-earner couples share the second shift. *Family Relations, 43,* 213-220.

Hawkins, J. D., Catalano, R. F., and Miller, J. Y. (1992). Risk and protective factors for alcohol and other drug problems in adolescence and early adulthood: Implications for substance abuse prevention. *Psychological Bulletin, 112,* 64-105.

Hochschild, A. R. (1997). *The time bind.* New York: Metropolitan.

House Ways and Means Committee (1994). *1994 Green Book.* Washington, DC: U. S. Government Printing Office.

Johnson, L. and Palm, G. (1992). *Working with fathers: Methods and perspectives.* Stillwater, MN: nu ink.

Kiselica, M. S., Stroud, J., and Rotzien, A. (1992). Counseling the forgotten client: The teen father. Special issue: Mental health counseling for men. *Journal of Mental Health Counseling, 14,* 338-350.

Knitzer, J. and Bernard, S. (1997). *Map and track: State initiatives to encourage responsible fatherhood.* New York: National Center on Children in Poverty.

Levant, R. F. (1995). Toward the reconstruction of masculinity. In R. F. Levant and W. S. Pollack (Eds.), *A new psychology of men* (pp. 229-251). New York: Basic Books.

Levant, R. F. and Kelly, J. (1989). *Between father and child.* New York: Viking.

Levine, J. A. and Pitt, E. W. (1995). *Community strategies for responsible fatherhood.* New York: Families and Work Institute.

Levine, J. A. and Pittinsky, T. L. (1997). *Working fathers: New strategies for balancing work and family.* Reading, MA: Addison-Wesley.

Loeber, R. and Dishion, T. J. (1987). Antisocial and delinquent youths: Methods for their early identification. In J. D. Burchard and S. N. Burchard (Eds.), *Prevention of delinquent behavior* (pp. 75-89). Newbury Park, CA: Sage Publications.

Maccoby, E. E. and Mnookin, R. H. (1992). *Dividing the child: Social and legal dilemmas of custody.* Cambridge, MA: Harvard University Press.

McBride, B. A. (1989). Stress and fathers' parental competence: Implications for family life and parent education. *Family Relations, 38,* 385-389.

McBride, B. A. (1990). The effects of a parent education/play group on father involvement in child rearing. *Family Relations, 39,* 250-256.

McBride, B. A. (1991). Parent education and support programs for fathers: Outcome effects on paternal involvement. *Early Child Development and Care, 67,* 73-85.

McLoyd, V. C. (1989). Socialization and development in a changing economy: The effects of paternal job loss and income loss on children. *American Psychologist, 44,* 293-302.

Miley, K. K., O'Melia, M., and DuBois, B. L. (1998). *Generalist social work practice: An empowering approach* (Second edition). Boston: Allyn & Bacon.

Morris, S. R., Dollahite, D. C., and Hawkins, A. J. (1999). A qualitative evaluation of the theoretical and ethical foundations of and practical implications of father education sites on the World Wide Web. *Family Relations, 47,* 23-24.

Nichols, M. P. and Schwartz, R. C. (1995). *Family therapy: Concepts and methods* (Third edition). Boston: Allyn & Bacon.

O'Connell, M. (1993). *Where's papa? Father's role in child care.* Washington, DC: Population Council.

Osherson, S. (1995). *The passions of fatherhood.* New York: Fawcett Columbine.

Palm, G. F. (1997). Promoting generative fathering through parent and family education. In A. J. Hawkins and D. C. Dollahite (Eds.), *Generative fathering: Beyond deficit perspectives* (pp. 167-182). Thousand Oaks, CA: Sage Publications.

Palm, G. F. (1998). "Developing a model of reflective practice for improving fathering practice (WP-98-01)." Philadelphia, PA: University of Pennsylvania, National Center on Fathers and Families.

Peterson, R. R. and Gerson, K. (1992). Determinants of responsibility for child care arrangements among dual-earner couples. *Journal of Marriage and the Family, 54,* 527-536.

Phares, V. (1997). Psychological adjustment, maladustment, and father-child relationships. In M. E. Lamb (Ed.), *The role of the father in child development* (Third edition, pp. 261-283). New York: John Wiley & Sons.

Pleck, J. (1983). Husbands' paid work and family roles. In H. Lopata and J. Pleck (Eds.), *Research in the interweave of social roles: Volume 3. Families and jobs* (pp. 251-333). Greenwich, CT: JAI Press.

Pleck, J. (1997). Paternal involvement: Levels, sources, and consequences. In M. E. Lamb (Ed.), *The role of the father in child development,* (Third edition, pp. 66-103). New York: John Wiley & Sons.

Pollock, V. E., Schneider, L. S., Gabrielli, W. F., and Goodwin, D. W. (1987). Sex of parent and offspring in the transmission of alcoholism: A meta-analysis. *Journal of Nervous and Mental Disease, 175,* 668-673.

Popenoe, D. (1996). *Life without father.* New York: Free Press.

Seltzer, J. A. (1991). Relationships between fathers and children who live apart: The father's role after separation. *Journal of Marriage and the Family, 53,* 79-101.

Seltzer, J. A. and Bianchi, S. M. (1988). Children's contact with absent parents. *Journal of Marriage and the Family, 50,* 663-677.

Shecket, P. (1995). Support for fathers: A model for hospital-based parenting programs. In J. L. Shapiro, M. J. Diamond, and M. Greenberg (Eds.), *Becoming a father* (pp. 135-143). New York: Springer Publishing.

Snarey, J. (1993). *How fathers care for the next generation.* Cambridge, MA: Harvard University Press.

Sorenson, E. (1997). A national profile of nonresident fathers and their ability to pay child support. *Journal of Marriage and the Family, 59,* 785-798.

Staples, R. and Johnson, L. B. (1993). *Black families at the crossroads: Challenges and prospects.* San Francisco: Jossey-Bass Publishers.

Starrels, M. E. (1992). The evolution of workplace family policy research. *Journal of Family Issues, 13,* 259-278.

Sternberg, K. J. (1997). Fathers, the missing parents in research on family violence. In M. E. Lamb (Ed.), *The role of the father in child development* (Third edition, pp. 284-308). New York: John Wiley & Sons.

Sternberg, K. J., Lamb, M. E., Greenbaum, C., Cicchetti, D., Dawud, S., Cortes, R. M., Krispin, O., and Lorey, F. (1993). Effects of domestic violence on children's behavior problems and depression. *Developmental Psychology, 29,* 44-52.

Toseland, R. W. and Rivas, R. F. (1998). *Group work practice* (Third edition). Boston: Allyn & Bacon.

Wilson, P. and Johnson, J. (1995). "Fatherhood development: A curriculum for young fathers." Unpublished manuscript. Philadelphia: Public/Private Ventures.

SECTION I:
CLINICAL INTERVENTIONS

Chapter 1

Tools for the Trade: Clinical Interventions with Fathers in Family Therapy

James L. Furrow

> In making the handle
> Of an axe
> By cutting wood with an axe
> The model is near at hand.

Snyder (1983)

Among the many metaphors used to describe a clinician's work with a client, I can think of no better analogy than "tools" to describe therapeutic interventions with fathers. While the instrumentality of the image oversimplifies many of the complexities inherent in a therapeutic relationship, it defines in direct terms what many men seek. One father, at the end of an initial session, expressed this sentiment when he replied, "Look, we've been talking for an hour and you haven't given me any tools to make this situation better. What am I supposed to do?" As a clinician, I learned that these appeals were to be distrusted. Too often they simply represented a plea for a "quick fix," thus avoiding the deeper issues for which therapy was designed. Yet, I too wished for a tool that I could hand over to this father to help him care for his children.

This search for tools is not simply an attempt to evade life's emotional complexities, but an expression of the pursuit of mastery, a search to set things right. Family therapist Eric McCollum (1990), in his essay titled "Tools," recounts the connection of men in his family to the tools and labors they shared. Drawing together his own experience and the poetry of Gary Snyder (1983) he portrays the profound relational ties bonding fathers and sons, even in the absence of more direct and spoken intimacies. Snyder's poem "Axe Handles" portrays the similarity between the shaping of a new axe handle and the developmental influence of a father's relationship to his child.

> The axe is an apt symbol, with both a constructive and a destructive aspect. A father's influence may be felt in many ways, as well; through affection and involvement at one moment and through absence and disregard at another. Either instance shapes a son. Snyder's description is complex and moving and reminds us that connections occur on many levels, some spoken, others not. (McCollum, 1990, p. 47)

This chapter describes a clinical approach to intervention with fathers. The narrative-oriented model proposed emphasizes the roles that paternal images and emotional interaction have in fathering. In support of this approach, several psychological and social issues facing fathers are reviewed. Attention is given to recent findings that inform an approach to assumptions about fatherhood in general. The chapter provides support for a narrative intervention as illustrated in the pivotal roles that paternal images play in the formation and practice of fathering. These images and their shaping represent in Snyder's poetry the axe handle, and in clinical practice they represent a tool of intervention.

FATHERS IN FAMILY THERAPY: PSYCHOLOGICAL AND SOCIAL ISSUES

An understanding of the issues faced by fathers entering therapy is necessary for increasing the effectiveness of clinical interventions with these men. A father's assumptions about masculinity often shape his experience of fatherhood, emotions, and therapy. The psychological wounds a father carries from his childhood are often present in his approach to parenthood.

Fatherhood and Masculinity

A father's definition of "good fathering" may consist of stories that bring up issues of conflict about the nature of the role he is supposed to play. For many men, their motivations as fathers are far better than the models of fatherhood they experienced. Caught between what they have known and what they hope to be as fathers, many men are confused about how to embrace this paternal role. Gary, a father of two, illustrates this struggle through the problems he has in communicating with his adolescent children. In the heat of the moment he disengages and distances from difficult interactions with the children. Later he recalls the parallel to his childhood, noting his father's frequent sarcastic comment to his mother, "How am I supposed to know? You are their mother; you need to figure it out." Gary was torn between his ideal image of an involved father, and his memory of his seemingly disinterested dad.

Concepts of fatherhood tie together assumptions about parenting roles and masculinity. Gary was uncertain how to engage his children since his desire to be more involved competed with the image of his own father's tough masculinity. His identification with a more nurturing parental role came from what he hoped for, and still wanted from, his father. Yet his childhood experience identified this care as maternal, which fostered his ambivalence, for to be nurturing meant that even as a male he was less like a father and more like a mother. Real (1995) observes that masculine identity is shaped more by a "disidentification" with maternal qualities than a purposeful identification with paternal ones. Sons learn that fathers are the emotional antithesis of mothers. Emotional commitments are discretionary, and emotional expressiveness is optional. Exploring the assumptions a man makes regarding masculinity and paternity is effective in resolving the uncertainty a father has in reconciling his images of masculinity and paternity.

Emotions and Masculinity

The effect of the polarization of masculine and feminine traits in parenthood is associated with the constriction of a father's emotional expression. This inexpressiveness is challenged by the presence of his child's emotional needs and pursuits (Balswick, 1988). Clarification of a father's beliefs and responses to emotional expression provides a means for assessing the effectiveness of his parenting and judging the impact that emotional constriction may have on the family as a whole.

Gottman (1998) describes the positive impact a father's response to his child's emotions has on the child's development. In his research, Gottman found that fathers who responded to their children's emotions and who were able to guide them through difficult emotional experiences were more effective fathers. Children who were "emotionally coached" by their parents demonstrated higher levels of development on social, affective, and cognitive indicators (Gottman, 1998).

A father's beliefs about emotion impact how his family responds to emotions as a whole. A father who responds to a difficult day at work by dismissing his own disappointment is likely to dismiss a similar negative sentiment that he encounters with his child at home. The parental task, however, requires that a child is responded to on the child's own emotional terms (Larson, 1993). When a father dismisses a child's emotion, he invalidates the child's experience and communicates an impression of his limited emotional availability. The repetition of this pattern results in the reduction of a child's emotional pursuit of the father. The family may create an unspoken rule that children should not bother their dad with emotional concerns. The rule, in effect, protects the father from emotions that the father has yet to resolve for himself.

Therapy and Masculinity

Just as traditional male socialization shapes a father's view of emotions, his beliefs about therapy are similarly impacted. In many therapy settings a father is expected to express his need for help, to address his own emotional reactions to this need, and to willingly participate in a conversation based upon emotional self-disclosure (Levant, 1996). Recent findings on conversation styles suggest a potential disjunction between the type of conversation that a therapist is trained to conduct and the type of conversation that a man may see as helpful. Tannen (1990) observes that men engage in a form of dialogue emphasizing the exchange of information and retention of status in social order, "report talk." Therapeutic conversations are guided by emphases that promote a working alliance or supportive relationship, and as a result are indicative of "rapport talk," Tannen's term for the typically feminine form of discourse. Therapeutic language is simply foreign to the vernacular of "real men" (Shay, 1996).

When men hold to a stereotypic view of therapy as feminine (i.e., nonmasculine) they are more likely to experience the client role as threatening. Tannen's observation that men seek to retain status in report talk implies that men in therapy may be reluctant to engage in a conversation with a professional who facilitates emotional disclosures that result in a loss of status. Brooks (1996) finds that a traditional male client is likely to retain his masculine identity by resisting feminine forms of expression and maintaining control over the interaction. A father's reserved approach to therapy can be understood as an attempt to support his family and at the same time preserve his masculine identity.

It is helpful for the therapist to understand the basis of a father's struggle in therapy to successively work with the gender-based assumptions that impact his participation in therapy and the family. Osherson and Krugman (1990) observe that a man's resistance to therapy may be influenced by his inner world of restricted emotions and rationality. Traditional masculine assumptions lead many fathers to question the benefit of talking about feelings and introspection as a solution to the family problem. They may believe that they have more to lose and less to gain by participating in treatment. The therapist who relies on a generic therapeutic approach to reach through this reluctance is likely to miss the issues that support the need for this reserved stance. Fischer and Good (1997) also suggest that a man's inexpressiveness is associated with limited social support, loneliness, and a history of short-term relationships. These men have been described as "strangers" to their emotions and as a result have greater difficulty articulating them. Therapists who simplify this struggle to one of repression alone have underestimated the estrangement that may exist between what a man knows to be true and what he feels.

Wounds of the Father

No father enters fatherhood without a model. Sons of absent fathers fill this void with stories of father figures, some real and others imagined. As Snyder's axe handle analogy illustrates, the task of shaping a child for the father draws upon the model of his own father and how it has shaped his own experience. A father's uncertainty in responding to his own emotions or to those of his child points back to a similar uncertainty that the father experiences of his own father (Pleck, 1995).

From generation to generation a child's emotional pursuit of his father pulls on that father's experience of emotional validation as a child.

These potential wounds may shape the legacy of fatherhood in a family. Hargrave (1994) points to the intergenerational impact of adult men distanced from their fathers in response to their childhood wounds, only to pass on these wounds to their children. In a tragic irony, the father separates himself from the pain of being fathered, only to find that this lack of resolution manifests itself in his relationship to his child. To face the wounds that he has imposed on his children, the father must begin with his own wounds as a son. This means that a man must heal the inner image of his father (Osherson, 1987). The healing begins as his childhood wounds are addressed and his wounding paternal actions are challenged (Real, 1995).

ASSUMPTIONS AND VALUES

A primary assumption of this intervention model is that fatherhood is best understood as a socially constructed role (Doherty, Kouneski, and Erickson, 1998). Fatherhood and its consequent role expectations are increasingly being shaped by cultural narratives or stories that hold the values of a particular time (Pleck and Pleck, 1997). Gender roles are constantly being constructed within the family and within the culture at large. Hoffman (1990) recognizes the importance of viewing therapeutic approaches with a "gender lens" to expose the premises and assumptions supporting psychological theories that are often working against the very women and men they intend to help. In the case of an inexpressive father, a therapist may treat the father's lack of emotional vulnerability as evidence of emotional withdrawal, thereby missing the ways in which a father is invested in his family. This does not excuse emotional inexpression. Instead, it highlights how a therapist's values in treatment are likely to shape not only what is treated in therapy, but also how the issues themselves are addressed. In some cases the therapist may think too much of what is missing, all the while ignoring the connections that do exist (McCollum, 1990).

A second assumption holds that a father's actions in relationship to his children are best defined by a set of multiple influences. Scholars have proposed models of parental behavior that identify several factors explaining paternal involvement (Belsky, 1984; Lamb et al., 1987). In

Belsky's model these factors include: parental factors (e.g., personality), child factors (e.g., temperament), and contextual factors (e.g., marital relationship, social support, and employment practices). Parke (1996) and Pleck (1997) provide substantive reviews of empirical support for the influence of these domains upon a father's paternal involvement. The contextual models balance the influence of social and family factors as well as the father's contribution to his role.

A third assumption presumes that fatherhood is influenced by developmental changes occurring across the life span (Carter and McGoldrick, 1989). A life-span perspective suggests that fathering will be influenced by the developmental progression of childhood and continuing changes in adulthood (Levinson, 1978). Several scholars propose a developmental approach to fatherhood that embodies fatherhood as an expression of Erik Erikson's stage of generativity (Dollahite, Hawkins, and Brotherson, 1997; Hawkins et al., 1993; Snarey, 1993; Snarey, 1997). These models underscore the dynamic change implicit in a parental role.

Galinsky (1987) proposes using a developmental framework to understand the changing nature of parental roles (see Table 1.1). Based upon her interview studies of parents, she argues that parents carry images of what their children, their parenting, and their relationships with their child will be like at each stage of development. These images are informed by the parent's life experience, including his or her experience of being parented as a child. Personal growth results from the changing images that emerge as the parent responds to the changing developmental needs of his or her child. For Galinsky, parenthood is an unfolding story, marked by different stages, which are informed by the developing child. These stages provide a model for anticipating the changes and challenges represented for fathers throughout the life course.

As mentioned previously, the proposed intervention emphasizes parental images. These images, or narratives, contain parental preconceptions of what the child will be like, what the parental role will be like, and what the parent-child relationship will be like at each stage of development. Developmental change requires adapting parental expectations of the child, the parental role, and the parent-child relationship. These changes result in gains and losses for parents and children.

Table 1.1. Galinsky's Six Stages of Parenthood

Stage	Developmental Milestones	Developmental Tasks of Parents
Image-Making: Pregnancy	Prenatal development	Preparing for birth and parenthood; Developing an attachment to the unborn child
Nurturing: Birth to Two Years	Developing a relationship with parents	Forming an attachment; Reconciling images of the birth, the child, and parental roles with actual experience
Authority: Preschool Age	Asserting independence; Beginning sense of identity	Accepting authority role and issues of control; Experience child as separate from parent
Interpretive: School Age	Moving out into the world beyond the family	Reevaluating and revising parental roles; Deciding level of parental involvement
Interdependent: Adolescence	Developing an identity; Dealing with sexuality	Adapting to changing adolescent, dealing with striving and criticism, midlife concerns
Departure Stage: Grown Child	Making it on their own yet remaining connected	Dealing with loss and changing images; Accepting separation from grown children

Source: Adapted from Galinsky, 1987.

The losses associated with developmental change often influence a father's identity and emotional well-being. Loss events for men are of "paramount importance" across the life span (Cochran and Rabinowitz, 1996). Losses may be tangible (e.g., death of a parent) or symbolic (e.g., such as a loss in status or prestige). An adolescent daughter (Interdependent Stage) may express greater criticism and independence in relationship to her father while the father facing losses associated with his own aging may be seeking a more significant role in her life. In response, the father may seek solace in focusing on personal achievement or impersonal problem solving (Cochran and Rabinowitz, 1996). His coping responses will negatively impact his relationship with his daughter and decrease the family's ability to adjust to developmental change.

"TOOLS" OF BEST PRACTICE WITH FATHERS

Therapists working with fathers need to understand the ways in which images of paternity and masculinity are influenced by developmental change. A review of the literature supports several practice strategies that facilitate this clinical direction. These practices are presented as they relate to the evolving therapeutic process.

Beginning Treatment: Building a Therapeutic Relationship

A father's adjustment to therapy is enhanced if the initial stages of therapy are strongly goal-directed. A therapist 's willingness to engage in cognitive strategies and examine problem-solving strategies in a goal-directed manner may be a necessary step to opening the way to other discussions of the problem (LeCroy, 1987). This may include validating a father's attempt to offer solutions, recognizing that the therapist must differentiate between an attempt to bring resolution and the imposition of the solution. Supporting a father's efforts to offer constructive solutions enables a more collaborative conversation, which lessens the status difference that is likely to escalate with a professional therapist. Wall and Levy (1994) support the use of less hierarchical terms (e.g., consultations, educational strategies) in therapy relationships with men to accomplish a similar purpose.

Therapy with fathers is more effective when the early stages are structured. This includes an intentional effort by the therapist to organize the treatment in evolving stages (LeCroy, 1987). Traditional masculine assumptions are often challenged by the common assumptions of a therapeutic process, and may contribute to a father's withdrawal from therapy (Feldman, 1990). Limiting the expectations of emotional vulnerability early in treatment is likely to produce less opportunity for a man to experience shame as a result of treatment (Shay, 1996). Instead, the therapist actively engages the father at points where he willingly discloses, reinforcing the disclosure and enabling the father to set the pace of disclosure. The initial therapeutic focus is upon finding areas where his interests converge with the goals of the therapy (Shay, 1996). A therapist can pursue this convergence by aligning with a father's stated goals, even if that may be to terminate treatment as soon as possible. Joining with a father's initiative enables the therapist to better assess his reluctance to disclose emotional material, which often is associated with unresolved issues related to his own father and family of origin (Levant, 1995; Osherson and Krugman, 1990). As the therapist gives attention to the father's presenting concerns, the therapist is better able to strengthen the father's investment in treatment despite the reluctance that often defines the early stage of therapy with men (Shay, 1996).

Intermediary Stages: Fathers and Emotional Expression

As initial goals are accomplished and the relationship between the father and the therapist is strengthened, the therapist is better able to facilitate discussions of the father's emotional experience and the family's experience of him. These interventions foster a deeper emotional engagement of the father with his family and himself. Two models illustrate strategies used to increase emotional responsiveness with fathers.

Levant and Kelly (1989) promote emotional self-awareness by helping men identify the "buzzing" (i.e., physiological arousal) they experience internally. The client is then challenged to develop an emotional vocabulary enabling him to name these feelings. This represents an intentional step toward increasing the range of his emotional expression. The next step in developing emotional self-awareness involves tracking the internal experiences that he encounters interacting with his child. Finally, the skill of using this emotional awareness with others is practiced in therapist-structured role-plays. Once the father has begun to identify his emotional responses to patterns of family interaction, the therapist asks the father to explore his responses to his child's emotion. Participation of the mother in these exercises is important for validating her experience of the child and the father, as well as minimizing the portrayal of the father's emotional nonresponsiveness as the basis of the family problem.

Gottman's (1998) model of "emotional coaching" instructs a father in how to recognize and respond to the emotions of his child at low levels of intensity. With this ability the father can better communicate validation, understanding, and problem solving with his child. The multistep process of coaching provides a useful focus on increasing a father's ability to respond to his child's emotions as well as his own. The components of "emotion coaching" include teaching the father awareness and recognition of lower-intensity emotions in his child to engage the child in this opportunity for intimacy and teaching. Approaching the emotional response from this stance enables the father to assist his child in labeling the emotional response, to provide support and validation to the child, and to discuss problem and solution strategies that will help the child learn from the experience.

These practical strategies provide a means for the therapist to work in a direct fashion with fathers. The therapist's use of validation with fathers is important in these task-oriented approaches (Cohen, 1998). Wall and Levy (1994) draw attention to a father's competency in providing nurture and comfort to his child. Reinforcement of these positive steps provides validation for the father seeking to enhance his emotional responsiveness.

Narratives of Fatherhood: Tools That Shape a Father's Experience

Interventions based upon paternal images offer the therapist a means to understand the social construction of a father's role in relationship to his child and himself. McAdams (1993) suggests that these images (i.e., imagoes) shape the life narrative of an individual. A father's actions and intentions reflect what that man desires for his child and family and these desires shape and are shaped by his imagoes. The images of fatherhood provide a means for understanding his paternity and a basis for change. Therapy provides a means by which a father can discover a better image and forgotten motivation necessary for becoming the father he desires to be (McAdams, 1993).

I propose a narrative-oriented approach to family therapy in response to the recognition that fatherhood is a socially constructed role rooted in the paternal images of a father. A narrative-based approach begins with the assumption that an individual or a family will organize their experience in storied form (Brunner, 1990). The impact of these stories and the images the stories are composed of can have a "totalizing" influence on the family, restricting the family's response to problematic interaction patterns and themes. The process of therapy from this narrative perspective involves helping the family begin to articulate an alternative story; one that expresses alternative preferences and possibilities (Freedman and Combs, 1996). These possibilities are indicative of the competencies that already exist within the family but are not acknowledged (Eron and Lund, 1999; Griffith and Griffith, 1992).

This approach suggests that the images a father has of his child, his paternal role, and his relationship with his child (Galinsky, 1987) will be informed by the imagoes that shape his fatherhood (McAdams, 1993). A narrative-based intervention provides a powerful means for helping fathers and their families identify alternative resources for the agency (work) and community (love) in fatherhood. Working with the preferred stories of fathers and their families enables the therapist to identify alternative accounts, to broaden paternal images, and to identify empowering resources (Eron and Lund, 1999). An emphasis upon strengths and competence with fathers in family therapy is consistent with the generative, narrative approach to clinical work with fathers used by Deinhart and Dollahite (1997). While the initial stages focus upon goal-directed problem resolution and the development of emotional awareness and responsiveness, a narrative approach extends the clinical work to reshaping narrative forms composing a father's image of fatherhood. Working together with the father and his family against the problem, the therapist deepens the conversation with the father and the opportunity to consider not only how a father practices, but also who he is.

Reimaging a Father's Presence: Joe's Story

The following case study is composed from a collection of family therapy cases where paternal issues were pivotal to the resolution of the treatment. Each case followed a similar pattern. The initial sessions addressed a child-related problem. Once the presenting complaint was addressed and a reduction in symptoms evident, remaining sessions addressed issues of the father's emotional engagement with his role and family.

Case Study

Karen and her two children described her husband Joe as lacking interest in the family. Joe tacitly confirmed the family's impression by remaining emotionally detached in therapy sessions or missing them all together. For Karen, Joe was "only interested in his career," which did not fit her image of a father's role in the family. Her frustration with his "workaholism" grew with his increased overtime schedule and recent reports of her daughter's oppositional behavior at school. Karen attributed Joe's overtime to an attempt to avoid the problems at home.

An individual interview with Joe revealed his own frustration with the family problems. He explained that his efforts to offer solutions were not accepted by the rest of the family. His admitted retreats to the office were out of his frustration and a sense of rejection. He described his work as the one thing he did for the family, and he felt that they didn't appear to want much else from him. Joe described the bind he experienced being torn between the responsibilities that he had in his job and his image of being a "good father." His voice choked when Karen described his fathering. "He is just like his own father, never having time for anyone but himself." She was quoting Joe's description of his father, and in doing so he felt her minimize the efforts he had made to be different from his distant, uncaring father. When questioned further, Joe withdrew emotionally, focusing instead on the more general challenges of managing the competing expectations of work and family.

His daughter's failing grades and behavior problems were the catalyst for family treatment. The family's self-description was marked by disempowerment: "out of control," "uncaring," and "disinterest." The family's "problematic story" did not reflect the efforts each person was taking to help the family. Reworking the family's story, including the father's absence and the daughter's rebellion, began with generating alternative accounts which recognize a father working to help the family succeed, a mother working to hold the family together, and a daughter seeking to be grown up. Highlighting these alternative stories increases the possibility of different actions and meanings, and empowers the family members to engage together against the problems they face (White and Epston, 1990; Eron and Lund, 1999).

The therapy progressed with attention given to the ways in which the family was working together against the "teenage trouble-making." Karen re-described her daughter's struggles as being somewhat typical of many high school students; as a result Karen found she used more supportive statements with her daughter and they both appeared less anxious. Joe described the daughter's behavior as improved, but he remained doubtful that any real change had occurred. He described his role in her life as a motivator, and he expressed concern that she did not seem to listen to him the way she did as a younger child.

In earlier sessions with the two parents, we discussed ways in which both parents could better communicate with their daughter. This involved focusing on accounts where either parent described their parental action as fitting or approaching their parenting ideal. Karen was able to name several instances where she felt she was acting consistently with her preferred maternal role. In contrast, Joe found this exercise troubling. He complained that too often he felt that he had no model of positive fathering. All he knew to do as a father was to criticize and give direction. It was what he had known as a son.

Joe's fatherhood was informed by competing images. His image of an involved parent was better characterized by the "authority stage" even though his daughter's developmental needs were in the "interdependent stage" (Galinsky, 1987). Joe held to power and control to define his role. As a result, he found it difficult to moderate his expectations and set effective limits with his daughter. He vacillated between remaining distant and aloof, until a problem emerged, and then he often responded in a harsh, critical style. The second influence on Joe's self-description was the image of his father. His best efforts to reform his paternal experience often betrayed him. The treatment objectives in response to these constructions involved first addressing the developmental issues and then discussing his relationship with his father.

Personal growth for Joe involved adapting his image of fathering to his experience of his daughter. Joe evaluated more developmentally appropriate expressions of parenting. Moving toward a parental image that embraced his daughter's needs for greater autonomy required helping Joe to identify his own emotional response to his daughter's transition to adulthood. Following leading questions that emphasized how he imagined responding to her as a young adult, Joe described alternative ways to relate to his daughter. Therapy focused on how Joe could enact his preferred paternal image in his relationship with his daughter. As a result, his efforts to father his daughter were reinforced in a manner that emphasized supporting her developing identity and at the same time filling her need to remain connected to him. Joe was asked to discuss his preferred view of fathering with his daughter in session and he was encouraged to express his intention to be the father he desires to be.

The second aspect of Joe's paternal image was explored with a similar narrative emphasis. In conversations with Joe and Karen, Joe's overly critical and often hostile outbursts were characterized as being just like his father. This frame of reference did not lead either parent to see the resources Joe had to offer as a father. His fathering was defined by the deficits he experienced in his relationship to his father. In conversation with the couple, I explored ways in which this "bad father image" impacted the way the family experienced Joe. Separating the narrative image of the bad father from Joe enabled the couple to have conversations about Joe's parenting that seemed to break this mold. Joe identified different relationships where he had received caring from older adult mentors and the resources that these experiences brought to his fathering. This was helpful to the couple in identifying additional influences that may explain how Joe is able to father in ways that were different than those modeled by his father.

Alternative explanations were developed for Joe's fathering behaviors that were inconsistent with his expressed intentions. The validation and support generated in the couple's discussion of alternative accounts provided a basis for exploring how these negative father images exerted influence over Joe's best intentions. These discussions depersonalized the influence of Joe's poor parenting model, and enabled the couple to discuss what happened when the "bad parenting took over." Joe described his irritation with his daughter's insolence. "She walls me off, and goes on making stupid choices. I get scared and try to take control." Joe's fear that his daughter will fail him is intolerable to him. The alternative explanation emphasized Joe's concern for his daughter's well-being along with his inability to express this care in a meaningful way. The "caring father" often became the "angry father."

I asked Joe if the same story might also be told of his father. Joe was concerned about how his daughter's potential failure would hurt her, but he was also afraid of how such a failure would reflect upon his fathering. This alternative explanation accounts for his response to his daughter, but does not explain his own fear. We explored the possibility that his "angry father" actions related to this personal fear. Joe had found little reason to believe that his father cared about him at all. He managed this relationship by maintaining both geographic and interpersonal distance. Joe began to weep as he pondered his father's care. He always wanted to believe that his father's intentions were caring, but his father's angry outbursts led him to a different conclusion. I extended the emerging possibility of the "caring father" by asking Joe what his father would say if Joe asked him for advice on how to raise a teenager. Joe was intrigued with the idea and skeptical about his father's ability to respond. Exploring this further, I asked him to consider the advice that he might give his daughter if she called one day with the same question. He responded in a tearful manner with his preferred view.

Joe's image of fathering changed as he considered his fears of fatherhood. He was afraid of the power his daughter had over his fatherhood, and he was afraid of the power his father had to discredit Joe as a man. Seeing this fear as, in part, a risk implicit in loving relationships where one must guide and one must release, Joe and Karen found the possibility of telling a different story of fatherhood in their family. For Joe, this meant seeing in the reflection of his own fatherhood the shape and impression of his father's. In Snyder's (1983) words, "The model was near at hand."

INCREASING FATHER INVOLVEMENT IN THERAPY

A father's participation in therapy is pivotal to this approach and several practical steps are recommended to support his involvement. Many fathers share beliefs that lead them away from seeking therapy as a resource. Practical strategies to address these beliefs involve the education of fathers and therapists.

Fathers often need to be prepared for family therapy. Fischer and Good (1997) propose the use of an introductory session for men so that the potential client is informed about what he can expect and what will be expected of him in treatment. Others support the use of psychoeducational groups to introduce men to heighten a man's interest as well as familiarize him with emotionally oriented conversations (Brooks, 1996; Levant, 1996). The use of educational courses is also considered a preparatory step to therapy for fathers. Fathering courses offered in conjunction with predictable developmental transitions (e.g., prenatal classes, promotion to a middle- or high-school campus) provide an opportunity to increase a father's awareness of the psychosocial needs of the parent and the family (Jordan, Stanley, and Markman, 1999). Other recommendations include encouraging fathers who have benefited from therapy to speak publicly about their experience (Guillebeaux, Storm, and Demaris, 1986). A therapist could create a brochure specifically designed to help the father understand what he might expect from therapy.

Therapists may need to reconsider their practice strategies to increase a father's involvement in treatment. Therapists have lowered their expectations of fathers and are less likely to seek their participation (Phares, 1996). Doherty (1981) holds that the therapist should advance the expectation that the father be involved in family sessions beginning with the first appointment. Brooks (1996) and Shay (1996) offer a variety of verbal approaches that a therapist may use to address the anticipation of reluctance on a father's part. A therapist's willingness to understand a father's tentative commitment and at the same time validate his effort to contribute to finding a solution to family problems is helpful in sustaining his ongoing participation. Emphasizing the expertise of a father's experience enables the therapist to avoid placing the father in a one-down relationship to the therapist (Gaines, 1981). Therapists also need to consider how their office hours might better accommodate the schedule of both parents.

OUTCOME AND EVALUATION

The goal of this therapeutic approach is to facilitate the expression and experience of alternative stories of fatherhood in a family context. Interventions addressing these paternal images are successful when a father's actions fit with his preferred views and those of his family. Therapy is enhanced by the inclusion of those who have a stake in this preferred view, and the generalization of the treatment effect to all family members is limited by the degree to which this preferred view is not shared. The efficacy of this approach is best judged by the degree to which a transformed paternal image offers a better fit in the family, social context, and the family's developmental needs. The case study of Joe and his family illustrates the successful application of this intervention approach. Systematic evaluation of these best practices with fathers is needed to validate this anecdotal report. Further research is needed to establish the appropriate application of these methods with fathers in diverse settings (e.g., ethnicity, divorce, and gay fathers).

In recent reviews of research on gender effects in psychotherapy a distinct relationship between a client's gender and therapeutic outcome is yet to be established (Garfield, 1994). It remains unclear how these comprehensive reviews account for the absence of fathers in family treatment or the reluctance of men in general to participate in psychotherapy. Among studies linking fathers' participation in therapy to positive outcomes, Shapiro and Budman (1973) found that family treatment was less likely to reach early termination when fathers were supportive of the therapy. Bennum (1989) found that positive outcomes were more likely when a father perceived the therapist as competent and the therapy as more directive. While paternal involvement in child and family therapy has been supported in clinical literature, Phares (1996) noted a rather significant gap between clinicians' recommendations and the overall strength of the empirical evidence for this support. Further empirical study is needed to establish the unique influence of a father in family therapy as well as factors that may inhibit and promote his participation.

CONCLUSION

Clinical interventions with fathers and their families intersect the social domains of paternity and masculinity. The images a father holds of paternity offer an important tool for referencing and shaping a father's actions and interests in his family. Therapeutic strategies which build on the narrative accounts of a father's work will offer new possibilities for a father to respond to the challenges of being a parent. Therapists need to revisit their paternal images. Family therapists often expect too little out of these men who want to make a difference in their families. A therapist's narratives of fatherhood may keep the clinician from recognizing the possibilities a father's presence brings to family therapy. In the case of fatherhood, Snyder (1983) and McCollum (1990) may offer some direction by recognizing that the images shaping the therapist are in turn the tools shaping the trade.

REFERENCES

Balswick, J. (1988). *The inexpressive male.* Lexington, MA: Lexington Books.

Belsky, J. (1984). The determinants of parenting: A process model. *Child Development, 55,* 83-96.

Bennum, I. (1989). Perceptions of the therapist in family therapy. *Journal of Family Therapy, 11,* 243-255.

Brooks, G. R. (1996). Treatment for therapy-resistant men. In M. P. Andronico (Ed.), *Men in groups: Insights, interventions, and psychoeducational work* (pp. 7-19). Washington, DC: American Psychological Association.

Brunner, J. (1990). *Acts of meaning*. Cambridge: Harvard University Press.

Carter, B. and McGoldrick, M. (1989). Overview: The changing family life cycle: A framework for family therapy. In B. Carter and M. McGoldrick (Eds.), *The changing family life cycle: A framework for family therapy* (Second edition, pp. 3-28). Boston: Allyn & Bacon.

Cochran, S. V. and Rabinowitz, F. E. (1996). Men, loss, and psychotherapy. *Psychotherapy, 33*, 593-600.

Cohen, O. (1998). Parental narcissism and the disengagement of the non-custodial father after divorce. *Clinical Social Work Journal, 26*(2), 195-215.

Dienhart, A. and Dollahite, D. C. (1997). A generative narrative approach to clinical work with fathers. In A. J. Hawkins and D. C. Dollahite (Eds.), *Generative fathering: Beyond deficit perspectives* (pp. 183-199). Thousand Oaks, CA: Sage.

Doherty, W. J. (1981). Involving the reluctant father in family therapy. In A. S. Gurman (Ed.), *Questions and answers in the practice of family therapy* (pp. 23-26), New York: Brunner/Mazel.

Doherty, W. J., Kouneski, E. F., and Erickson, M. F. (1998). Responsible fathering: An overview and conceptual framework. *Journal of Marriage and Family, 60*, 277-292.

Dollahite, D. C., Hawkins, A. J., and Brotherson, S. E. (1997). Fatherwork: A conceptual ethic of fathering as generative work. In A. J. Hawkins and D. C. Dollahite (Eds.), *Generative fathering: Beyond deficit perspectives* (pp. 17-35). Thousand Oaks, CA: Sage.

Eron, J. B. and Lund, T. W. (1999). *Narrative solutions in brief therapy*. New York: Guilford.

Feldman, L. B. (1990). Fathers and fathering. In R. Meth and R. Pasik (Eds.), *Men in therapy: The challenge of change* (pp. 88-107). New York: Guilford Press.

Fischer, A. R. and Good, G. E. (1997). Men and psychotherapy: An investigation of Alexithymia, intimacy and masculine gender roles. *Psychotherapy, 34*, 160-170.

Freedman, J. and Combs, G. (1996). *Narrative therapy: The social construction of preferred realities*. New York: Norton.

Gaines, T. (1981). Engaging the father in family therapy. In A. S. Gurman (Ed.), *Questions and answers in the practice of family therapy* (pp. 20-22). New York: Brunner/Mazel.

Galinsky, E. (1987). *The six stages of parenthood*. Reading, MA: Perseus.

Garfield, S. L. (1994). Research on client variables in psychotherapy. In A. Bergin and S. Garfield (Eds.), *Handbook on psychotherapy and behavior change* (pp. 190-228). New York: Wiley.

Gottman, J. M. (1998). Toward a process model on men in marriages and families. In A. Booth and A. C. Crouter (Eds.), *Men in families* (pp. 149-192). Mahwah, NJ: Erlbaum.

Griffith, J. and Griffith, M. (1992). Speaking the unspeakable: Use of the reflecting position therapies for somatic symptoms. *Family Systems Medicine, 10*(1), 41-52.

Guillebeaux, F., Storm, C. L., and Demaris, A. (1986). Luring the reluctant male: A study of males participating in marriage and family therapy. *Family Therapy, 13*(2), 215-225.

Hargrave, T. (1994). *Families and forgiveness*. New York: Brunner/Mazel.

Hawkins, A. J., Christiansen, S. L., Sargent, K. P., and Hill, E. J. (1993). Rethinking fathers' involvement in child care: A developmental perspective. *Journal of Family Issues, 14,* 531-549.

Hoffman, L. (1990). Constructing reality: An art of lens. *Family Process, 29,* 1-12.

Jordan, P. L., Stanley, S. M., and Markman, H. J. (1999). *Becoming parents: How to strengthen your marriage as your family grows*. San Fransisco: Jossey-Bass.

Lamb, M. E., Pleck, J. H., Charnov, E. L., and Levine, J. A. (1987). A biosocial perspective on paternal behavior and involvement. In J. B. Lancaster, J. Altman, A. Rossi, and L. R. Sherrod (Eds.), *Parenting across the lifespan: Biosocial perspectives* (pp. 11-42). Hawthorne, NY: Adeline Publishing.

Larson, R. W. (1993). Finding time for fatherhood: The emotional ecology of adolescent-father interactions. In S. Shulman and A. Collins (Eds.), *Father-adolescent relationships* (pp. 7-25). San Francisco: Jossey-Bass.

LeCroy, C. W. (1987). A model for involving fathers in treatment. *Family Therapy, 14*(3), 237-245.

Levant, R. F. (1995). Fatherhood, numbness, and emotional self-awareness. In J. L. Shapiro, M. Diamond, and M. Greenberg (Eds.), *Becoming a father: Contemporary, social, developmental, and clinical perspectives* (pp. 144-153). New York: Springer.

Levant, R. F. (1996). The male code and parenting: A psychoeducational approach. In M. P. Andronico (Ed.), *Men in groups: Insights, interventions, and psychoeducational work* (pp. 229-241). Washington, DC: American Psychological Association.

Levant, R. F. and Kelly, J. (1989). *Between father and child*. New York: Viking/Penguin.

Levinson, D. (1978). *The seasons of a man's life*. New York: Knopf.

McAdams, D. (1993). *The stories we live by: Personal myths and the making of the self.* New York: Guilford Press.

McCollum, E. (1990). Tools. *North American Review, 274,* December, 47-49.

Osherson, S. (1987). *Finding our fathers: How a man's life is shaped by the relationship with his father*. New York: Fawcett.

Osherson, S. and Krugman, S. (1990). Men, shame, and psychotherapy, *Psychotherapy, 27,* 327-339.

Parke, R. D. (1996). *Fatherhood*. Cambridge: Harvard University Press.

Phares, V. (1996). *Fathers and developmental psychopathology*. New York: Wiley.

Pleck, E. H. and Pleck, J. H. (1997). Fatherhood ideals in the United States: Historical dimensions. In M. E. Lamb (Ed.), *The role of the father in child development* (Third edition, pp. 33-48). New York: Wiley.

Pleck, J. H. (1995). The father wound: Implications for expectant fathers. In J. L. Shapiro, M. Diamond, and M. Greenberg (Eds.), *Becoming a father* (pp. 210-223). New York: Springer.

Pleck, J. H. (1997). Paternal involvement: Levels, sources, and consequences. In M. E. Lamb (Ed.), *The role of the father in child development* (Third edition, pp. 66-103). New York: Wiley.

Real, T. (1995). Fathering our sons; Refathering ourselves: Thoughts on transforming masculine legacies. In K. Weingarten (Ed.), *Cultural resistance: Challenging beliefs about men, women, and therapy* (pp. 27-43). Binghamton, New York: The Haworth Press.

Shapiro, R. J. and Budman, S. H. (1973). Defection, termination and continuation in family and individual therapy. *Family Process, 12,* 55-67.

Shay, J. J. (1996). "Okay, I'm here, but I'm not talking!" Psychotherapy with the reluctant male. *Psychotherapy, 33,* 503-513.

Snarey, J. (1993). *How fathers care for the next generation.* Cambridge, MA: Harvard University Press.

Snarey, J. (1997). Foreword: The next generation of work on fathering. In A. J. Hawkins and D. C. Dollahite (Eds.), *Generative fathering: Beyond deficit perspectives* (pp. ix-xii). Thousand Oaks, CA: Sage.

Snyder, G. (1983). *Axe Handles.* San Francisco: North Point Press.

Tannen, D. (1990). *You just don't understand: Women and men in conversation.* New York: Ballantine.

Wall, J. C. and Levy, A. J. (1994). Treatment of noncustodial fathers: Gender issues and clinical dilemmas. *Child and Adolescent Social Work Journal, 11*(4), 295-313.

White, M. and Epston, D. (1990). *Narrative means to therapeutic ends.* New York: Norton.

Chapter 2

Therapeutic Support Groups As a Primary Intervention for Issues of Fatherhood with African-American Men

Anderson J. Franklin
Tommy Davis III

Fatherhood for African-American men is one of the most complex topics to discuss because it raises emotions about the adequacy of black men fulfilling the father role. The statistics indicating the number of African-American fathers absent from the home, the personal reports of emotional inaccessibility of those fathers at home, and the general understanding that fatherhood in the black community is in crisis, are all a part of the controversial discourse on black male survival. These issues take their toll upon the self-esteem and dignity of many black men.

In this chapter we discuss the use of therapeutic support groups as a primary intervention for African-American men working to fulfill their commitments and responsibilities as fathers. A goal of the support group is to help African-American men gain better insight into and control of their behavior in emotionally provocative circumstances. This is linked to a larger objective, and that is to help men achieve better outcomes for the way they feel in general. We consider such groups to be effective in assisting men to handle the challenges of being a father, managing the expectations of being a man, and confronting unique social circumstances presented to the development of their manhood by virtue of being of African descent.

We want to discuss three areas important to the success of using therapeutic support groups as a primary intervention: (1) underlying psychological factors influencing African-American men's view of the world and their potential use of professional services, (2) major themes to promote in conducting support groups for African-American men, and (3) various issues involving the formation and implementation of support groups.

SOME UNDERLYING PSYCHOLOGICAL FACTORS

When given the opportunity to engage in open dialogue, in a safe place, many African-American men have voiced their struggles with being competent fathers. They struggle with the challenges faced in contemporary times with evolving changes in gender-role expectations. In addition, underrepresented and invisible from public view, are those African-American men who are highly involved fathers and responsible family men. Their lack of visibility as public role models poses a dilemma for young black men needing to learn how to be resilient black men and fathers (Franklin, 1999a). Black fathers who are making conscientious efforts become disillusioned by the pervasive references to failure, feeling as though they are expected to fail.

There are a number of issues that practitioners and scholars need to address to design effective interventions with African-American fathers.

Understanding Race and Gender Issues

Bowman and Forman (1997) note that there are both instrumental and expressive family roles among African-American fathers. These parental roles consist of five interrelated functions, responsibilities, or expectations:

1. an economic provider role to ensure the material well-being of children;
2. a caregiver role to provide child nurturing, socioemotional well-being, and socialization;

3. a homemaker role to maintain an orderly and healthy home environment;
4. a security role to protect children and the home from external threats; and
5. an interface role to guide and advocate for children in the community and society.

The role of breadwinner in African-American households, while frequently shared with mothers, is often believed by many fathers to be their primary role. For many African-American fathers, being employed supercedes other family responsibilities. However, there has also been a tradition among some black fathers of helping with children and especially of cooking for the family. A number of participants in our groups could recall their fathers, or uncles, or men in the church, for example, who would routinely prepare meals for the family or church affairs. Some remembered summers with grandfathers who did a lot of caretaking of them and nurturing of their self-confidence. The flexibility of African-American men and women to switch roles on occasions and help each other with family responsibilities has been identified by some scholars as a strength of black families (Billingsley, 1992; Boyd-Franklin, 1989).

For African-American men the successful fulfillment of these various roles requires that there also be opportunities for further education and good jobs. The success level in both education and job opportunities for most African-American men remains disproportionately lower than for white men. Therefore, many of their ideals for fatherhood are compromised. Joblessness and underemployment are common and greatly erode black men's confidence in being able to be providers and to be respected within the family and community. Moreover, there is wide speculation that the decline in marriage rates is related to male joblessness; male joblessness also exacerbates black men's relationships with black women (Tucker and Mitchell-Kernan, 1995). One of the first challenges for African-American men in our support groups is to evaluate their personal competence in the areas of employment and education using criteria that are both realistic and honest. The next challenge is to accept one's conclusions drawn from self-assessment or to devise viable alternatives if there is dissatisfaction with the direction one's life is taking.

Masculinity is no longer a simple matter in contemporary society. It is conceptually framed now as a matter of gender-role strain. Despite changing concepts of masculinity, African-American men still live in a society in which there is defensive overconformity to gender stereotypes (Pleck, 1995). Moreover, African-American men are often faced with the imposition of traditional gender identities, coupled with the threat of severe consequences such as being ostracized or ridiculed by the brotherhood of black men when one deviates from expectations (Pleck, 1995).

African-American men continue to contend with unique racial and gender stereotypes. Feelings of victimization caused by experiences of recurring racial indignities, or what Franklin (1993, 1999c) describes as "microaggressions" (e.g., subtle rejections, such as being passed by when hailing a taxi to being discriminated against in employment interviews), are the source of many barriers to success for black males. The gender-role-strain paradigm for African-American men must therefore also be viewed from the perspective of how racism serves as a unifying life theme (Jones, 1997). In this way, gender-role expectations are derived from adaptive responses to life circumstances shaped by the prejudice and discrimination experienced by African-American men. This might be seen, for example, in the cool, "I have it under control," posture of black youth described by Majors and Billson (1992). Fulfillment of male roles is especially complex for African-American men. This is evident in discerning how and when to display appropriate aggressive and assertive behavior, or in choosing which jobs bring dignity to being a family provider and man. Moreover for some African-American men the responsibility of being the family provider can be overwhelmed by the stress of managing and sorting out emotional demands, and the insidiousness of race-coded circumstances that undermine the fulfillment of that role (e.g., the common complaint by African-American men of being passed over for promotion in the workplace because of their race).

Therapeutic support groups can assist black men to better understand and self-manage external social factors, such as racism, as well as internal psychological factors such as disillusionment and self-doubt. Support groups can help the individual to sort out when to hold society accountable for their low level of success and when to hold themselves responsible.

Managing the Invisibility Syndrome

Many African-American men believe that for programs to be effective, they must address what it means to be black and male in today's society. For example, the recurrent theme of "psychological invisibility" experienced by the African-American community in its transactions with the larger society leads to a variety of inner personal conflicts that put the health and well-being of black men at risk. Invisibility is defined as the feeling that one's abilities are not valued or even recognized in the larger society because of prejudice and racism (Franklin, 1993, 1998, 1999c). Respectability and dignity can and do thrive within the African-American community when they are defined by the African-American community. But, when fulfilling family responsibilities depends more upon criteria and opportunities controlled by white, male-dominated institutions, invisibility plays a more prominent, if not insidious, role. In the therapeutic support groups this invisibility paradigm is used to provide a theoretical framework toward formulating clinical insights about issues and treatment strategies for African-American men (Franklin, 1998; 1999c).

Rejecting Negative Stereotypes

African-American men who feel competent as fathers reject the negative societal images that often portray black fathers as uninvolved, unreliable, and uncaring. As Franklin (1999c) concludes from his "Invisibility Syndrome" model, the men who do not conform to those negative portrayals, but are model citizens and fathers, may be discouraged by the negative press. This puts an added burden upon those committed and conscientious fathers of African descent because they experience fewer sources of validation. Many of these fathers voice considerable resentment at being victimized by the public view of black fathers. For example, they complain that they are so often presumed to be uninvolved fathers that school authorities routinely engage mothers about their son's behavior without considering that they would like to be contacted also.

The process of rejecting negative stereotypes is complex, multifaceted, and varies among African-American fathers. However, one necessary component of this "rejection of rejection" process is the availability of defying sets of beliefs, experiences, and examples that contradict those negative stereotypes. In the absence of such alternatives, aspiring fathers are vulnerable to the negative perceptions of black men. Soon a vicious cycle emerges in which both the African-American male and society collude to maintain maladaptive behavior patterns (Davis, 1997). Sociopolitical factors are significant influences in the development of African-American men's views of themselves and fatherhood.

Resistance to Seeking Help

Many African-American men resist seeking help for themselves because their beliefs about masculinity include the idea that real men must solve their problems alone. Therefore, seeking professional services to facilitate self-understanding and better parenting can be identity-threatening. Although black men are consequently often resistant to such services, family and friends often recognize their needs and urge them to get help from these sources. Yet, when men announce that they are going to get help, they may also get conflicting messages from their partners, family, and friends who continue to buy into the idea that real men don't need personal help.

These beliefs about masculinity can undermine motivation and make the few services targeted for African-American men that much more difficult to effect. For example, in some cases men's partners and spouses criticized the establishment of men's support groups, although earlier they had supported them. Some felt there was a greater need for couples' groups dealing with relationship issues. Others felt that the group's discussion would not genuinely touch issues they felt men needed to resolve around trust, power, and control. Family and friends often acted out their apprehensions about men participating in the group, possibly because such participation threatened their feelings of comfort with the status quo. For example, family members would foster men's ambivalence about joining a group by suddenly elevating in importance other family priorities. Consequently, it is not only important to address each man's reasons to resist seeking help but also to be mindful of the ways in which they can be inadvertently undermined by their advocates for getting help.

THERAPEUTIC SUPPORT GROUPS
FOR AFRICAN-AMERICAN FATHERS

We believe the therapeutic support group holds much promise for helping African-American fathers to address some of the issues described in the previous section of this chapter. African-American men can be engaged more readily in this form of intervention by targeting the initial focus of groups on specific concrete tasks and problem-solving issues that are familiar to men. Most African-American men still hold conventional views of fatherhood, even as the gender role change movement strives to challenge traditional paternal attitudes.

A primary objective of therapeutic support groups is to help participants learn that sharing experiences in a mutually supportive way is valuable. Once the group members create a safe environment, sharing can validate or challenge their thinking. Group members can keep one another honest in how they represent themselves.

Case Illustration

A group of twelve men assembled to discuss their efforts to advance their children's chances of success. The group was started because the fathers wanted to become more nontraditional in disciplining and relating to their children. In the group process the men's strengths were deliberately identified. The commonly accepted belief that the man is as responsible for teaching and nurturing the child as is his partner, was also mentioned by many of the fathers. This belief was the source of much confusion over men's roles, as mothers typically take primary responsibility for carrying out daily caretaking tasks for their children. Further complicating these issues, the men observed that assuming a different interest in their children requires a new understanding with their spouses and partners.

The experience of many of these men with their own fathers in the home was that of disciplinarian and provider. This is a traditional paternal role that most of them were familiar with and practiced. However, it was also a role they said they wanted to change, given their childhood experiences. For some of the men, the absence of their own fathers and lack of paternal role models made them feel ignorant about parenting skills. Many of the men questioned whether their knowledge of how to be a father was appropriate.

For example, some of the men identified with the "no nonsense" type of father because it appealed to their sense of being in control of chaotic household circumstances and their children's behavior. It also supported a belief that fathers should be respected by being held in awe. They believed this was the way a father helps balance the mother's more nurturing and indulging role with the children. One of the men in the group, who was inclined to model his behavior after his father, reminisced about his experiences. His tale matched similar stories heard from the other men about their childhood. The following excerpt from a group session captures Mr. Abdul's ambivalence about the parenting style of his childhood, and how it distanced him from his own father.

> **Mr. Abdul:** My old man didn't say much, but you knew when he meant business and not to make him angry.
>
> **Group Leader:** What would happen?
>
> **Mr. Abdul:** He would tear into you. (Several group members nodded and smiled.) I didn't understand then. I just wanted to get from around him. That's why I left home as soon as I got old enough.
>
> **Group Leader:** Sounds like there are a lot of hurt feelings about your father.
>
> **Mr. Abdul:** I know he loved us. That's just the kind of man he was. He didn't take no mess. I try to be different with my boys. I want them to be able to talk to me. We hug a lot. I'll be watching TV, and my boy just come and sit on my lap. I'm a very different dad.

What contributes to acceptance of this father's form of parenting is its consistency with what he learned from the brotherhood in the streets. The understanding is that a brother "takes no mess off of anybody" if he is truly a man. This lesson in male-to-male relations is transferred to the home as a parental stance to control children's behavior, and particularly to parent black male children. Being a man of few words who is held in awe and feared is consistent with the defiant, self-confident street image of "cool" brothers necessary to survival on the streets. Therefore, there is little disagreement about the appropriateness of this paternal style, given its correspondence with conventional wisdom about how black men are to elicit respect from others. Some men see projecting the stern and intimidating father image as a way of conveying strength. The problem faced by Mr. Abdul and others like him is how this paternal style engenders the proper attachment between black fathers and their sons and daughters. Exactly how does a father acting in this manner make children feel toward him, and what does it teach black children about African-American men?

The sharing of experiences between fathers in this group session helped them to learn about similarities and differences in their childhoods that influenced the way they want to be as fathers. They learned how to help one another resolve delicate personal concerns about fatherhood, in particular putting fatherhood into perspective for black men. Their comfort with disclosures as well as their understanding of group process was nurtured when the group leader knowingly voiced unspoken feelings of the fathers. In these early sessions, the support group is as much instructive about appropriate group process as it is a forum to share and discuss intimate vulnerabilities. In the group process the men try to help one another understand by sharing their views and experiences without being defensive. The importance of this process is that with a skilled and sensitive group leader, very personal experiences can be explored and put into a proper perspective, and ultimately elevate the value of the support-group experience.

MAJOR THEMES
TO PROMOTE IN THERAPY

Using Empathy and Tenderness to Promote Resilience

Being able to overcome risks and bounce back from adverse situations and challenges to well-being is what we call resilience. The typical masculine response to adversity is to tough it out with bravado. However, there are other means of managing difficult times. They involve the capacity to be open to others and to feel connected to what others are feeling and thinking. When men display interpersonal openness, which is a manifestation of their own comfort with self, they also attract others to them. We have seen men rely on their empathic nature and consequently draw others to them for supportive advice, learning how to rely upon their own inner strength to weather life's storms and challenges (Franklin, 1999a). For example we have seen men in groups who have endured job layoffs, marital trouble, and trouble with children, who seem to draw on an array of supports that help them through their troubled times. We believe there is something in this capacity to be "empathic" that can act as a curative agent to buffer psychic injury and facilitate the person's ability to bounce back from adversity. Consequently, in our work with men we develop the empathic side of the man and scrutinize the assumed merits of the "macho" side.

Resisting Disengagement from Children

When marriages and relationships have problems and perhaps lead to divorce, resisting disengagement from their children becomes a challenge for African-American men. There are numerous issues black men have about wanting to maintain relationships with their children, and a goal of the support group is to encourage them to keep this commitment and responsibility. The support group becomes an important place, permitting men to explore their attitudes and feelings about fatherhood when they no longer have an intimate relationship with their children's mother. It allows them to address trust, power, and control needs that often get represented as traditional conflicts between African-American men and women but now become manifested in parental concerns. These include, for example, such issues as child support, discipline, visitation rights and expectations, how to raise a male child, being treating with respect, and exposing the children to new relationships. These parenting issues for African-American men are intertwined with the complex relationship issues between black men and women. This includes how the man views his competency in managing the life challenges presented to men of African descent, such as contending with stereotypes about black men and fathers.

Anger is often the source feeding much of the men's resistance to adequately engaging their children. They are mad at the circumstances, frustrated at not being able to control and completely dictate their own terms; they often feel victimized, uncertain about the future of parental commitment and responsibility given the decisions about child custody, the risk of conflicts with their children's mother, and uncertainty of being able to meet parental demands when caring for the children alone. Anger is at the source of too many outcomes from African-American male behavior, and the tendency to disengage from their children is frequently another example of it.

Developing a Family-Oriented Masculinity

Being in roles of helping other people facilitates developing family-oriented masculinity. That is, the helping process fosters values and skills about the importance of assisting others that contribute to restructuring the attributes of masculinity. This is one of the major goals of therapeutic support groups for African-American men, re-structuring the way black men provide support for one another. Men must learn that being seen as resourceful, knowledgeable, and wise (e.g., the way elders are supposed to be perceived) means speaking from a position of strength. This is part of being a strong black man in addition to, and just as important as, being the provider and protector. Such a process begins to reframe and challenge old notions of what it means to be a man.

We have focused on helping fathers view their role as teachers and mentors of the future generation. Their contribution to family must extend beyond providing and protecting. They need to feel that masculinity is about preparing the next generation for leadership roles, elevating the family status, and bettering the future for people of African descent. Some of the traditional ideas about fatherhood still have currency in father training, but they must be adapted to evolving twenty-first century family socialization goals. Emphasis should be on redefining the brotherhood code toward specific empowerment values (i.e., of self and others, particularly family members).

These goals are consistent with fatherhood as a generative activity. Erik Erikson considered generativity as a level of personal development we must achieve to mentor future generations meaningfully. Contemporary views of generative fathering support Erikson's essential beliefs but acknowledge the importance of present-day demands upon gender roles. In this regard, generative fathering presented as a goal to African-American men is tied to their social and psychological realities. Any appropriate interventions must take such realities into consideration to be effective in helping black men to be successful fathers (Allen and Connor, 1997).

Rites-of-passage programs are an example of redefining and encapsulating manhood within African and African-American history and traditions, from which contemporary cultural values have evolved. At the heart of these mentoring and tutoring programs, as well as programs to reconnect fathers with families and children when fathers return from incarceration, is an emphasis on the importance of the role of black fathers. There are a number of small demonstration projects to help the inordinate number of black fathers in jail to maintain a relationship with their children while incarcerated.

We particularly advocate that developing a family-oriented masculinity involves changing the notion that to be a man and father one must have all the authority, power, and control in the family system. The family system will be more effective when authority rests in working partnerships between responsible adults who employ democratic process and prudent child care decision-making. Therefore, one of our objectives in advocating therapeutic support groups for African-American men is to broaden the gender understanding of what a man is supposed to do in the family, so that being a man as well as a father is not so narrowly defined.

Maintaining Positive Self-Views

A positive attitude and outlook on life is essential to being a resilient person. The attitudes that promote resilience are internal, but also are derived from interpersonal encounters. These attitudes or resources seem rooted in the basic human tendency to seek out positive self-views (Sullivan, 1956). Many African-American males construct self-theories that directly oppose the esteem-damaging images imposed by the larger society (Franklin, 1993, 1998, 1999c; Paster, 1994). A number of researchers and theorists have noted this human capacity to evolve and sustain positive self-images (Markus, 1977; Markus and Nurius, 1986; Markus and Wurf, 1987).

One strategy employed in our therapeutic support groups to promote and protect positive self-views is "selective inattention" (Markus, 1977; Sullivan, 1956). Davis (1997) defines selective inattention as the tendency to divert attention away from anxiety-provoking perceptions toward security-enhancing perceptions, as a buffer against racism. We often coach men in our group to take the "glass-half-full" view of life rather than the "glass-half-empty" perspective. It allows the individual to escape preoccupation with the impact of racism long enough to identify and then mobilize other survival resources. Selective inattention generally ameliorates some of the effects of racism but does not eliminate the reality of its existence or its potential emotional consequences. However, redirecting the focus away from the emotional energy needed to buffer racism and toward positive emotional experiences and examples of resilient behavior, is curative.

African-American fathers in our groups have been receptive and at times eager to explore their emotional selves once their attention is focused on positive outcomes. Many quickly refer to episodes in their childhood that characterize their sensitive selves—times when some were painfully labeled as "crybabies," but other times when that sensitivity endeared them to their mother or favorite surrogate parent, or proved useful during their youthful womanizing days. For most of the men, their self-views were tied to their relationship with their fathers as well as their mothers. Whether the men described a limited emotional connection or a close and rewarding relationship with their fathers, they generally concluded from their experiences that emotional intimacy is important in their relationships with their own children. Therefore, regardless of whether they were skillful communicators of their emotions in relation to their children, they worked to remain engaged in the daily routines of their children and to be emotionally accessible. They found it was another way of learning about how they dealt with the world.

These fathers' curiosity about family functioning emerges as another distinguishing feature that strengthens their resistance to the seductions of institutional and cultural racism. This curiosity is the seed that bears a willingness to take emotional and decision-making risks in the performance of paternal duties. African-American fathers with this attitude reach out for external support and develop a social support network that assists them in personal and family problem solving. The social support network, in turn, helps the fathers decipher the secret codes of racism through comparisons, group validation of experiences, and exposure to diverse viewpoints.

"BEST PRACTICES"
FOR IMPLEMENTING SUPPORT GROUPS

There are many African-American men and women who privately acknowledge the need for a support group for black men but do not know how to get men to participate. Most African-American men do not talk about intimate personal issues with one another, and if they do, it is done superficially (Ridley, 1984). This, in many respects, is no different from all other men (Meth and Passick, 1990; Levant and Pollack, 1995). Black men will talk about circumstances that reflect inequities and the ways they feel mistreated in the workplace, at home, or in society. Many African-American men believe that success requires efforts that are far greater for them than for many other groups of men—particularly white men—in spite of competencies and experience. We believe that therapeutic support groups can be a primary intervention in helping African-American men explore these common thoughts and discuss strategies on how to become a more effective parent, partner, and role model in spite of the deep feelings that racism conspires against them. In the following sections, we present our thoughts about "best practices" for developing and implementing these groups.

Starting Therapeutic Support Groups

Group members can come from several sources. For example, an excellent starting point is with an existing program in one's organization or agency in which men are directly or tangentially involved. Building therapeutic support groups for African-American men from a program that they already deem useful capitalizes on consistency with a program's larger mission. Both of the authors have developed groups using this strategy. In an educational enrichment program for middle-school children, fathers who attended achievement events or parent-teacher meetings were encouraged to follow up their voiced concerns about being a "good father" by participating in a group on this issue. Several "rites-of-passage" programs for African-American adolescents used the curiosity of fathers about the experiences their sons were going through to establish special support groups for the fathers. We encourage leaders of programs and services to examine ways in which groups for fathers can be systematically evolved from, and become a part of the routine activity or services provided. One of the best ways is to build on the expressed interests of fathers. Identify and enlist interested fathers to advocate and market the idea of groups to other potential participants.

In those circumstances where there are no existing programs or services out of which groups can be formed, establish them independently on their own merits. This effort may require marketing the value of group to potential participants whose coming must arise more out of their own individual needs. The authors have each initiated groups for African-American men by making professional appeals to individuals, colleagues, and organizations (e.g., churches, places of work, and schools) for persons interested in joining a support group. In some instances other practitioners referred patients in individual or couples treatment for this type of group experience as an important adjunct to therapy. Spousal or partner referrals played a significant part since many black women, sensitive to the struggles of their men, saw the group as relevant for them. Utilizing a male peer network of friends and acquaintances as advocates was also very useful.

Making Group Purpose Relevant

In spite of the numerous legitimate issues for black men to discuss in a group, resistance to participation is high because of the stigma of therapy and mental health services among African-American men. Moreover, resistance to therapeutic support groups also stems from the belief that the need for any therapy-like intervention is a sign of weakness and lessens masculine identity. Therapy suggests that the man cannot manage and solve his own personal problems. To reduce the negativity associated with therapy-like interventions we often frame the groups as dealing directly with the challenges society poses to fatherhood and masculine identity for men of African descent. For example, it was decided in one instance that interest and participation from black men would best be cultivated by forming the group around the stated perspective that since society's treatment and response to the black male's race and gender was a major factor in their life success, it was important that we as African-American men bond together, like village elders, to be able to successfully handle these common but complex issues.

An appeal is often deliberately made to their sense of "brother-hood" and an orientation toward viewing a need for a new approach to fraternal values and fraternal support. One of the primary stated pur-poses of our groups is to empower black men to achieve their personal life goals and to remove personal barriers blocking that objective. Our groups are designed to get black men to pierce superficiality and start genuinely talking and sharing with each other for the welfare of the "village community" and their own.

Screening Candidates

Candidates for these groups should be screened according to some criteria that will maximize the launching and establishment of the groups. We recommend and often meet potential participants in several individual consultation sessions to determine their genuine interest, commitment, and view of how this group will assist them. For exam-ple, in the formation of one group each potential participant was encouraged to discuss the following issues:

1. How have their experiences as black men in society affected them?
2. What do they see as specific issues for black men?
3. Has their race and gender influenced their ability to achieve, and, if so, could they offer personal life examples? and
4. Why do they want to join such a group and what do they expect to gain from it?

They were also asked whether they had any prior experience with individual or group therapy. Persons with chronic mental disorders or substance abuse history must be carefully evaluated to determine whether their illness will unduly dominate and restructure the process and outcomes of the group.

Confidentiality and Commitment

Consultation sessions also focused on the importance of confiden-tiality between group members and voicing commitment to one another to make the group work. Since trust is seen as a sensitive issue between black men, discussing the vital role that confidentiality plays in permitting uninhibited participation from each member is carefully reviewed and assurances about confidentiality must be made.

Candidates are guided to understand that each member must be committed to attend group meetings regularly and to view their commitment to the group as a barometer of their behavior in life. Each group member must pledge to the others to keep the group's commitments and to hold one another accountable.

Establishing Ground Rules and Educating About Process

Since trust, power, and control are fundamental gender and racial issues in the lives of African-American men, agreements were developed about disclosures and sharing of personal information. Ground rules become important in establishing a group experience for black men. They must also address the assumed community wisdom that "we don't air our dirty laundry in public." Rules about disclosures to loved ones, friends, or acquaintances were agreed upon. When a new member joins an existing group we recommend that old members reaffirm the group's rules on confidentiality and be given a chance to discuss their understanding, expectations, and misgivings about how their fellow group members will protect their personal life experiences and how they will be equally responsible.

The meaning and expectations of "commitment" should also be discussed in initial meetings. Early discussions of what commitment means, how each participant understands fulfillment of commitments, and how they have experienced fulfillment of commitments as men of African descent are a good way of achieving consensus to honor the pledge to attend meetings regularly and on time. We have also found that talking about the group process and gaining a collective understanding about the group purpose, goals, and personal interpretations of them during initial meetings facilitates development of group cohesion.

The men should be guided into sharing their particular apprehensions about making disclosures, and the difference between sharing facts and personal vulnerabilities. Carefully explain that the group must have time to coalesce and form a bond before some "serious" issues can be confronted. Often, male participants start groups and expect to plunge into their own fantasies about "problem-solving" the stated goals of the group without realizing the necessity for the group process to evolve. A therapist-led discussion about group process and outcomes is important to maintain reasonable levels of expectations. We also recommend discussing the importance of integrity, and how it determines what each man will personally get out of the experience.

This initial set of focused discussions will educate the men on this type of group process. Our assumption and experience is that most African-American men have not been involved in therapeutic support groups. This education process also lessens the mystique about therapy as a form of "mind reading," or a disarming process that exposes you and makes you vulnerable. For black men, sharing intimate vulnerabilities is not only a great gender taboo but also a taboo of "the brotherhood" because by "opening-up" you are putting your survival skills within a racist society at risk for scrutiny.

Group Leader and Orientation

We have found that having a group leader or therapist who is of African descent is important when working with African-American men in groups (Davis, 1984; Sutton, 1996). For example, a group leader of African descent with particular knowledge and insights into black slang and idiomatic expressions can be mindful of how intentions might be masked in what is commonly known among African Americans as "getting over" behavior (Hecht, Collier, and Ribeau, 1993).

It is also our experience that, for a variety of reasons, using an integrative psychotherapeutic approach in guiding the group process has been most successful. An integrative approach to psychotherapy draws upon different modalities considered most effective for particular presenting issues in treatment (Stricker and Gold, 1993). For example, when the group focused on restructuring interpersonal skills about trust, communication, expressing anger, or stress management, cognitive behavioral techniques were employed. When exploring such issues as source of anger, self-esteem, immobility in career, and relationship commitment the group process followed a more psychodynamic approach. Therefore a particular learned skill of the therapist was relying upon clinical judgment, often consistent with conventions of treatment modalities, for both active and passive interventions.

In addition, understanding the interface of culture and ethnicity with treatment modalities is essential when using an integrative psychotherapeutic approach, and in particular for our work with African-American men. For example, we consider black racial identity development of the men as mediating some of the group process (Franklin, 1999b; Franklin, Carter, and Grace, 1993). This, in general, refers to the degree the men identify with being of African descent, as well as their level of black consciousness or "Africentricity." Variation in levels of identification among the men not only structures their responses to each other and the issues presented, but also their openness to forms of intervention. An internalized ethnic pride and defense of the African-American community, which evolved from contending with racial indignities, contributes to the men's suspicion about the trustworthiness of therapy. Many of the men were initially leery of the therapeutic process and how it would represent them or dispel stereotypes. Starting with these concerns of the men is an example of using a structured-focus approach. As the group process unfolds, utilization of other conventional modalities is adopted as they help achieve the group's goals.

The race and gender match of the group leader can facilitate the process of a group but it does not preclude group leaders with different personal or racial attributes from working effectively with black fathers in groups. Genuineness, commitment, and personal comfort along with professional skill are essential group leader attributes that ultimately determine effective work with black men.

EVALUATION

Evaluation of our groups and approach has been met by several criteria. The first is commitment, as determined by the frequency and duration of attendance by the men in the group. Second is involvement and participation as determined by the degree to which each man engages the group process to resolve their personal issues and becomes more self-empowered. The third is movement of the group process through anticipated evolutionary phases of growth, such as toward group cohesion. And finally, the feedback either directly from group members or indirectly by comments conveyed from significant others that the group member is gaining something from the experience. In some instances our groups are a part of larger programs which allow feedback from other professionals, who, in their interactions with group members, can provide observations about individual growth.

CONCLUSION

In conclusion, working with African-American men in therapeutic support groups to assist them in managing the multitude of challenges they face as fathers as well as men is strongly recommended as an effective intervention. Developing groups within existing services and programs can capitalize on the involvement of fathers or their potential to get involved as a natural extension of programmatic goals. However, establishing groups for black fathers can be creatively achieved in a variety of settings and under a variety of circumstances if the purpose and goals fulfill a need that African-American fathers can identify with. Our success with establishing groups has been built on the general concerns of black fathers and men. For example, many African-American fathers are as sensitive to being misrepresented as a father as they are to being victimized by stereotypes of black men. It is not that most do not want to be "good fathers," but that fathers of African descent often are presented with special challenges, require special skills, and must frequently draw upon inner, many times spiritual, resources to be successful. In learning to be effective fathers, African-American men have suffered from insufficient role models and community guidance along with the burden of the label of irresponsibility.

Much of the claim for African-American fathers' irresponsibility is developed from trend data that show their increasing physical absence from the household (Anderson, 1989). Depending upon the source one uses, approximately two out of three African-American families with children are without a father present. This raises concerns about black men as providers, their ability to support children when in the home and separated. Child support for female, single-parent households among African-American families is low. Marketable skills and employment for African-American men are reflective of educational achievement and workplace opportunities that remain problematic. A disproportionate number of African-American men within the judicial system, where estimates that one out of three black men are either in jail, on parole, or on probation helps shape a cynical and victim world-view in the minds of these men. Incarcerated fathers make up a significant proportion of African-American fathers and create special parenting issues. Many publicly debated circumstances of black men also create the impression and reality that African-American men are filled with anger, suspicion, and feelings of victimization. We believe that our therapeutic interventions with African-American men should be mindful of these issues for black men but not so overpowered by them that we overlook strengths, diversity, and presence of responsible and committed fathers in the community.

REFERENCES

Allen, W. and Connor, M. (1997). An African American perspective on generative fathering. In A. J. Hawkins and D. C. Dollahite (Eds)., *Generative fathering: Beyond deficit perspectives* (pp. 52-70). Newbury Park, CA: Sage Publications.

Anderson, E. (1989). Sex codes and family life among poor inner-city youth. *Annals of the American Academy of Political and Social Science, 501,* 59-78.

Billingsley, A. (1992). *Climbing Jacob's ladder: The enduring legacy of African-American families.* New York: Simon & Schuster.

Bowman, P. J. (1990). Coping with provider role strain: Adaptive cultural resources among black husband-fathers. *Journal of Black Psychology, 16*(2), 1-21.

Bowman, P. J. and Forman, T. A. (1997). Instrumental and expressive family roles among African-American fathers. In R. J. Taylor, J. S. Jackson, and L. M. Chatters (Eds.), *Family life in Black America* (pp. 216-247). Thousand Oaks, CA: Sage Publications.

Boyd-Franklin, N. (1989). *Black families in therapy: A multisystems approach.* New York: Guilford.

Davis, L. E. (1984). Essential components of group work with Black Americans. *Social Work With Groups, 7*(3), 97-109.

Davis, T. (1997). Male engagement: Implications for practice. In A. Carten and J. R. Dumpson (Eds.), *Removing risk from children: Shifting the paradigm* (pp. 243-258). Silver Spring, MD: Beckham House Publishers.

Franklin, A. J. (1993). The invisibility syndrome. *The Family Therapy Networker, 17*(4), 32-39.

Franklin, A. J. (1998). Treating anger in a therapeutic support group for African-American men. In W. S. Pollack and R. F. Levant (Eds.), *New psychotherapy for men: Case studies* (pp. 239-258). New York: John Wiley & Sons.

Franklin, A. J. (1999a). "Insights into resilience by Mississippi African-American male elders." Paper presented at the 107th Annual Convention of the American Psychological Association, Boston, MA.

Franklin, A. J. (1999b). Invisibility syndrome and racial identity development in psychotherapy and counseling African-American men. *The Counseling Psychologist, 27,* 761-793.

Franklin, A. J. (1999c). Therapeutic support groups for African-American men. In L. E. Davis (Ed.), *Working with African American males* (pp. 5-14). Thousand Oaks, CA: Sage Publications.

Franklin, A. J., Carter, R. T., and Grace, C. (1993). An integrative approach to psychotherapy with black/African Americans: The relevance of race and culture. In G. Stricker and J. Gold (Eds.), *Comprehensive handbook of psychotherapy integration* (pp. 465-479). New York: Plenum Publishers.

Hecht, M. L., Collier, M. J., and Ribeau, S. A. (1993). *African American communication: Ethnic identity and cultural interpretation.* Thousand Oaks, CA: Sage Publications.

Jones, J. M. (1997). *Prejudice and racism* (Second edition). New York: McGraw-Hill.

Levant, R. F. and Pollack, W. S. (Eds.). (1995). *A new psychology of men.* New York: Basic Books.

Majors, R. and Billson, J. M. (1992). *Cool pose: The dilemmas of black manhood in America.* New York: Lexington Books.

Markus, H. (1977). Self-schemata and processing information about the self. *Journal of Personality and Social Psychology, 51,* 1293-1299.

Markus, H. and Nurius, P. S. (1986). Possible selves. *American Psychologist, 41,* 954-969.

Markus, H. and Wurf, E. (1987). The dynamics of self-concept: A social psychological perspective. *Annual Review of Psychology, 38,* 296-337.

Meth, R. L. and Passick, R. S. (1990). *Men in therapy: The challenge of change.* New York: Guilford Press.

Paster, V. S. (1994). The psychosocial development and coping of black male adolescents: Clinical implications. In R. Majors and J. U. Gordon (Eds.), *The American black male: His presence, status, and future* (pp. 215-229). Chicago: Nelson-Hall Publishers.

Pleck, J. H. (1995). The gender role strain paradigm: An update. In R. F. Levant and W. S. Pollack (Eds.), *A new psychology of men* (pp. 11-32). New York: Basic Books.

Ridley, C. R. (1984). Clinical treatment of the nondisclosing black client: A therapeutic paradox. *American Psychologist, 39*(11), 1234-1244.

Stricker, G. and Gold, J. (Eds.) (1993). *Comprehensive handbook of psychotherapy integration.* New York: Plenum.

Sullivan, H. S. (1956). *Clinical studies in psychiatry.* New York: W. W. Norton & Company.

Sutton, A. (1996). African American men in group therapy. In M. Andronico (Ed.), *Men in groups: Insights, interventions, psychoeducational work* (pp. 131-149). Washington, DC: American Psychological Association.

Tucker, B. T. and Mitchell-Kernan, C. (Eds.) (1995). *The decline in marriage among African Americans.* New York: Russell Sage Foundation.

Chapter 3

When a Divorced Father Does Not Visit

Geoffrey L. Greif

Father·absence has drawn the attention of social policy analysts, welfare experts, mental health professionals, politicians, and the media. The concerns it raises are numerous and complex. On one hand are child support issues, such as when a single mother and her children land in the welfare system if the father's absence results in his not paying support; on the other hand are the myriad personal and emotional issues that affect children who do not have contact with one of their living parents. The absence of the father also can take a toll on the mother, who must fulfill a number of roles on her own. The purpose of this chapter is to describe one subset of father-absent families—those in which the father does not have contact with his children following a divorce—and to provide potential interventions for working with this "out of touch" father, his children, and the mother.

By the end of the twentieth century, the precipitous rise in single-parent families began to slow. According to the U.S. Bureau of the Census in 1998, single-parent families comprised 27.3 percent of family households, only a slightly higher percentage than in 1990, when the figure was 24 percent, and a much higher percentage than in 1970, when it was 11 percent. Also in 1998, according to the same source, there were 7.7 million single-mother households and 1.8 million single-father households with children under eighteen years of age. Many of these single mothers are raising children who have no contact with their fathers. Estimates as to the number of all fathers who do not visit range from one in ten to two in three (see Furstenberg et al., 1983; Minton and Pasley, 1996) with the Census Bureau placing the figure at approximately one in two (Scoon-Rogers, 1996). Such estimates are usually based on interviews with mothers and occasionally their children, and can be fluid. Respondents may underrepresent or overrepresent contact or not know about clandestine contact between the father and his children. The father's involvement with his children also can change rapidly. Significant family events, such as birthdays, deaths, graduations, remarriages, and weddings can spark new contact and render a previous statement unreliable. Changes in child support payment (sometimes the result of legal enforcement) can also result in a father reestablishing contact with his children.

PSYCHOLOGICAL, SOCIAL, AND ECONOMIC ISSUES FACED BY DIVORCED FATHERS

The issues that the divorced father presents are different in many ways from those presented by the never-married father, who often is less emotionally or financially involved with his children. Divorced fathers, as described in this chapter, have been married to the mothers and have lived in the home with their children. There is usually a strong emotional tie to these family members, as well as to the home and neighborhood. This connection can extend to the school, religious institutions, workplace, and the broader community and is often maintained through financial support of the family. The father's identity and a sense of fatherhood are established in the children's lives through his earlier presence and through his participation in activities with them. Moreover, the children usually have come to rely on him. Although the extent of this reliance can vary by the age of the child and the quality of the relationship, his absence can reverberate through many systems.

In the introduction, Fagan and Hawkins outlined some of the problems experienced by children and mothers due to a father's absence. One overarching problem is poverty, which has been linked to school dropout, teenage pregnancy, and delinquent behavior (see also Smock and Manning, 1997). Emotional problems also may appear. Children need consistency in their lives to develop optimally (Nord and Zill, 1996). When an involved father stops contact, it interrupts that continuity. With very young children, who may not have had a great deal of involvement with a father, his absence may cause less of an immediate problem than with older children who have formed a stronger bond. However, the model that a father provides a child can be an important buffer throughout childhood against the normal stresses of life. When that model is absent, so is a potential source of support.

Once the father leaves the home, he is likely to visit less often over time (Seltzer, 1991). But if he is visiting at one year postbreakup and feels competent as a visitor (i.e., he feels needed), he is apt, according to one source, to be visiting at the three-year mark (Tepp, 1983). Other research confirms that the stronger the father-child relationship, the greater the likelihood of postdivorce involvement (King, 1994). Despite what we know about a child's need for a father from a developmental standpoint, the research is not unanimous regarding the positive influence of a visiting father. One review of thirty-three studies found eighteen studies supporting the hypothesis that children's well-being is positively associated with contact with the visiting father, while nine studies found no correlation, and six found a negative association (Amato and Rezac, 1994). Despite discrepancies in some of the research, experts generally agree that children adjust better to divorce when they have contact with both parents *and* those parents are not in conflict with each other.

In considering the question of contact between father and child, the assumption here is that the father is a competent parent whose presence would be beneficial to the child. I am not advocating that all fathers who have been absent should have contact with their children. Some men are abusive, neglectful, or unwilling to change a self-destructive lifestyle. I am only referring in this chapter to the benefits that can accrue to children of fathers who are interested in reconnecting with their children and are willing to work in adaptive ways toward such a goal.

Men who do not see their children often experience great pain from the loss. Three-quarters of the fathers in the study that forms the basis for this chapter recount feeling angry, guilty, lonely, and abandoned (Greif, 1997). Living away from their children is wrenching for most. These fathers primarily experience role ambiguity, the sense that expectations associated with the role of father are unclear. People who feel unsure of the expectations for their behaviors may experience depression, anxiety, and low self-esteem (Sarbin and Allen, 1968; Van Sell, Brief, and Shuler, 1981). These fathers are constantly faced with doubts about their performance as fathers, an issue of importance to them when they have no contact with their children.

This "nonrole" gets played out every day in different ways. How do they answer one of the commonly asked social questions, "Do you have children?" when they can anticipate that the next question will be asking for specifics about the children? Are they willing to explain to their family, friends, and acquaintances that they are not seeing their children when society stigmatizes such behavior?

The economic issues these fathers face vary greatly. Some are paying child support but not visiting their children, either by choice or because they have been refused visitation. Others are refusing to pay, while still others are not asked to pay. Some fathers want to provide child support but cannot. As mentioned earlier, the role of father has traditionally been packaged with the role of financial provider. Money takes on enormous meaning for these fathers—it can be either a measure of self-worth or a weapon if the family relationships are conflictual.

How Divorced Fathers Lose Contact

When considering interventions with fathers, their children, and ex-wives, we must understand why contact was lost and what is making connection problematic. For the purposes of this discussion, a father with no contact is defined as someone who has not seen or spoken with his children in at least six months. Divorce is often a difficult event that signals a time of transition. New routines must be established. Many issues arise and have to be worked through. These include changing parent-child relationships, physical visitation, telephone contact, potential interparental conflict, and differences in parenting styles (Greif, 1997). When looking briefly at each of these areas, it is possible to understand why a father may cease to have contact with his child.

Parent-Child Relationships

Once the father moves out of the home, he and his children have to establish a new way of relating. This is a major task. It is likely that neither the father nor the children have ever been in the situation before where their interactions have to be scheduled in advance and where time together is limited. In the past, the father and child could spontaneously decide to play catch, go for a walk, or watch a TV show together. Now they must work to find commonalities. Interactions that were happenstance take on new meaning. They need to encapsulate "fun time," serious "talk time," and unstructured time (where they may be in the same home or apartment but engaged in separate activities).

What if the father and child have trouble continuing a relationship under these circumstances? Suppose the father or child is uncomfortable with this level of intensity? If they have not been close, they have little on which to build. As Tepp (1983) suggests, a father who feels competent and needed as a father figure is more apt to stay involved. Yet, the older the child is, the less apt he or she is to openly demonstrate a need for the father. Extrafamilial activities will draw the older child's attention. By the time the child is a teen, the peer group looms as an attractive alternative to spending time with either parent. If teens are distancing themselves developmentally from parents with whom they are sharing a residence, such a separation is more extreme with a visiting parent. Stress or discomfort in the father-child relationship can lead to a further diminution in contact.

Physical Visitation

Linked to the emotional issues of the father-child relationship are issues related to arranging time together. Many barriers can arise. Schedules may conflict as work and homework crises develop, or as social opportunities appear. For example, if the child is invited to a party on a Friday night when visitation with her father is slated, does the father get to see her at a different time? If the father and child are living in different cities, a disabled car or a mechanical glitch on an airplane can wreak havoc in a carefully planned visitation weekend. If interruptions happen frequently, they will affect the relationship, particularly if each missed visitation takes on great emotional meaning as a metaphor for other losses in the relationship.

Struggles Concerning Telephone Contact

Many people are uncomfortable with the phone or only wish to use it on certain occasions, yet this is often a primary means of communication. Some families may only have one telephone line into the home with multiple users for that line. Some homes do not allow for a quiet space where meaningful conversations can take place. If a father and child are feeling uncomfortable with each other, trying to work out a relationship on the phone can add to the discomfort. Telephone contact that was court mandated or informally agreed upon easily begins to feel stilted or forced, and may leave both parties feeling neglected or rejected.

Interparental Conflict

Any struggles a father and his children are having can be affected by the custodial mother. The mother can simplify or complicate the visiting father's relationship with his children. Does she foster visitation? Or does she overtly or covertly impede it by speaking disparagingly of the father, "forgetting" when he is coming to pick up the child, or not preparing the child for an overnight by helping to pack a suitcase? Child support can further complicate the father's relationship with his children. For example, if the father is in arrears, the mother may prevent visitation even though this is illegal in many states (Czpanskiy, 1989). If the child gets drawn into a battle over support payments, the money paid or withheld may become equated with love in the child's mind. For example, when a payment is not made a child may feel that if he or she were worthy of love, the father would be paying support.

Interparental conflict is often fueled by unresolved feelings that divorced parents have for each other. Decisions about visitation and childrearing are viewed through the lens of these unresolved feelings so that, for example, when a father is financially withholding from the children, the mother is reminded of how financially withholding he was with her. The father's purchase of gifts for the children may be seen as an attempt to buy love if that is the way the mother viewed his behavior in their marital relationship. If the marital relationship was verbally abusive, the father may be especially sensitive if the mother shouts at the children. In essence, past unresolved issues affect the present parenting of the children.

When these issues are allowed free reign, contact between the father and child can be jeopardized. The father may find it too upsetting to visit, while the child will sense conflict and may want to avoid this triangle by not visiting his or her father.

Differences in Parenting Styles

Disagreements about parenting are common even in the strongest marriages. If the marriage has dissolved, the chances are great that the parents' abilities to communicate effectively have been greatly diminished. Significant differences concerning expectations, rules for children, schooling, and religious upbringing can be even more troublesome between divorced parents.

It is especially difficult for parents who have an acrimonious relationship to agree as children's developmental needs change—what they need from their father or mother at one age is quite different from what they need at another age. Parents must adjust to these changes and this may be more difficult for them. For example, a father might be very good at raising a preadolescent daughter but become increasingly uncomfortable being physically close to her during adolescence. In addition, a parent who knows how to discipline a six-year-old may have no idea how to discipline a sixteen-year-old. The result is that the parents may agree on how to raise a six-year-old but not the teenager and have no sound basis of communication to resolve issues that arise.

DIVORCED FATHERS AND CONTACT

My research on 109 divorced fathers who had no contact with their children for at least six months revealed a number of specific reasons for this cut-off (Greif, 1997). The sample of fathers was obtained from members of Parents Without Partners who responded to a survey targeting parents who had not had contact with their children following divorce. Over twenty fathers were interviewed in depth. The sample is not representative of all divorced fathers, and other family members were not interviewed to learn about their experiences. The sample did provide insight into fathers who are interested in discussing parenting issues. It also may have been representative of the kinds of fathers who seek assistance from mental health practitioners.

The most common reason for the lack of contact, according to the fathers, was that the mother was interfering with his relationship with the children. Many fathers believed their ex-wives were poisoning the children against them or that they were blocking their access to the children by making physical or telephone contact difficult. Richard Gardner (1987) has coined the term "parental alienation syndrome" to characterize the systematic turning of the children against the other parent. It is this interference that leads to or is the result of interparental conflict and differences in parenting styles.

Fathers also withdrew from their children because they felt they were inadequate parents. A father battling substance abuse may believe his children are better off without him. An unemployed father may withdraw because he believes fathers are only worthwhile to their family if they can be financial providers. There are also fathers who withdraw when the mother of the children remarries. If the stepfather appears more competent or successful, the father may feel inadequate. An inability to pay child support may also cause a father to drop out.

Geographical distance was also mentioned as a reason for withdrawing (see also Arditti and Prouty, 1999). After divorce, parents' lives go on. Either parent may remarry or relocate for work. Such moves make visitation more difficult to arrange. If other problems already exist for the family (interparental conflict, differences in parenting, etc.), contact can wither on the vine.

Fathers sometimes stop contact because of accusations of child abuse. In these extremely upsetting situations, a father may have been falsely accused of physical or sexual abuse or correctly identified as an abuser. Abuse is, unfortunately, all too common. Among the fathers I interviewed, however, many claimed to have been falsely accused. As this is not a random sample of all divorced fathers but one drawn from the membership of Parents Without Partners who voluntarily responded to a questionnaire, it is difficult to interpret the meaning of the frequency of such accusations. It may be that fathers who are falsely accused are more apt to try to prove to themselves and others that they are good parents and join such groups for that approval. A typical situation, I was told, would be that the mother would make the accusation because she was angry with the father. Sometimes there would be corroboration by the child. An investigation would follow, during which time the father would be unable to visit. The investigation would take a few months and conclude with the father being exonerated. However, enough of an emotional wedge would have been driven between the child and father by the accusation and the separation that the resumption of a relationship would be difficult. (For more on this issue, see Chapter 9.)

Finally, contact with the father can cease because the children are not interested in seeing him. As children's needs change (Nord and Zill, 1996), their perceptions about their parents shift as well. They may not want to be with a father whom they perceive to be unfaithful, unloving, or unsupportive. At the same time, their connections to peers take on new meaning. In some cases the mother may be encouraging contact but to no avail. Some fathers I have interviewed are cut off from one child while maintaining contact with others, thus emphasizing the importance of the children's perspective in the question of father-child contact. As children reach their teens in particular, they make individual decisions about the noncustodial father. Many parents overtly or covertly show favoritism for one child over another. A child who feels unloved may be less willing to go out of the way for contact with the father. Others feel more intensely the tension and acrimony between their parents. A sibling who feels more favored and unfazed by parental acrimony may choose to stay involved.

Many fathers do not stay involved. A social exchange approach is one way to theoretically conceptualize the father's lack of involvement with his children. Braver and associates (1993) contend that when the costs outweigh the benefits for a certain pattern of behavior, that pattern will stop. Thus, when a father is finding that the "costs" of staying involved are too great, he may stop visiting. It takes a committed, loving, and loved father to overcome the obstacles to contact. It takes a mother who is invested in the father's remaining involved with the child, and it takes a child who communicates that the father is valued.

CLINICAL ISSUES IN RECONNECTING DIVORCED FATHERS TO THEIR CHILDREN

How can the absent divorced father be reconnected to his children in an adaptive way? A number of interventions can be considered to involve him, if he is interested. Two such case examples, those of

John, who ceased contact because of alcoholism, and Sylvester, who was accused of being abusive and denied contact, illustrate common situations confronting the mental health practitioner. Versions of these cases appear in my book, *Out of Touch: When Parents and Children Lose Contact After Divorce.*

Case Example Number 1

John had a résumé that read like that of a regional star in management—a PhD in education, and an exemplary work history. He was articulate, bright, and presented himself as warm and supportive to his staff. But there was one major problem. He was an alcoholic. He told me that before he sobered up he lived in constant fear. That fear affected his relationship with his co-workers, his wife, and his son. He arranged his work schedule around his drinking. He tried to arrange his home schedule around his drinking, too, but that was impossible.

John's wife divorced him, and because of the fear that was now ruling his life, John withdrew. As he needed his son's approval, he refused to see him for three years. He didn't want to be seen as an alcoholic: "I was ashamed of who I was so I stayed away." It was not until he went to AA that he began to consider visiting again.

John fits the stereotype of the father who voluntarily drops out and stops seeing his children, with one key exception—he did care about his son. It was, in part, this caring that convinced John that his son would be better off without him. This could be construed as a loving, even generative stance—protecting his child from the problems caused by his alcoholism. John also could have been operating under the misguided perception that fathers do not play a significant role in the lives of their children. Parents with problems, such as alcoholism, often feel that they are unlovable. Rather than be rejected by their children, they withdraw first.

With time and sobriety, John has begun to see his son again. But it is an uncomfortable reconciliation and one that is still troubled. John's son, with whom I spoke briefly, is not ready to talk about his view of his father.

Case Example Number 2

Sylvester met his wife, Sharon, in high school. They did not marry until they were in their mid-twenties, after he finished a stint in the army and began working as a machine operator and she as a teacher. "The marriage was great at first. But after a year, I had a spinal cord injury that put pressure on the relationship. Then she discovered she had an infertility problem, which put further pressure on us. We decided to adopt, and the adoption process placed an additional strain on the marriage because of the anxiety of waiting. There was also a problem with adoption fraud where we lost money."

The couple finally was able to adopt, and both bonded very easily with their first daughter. They adopted a second daughter a year later but experienced problems bonding with her. She was cranky, slept little, and cried a great deal, which further stressed their relationship. Then Sylvester's health deteriorated once more: "I had another catastrophic injury which required major surgery. I was unable to work much, and, while that permitted me time with the children, it was a financial strain on the family."

The number of problems the family was facing began building to the breaking point. Marriage counseling was attempted from time to time, but when their youngest child was two, Sylvester came home and found that Sharon had left with the children. Her parents were in town for a visit, and Sylvester concluded that they had been planning this move for some time.

Sylvester sounds like many divorced men I have interviewed. He was unaware of the problems brewing or never took them seriously because he was focusing on the external issues of trying to support the family rather than the internal issues of trying to improve the marriage. "I was too busy trying to make the bills and didn't know what was happening between us."

Sharon hired a lawyer, removed money from the bank account, and began custody proceedings. Sylvester sought joint custody because his lawyer advised him he had no chance of winning sole custody. He won and began paying child support, but, despite the court order, had trouble arranging visitation. Sharon complained that the children were having adjustment difficulties when they spent the night with him. Sylvester, who still lived in the family's original home, avoided taking the children there during visitation because he believed that would be too upsetting for them. "It was hard spending time with them in someone else's home, though at least at my parents' it wasn't too bad. It began to affect the closeness I had with my daughters. It became extremely upsetting for me. I would call every night, and then it was decreed I was calling too much, so it was reduced to three times a week. Sometimes Sharon would even block that."

Sharon's efforts to impede Sylvester's contact with the children escalated. "She accused me of sexually abusing the children. She had tried to modify visitation—she had a medical background and it was easy for her to draw from this with the false accusations. She tried a number of times until it was successful. I went for a long time without seeing them while the court straightened things out. I finally got the abuse charge dismissed at the grand jury level. By this time, they needed to see a psychologist to figure out if it was okay for them to see me after going for two years without us having contact. I got to see them once before she moved to a new state and started new allegations of sexual abuse."

I questioned Sylvester about why she would plant ideas in the children's heads about abuse. "I don't know if she wanted to punish me or gain control. She always had issues of control. It was always a women-against-men kind of thing in her family." At my request, he sent me copies of court documents covering a seven-year period. Evaluations of the children included a review of seventy-four separate documents, projective tests, and interviews. The significant conclusions drawn from the review include two findings: (1) Both children are firmly convinced that their father molested one of them; and (2) Sharon contributed intentionally or unintentionally to their alienation from Sylvester.

The recommendation was that Sylvester and the children, with the assistance of a therapist, begin supervised visitation for short periods of time and that both parents receive counseling.

Working with fathers in these two situations entails following clear theoretical guidelines constructed on practice experience. Wisdom must guide the practice, as the cases are often quite complex. I have included these two cases in my discussion because they encompass many of the issues that fathers face when they are not visiting.

Intervention Strategies

I have found that when family members are interested in reconnection, a Structural Family Therapy approach coupled with a Bowenian approach can be effective. Each approach focuses on different aspects of family functioning.

The Structural Family Therapy approach, stemming from the seminal work of Salvador Minuchin (see, for example, Minuchin, 1974; Minuchin and Fishman, 1981), is based on the belief that families function the most effectively when there is a parental (or other adult) subsystem in charge of the family. In addition, the family needs to have boundaries around it that make it distinct from other families. The concept of boundaries is also used to describe the space between family members. Minuchin conceptualizes boundaries as being on a continuum between enmeshed at one extreme and disengaged at the other. When families are enmeshed, they are tightly linked and there is little individual autonomy. Disengaged families tend to provide little sense of connection and nurturance. If a family does not have a parental subsystem with a clear boundary around it, children can be pulled into parental conflict and become triangulated with the parents.

Interventions in Structural Family Therapy are geared toward putting a parental hierarchy in place and building boundaries that allow for the growth and development of family members. The past is not explored in depth, as Minuchin believes that the past is manifest in the behaviors displayed by the family. The focus is on the present (Minuchin, 1974). Family problems are brought into the therapy session when family members are asked to reenact the conflict before the practitioner. The practitioner then introduces new possibilities for resolving the problem, while also attempting to build a family system in which the adults are in charge.

Murray Bowen's (1976) Family Systems approach takes a slightly different tack. Bowen believes that family members are most functional when there is a good balance between their thinking and feeling, so that a person is not driven by emotions (Nichols and Schwartz, 1998; Kerr and Bowen, 1988). Minuchin explores enmeshment and disengagement, while Bowen considers the similar concepts of fusion and differentiation. However, the goal for Bowen is differentiation, the ability to act independently of one's family history and separate thinking from feeling. Triangulation is a manifestation of a lack of differentiation.

Interventions in Bowenian theory are geared toward reducing anxiety and aiding differentiation. Family members are asked to consider their family history in light of repeating patterns of behavior from previous generations. These include the tendencies to triangulate (Nichols and Schwartz, 1998). The couple, rather than the whole family, is the target of change. Once the couple differentiates itself from each of their families of origin, they can deal more effectively with the children.

Using these two theories, work with the father who wants to reconnect with his children can focus both on boundary issues and the inherited patterns of behavior that may be affecting the father's behavior with his children and his ex-wife. In most of the 109 cases on which I have data, the father was interested in reconnecting. Eighty percent described themselves as "very involved" or "involved" with the children during the marriage, and within this group almost the same number said they were unhappy about not seeing the children (Greif, 1997). When asked specifically about reconnecting with their children, 87 percent of the fathers said they were interested in having contact (Greif, 1995). Obviously, a desire by the father is a prerequisite for intervention.

Basic Assumptions and Values Informing This Approach

John Snarey's view of generative fathering is instructive in considering father-child contact. In Snarey's view, generative fathers are "men who contribute to and renew the ongoing cycle of the generations through the care they provide as birth fathers [biological generativity], childrearing fathers [parental generativity], and cultural fathers [social generativity]" (1993, p. 1). Drawing on Eriksonian theory, Snarey believes that parental generativity, a particularly important link here, entails "carrying out childrearing activities that promote children's ability to develop their full potential in terms of realizing a favorable balance of autonomy . . . initiative . . . industry . . . and identity" (1993, p. 21). Healthy father-child involvement is beneficial not only to the father and child but also to society as a whole—to present and future generations. As the father grows comfortable in his role, his children will prosper. Another benefit of the father's comfort with his children may be the enhanced psychological welfare of the mother (Doherty, Kouneski, and Erickson, 1998), who benefits through seeing her children thrive. Ideally, all family members gain. The goal of interventions for this population of divorced fathers who do not have contact with their children is to reestablish contact so that the fathers can achieve this generativity.

A second key assumption is that divorce forces parents and children into a terrain for which they have little preparation and, by its very nature, is usually quite stressful. As Maccoby and Mnookin (1992) point out, the crumbling of the family has often started prior to the separation and divorce. The divorce and subsequent attempts to co-parent may be marked by the continuation of a dysfunctional situation that has been ripping the family apart for months or years. Two new and untested family structures (the single mother-child and the noncustodial father) replace the old one. If the family disintegrates to the point at which the father is no longer contacting his children, significant events must have occurred that have caused the family great pain. Therefore, interventions should be attempted with great care.

As Ihinger-Tallman, Pasley, and Buehler (1995) suggest, some role saliency has to be established for the father to feel comfortable. They state, "When a father loses the daily, routinized, familiar opportunities to parent after divorce, his identity as a father is expected to be affected" (p. 68). The father who wants to reestablish contact needs to have meaningful interactions with the children that result in his and their believing that his presence is necessary and beneficial. If the contact is only related to providing financial assistance, role saliency is less likely to be established.

Structural Family Therapy, with its assumptions about dysfunction stemming from a lack of hierarchy and boundaries, is especially useful in these situations. As it is the welfare of the children that drives the treatment, it is a realignment of the parental relationship that becomes the cornerstone. The goal is for parents to present a united front and prohibit any triangulation. What is valued in both this and Bowen's model is clear, emotionally unencumbered communication. Although the Structural Family Therapy technique approaches communication behaviorally, working in the present, Bowen's Family Systems Therapy approaches it, in part, by asking each adult to gain insight from the past.

In sum, work with these families is based on the recognition of the importance of the father to the well-being of the family. It also appreciates the stressful nature under which interventions occur and the need for the interventions to build family leadership, communication, and an appreciation of the many responsibilities that a father has beyond economic providing.

Explicit Approaches and "Best Practices" Used to Work with Noncustodial Fathers

The approaches will vary based on a full-family assessment, the father's desire to see the children, the children's desire to see the father, and the history of their relationship. As mentioned, a Structural Family Therapy approach is recommended for its emphasis on clearly defined boundaries and hierarchy. In this therapy model, families are believed to progress best when the parental subsystem is united and closed to intergenerational (child) interference. With single-parent families, children of divorce will fare better if their parents agree on expectations for the children and can work in tandem to teach those expectations to the children as well as enforce them. With this model as a guide, a number of key interventions can be attempted, given a willingness of the family members to reconnect with or attempt to reach out to the other party.

First, the practitioner, depending on the animosity between the father and the child (and the age of the child), should encourage written communication. Ideally, the father, as the adult—even if it has been the child who has refused contact—should initially write (reestablishing hierarchy). This can be by e-mail or letter. The communication should be age appropriate, should not comment on the role of the mother in the relationship (boundary issue) and should avoid touching on emotional issues. Contact may initially have to go through the mother, depending on the situation. A statement could be, "I know we have not seen each other for awhile and for a number of reasons. I would like to meet with you to talk about these things and to discuss how our relationship can improve in the future. Would you be willing to speak with me and arrange a meeting if I call?" (If the father has absented himself, the child may be writing first and may need help with expressing feelings.)

The next step is to arrange a meeting. It is common for some level of animosity to exist between once-married parents. Given the nature of these particular relationships, in which the father has had little contact with the children, the likelihood is that the animosity might be quite significant. The practitioner working with any of the parties involved can help those parties to "tune in" to what each family member is feeling. This is preparatory work and involves asking the person present to talk about feelings. This is followed by asking that person to consider what the ex-spouse may be feeling prior to and during the meeting. Helping each family member to "think through" his or her position and the position of the ex-spouse is a way to tap into the less emotional sides of the conflict. Madden-Derdich and Arditti (1999) suggest asking divorced spouses to consider what their relationship "should" look like as a way to explore congruency in expectations. If their expectations are not similar, efforts at reconciliation may be impaired.

The wounds from the relationship may be quite deep and it is incumbent upon the practitioner to help the family member consider the range of issues that might be raised during any reconciliation meeting. Some practitioners use the concept of forgiveness to help a client who has been hurt by another person to put the hurt in the past (DiBlasio, 1998). This technique may be appropriate here. With proper anticipation and preparation, it is less likely that a meeting will get out of control. Legal issues also may need to be clarified in advance, so that alimony, child support, and visitation rights do not become barriers to discussion at a time when reestablishing contact with the children is the primary purpose.

At the meeting, all parties should be coached in how to talk to each other without being accusatory. Role playing in advance can help with this. Past issues do not have to be resolved—the focus should be on the present and future. Expectations should be kept low for the meeting and each party should not expect a great deal of physical touching or verbal expressions of love. If a great deal of time has elapsed since the father and children have seen one another, each should be aware of the enormous physical changes that have occurred since they last met. The mental health practitioner should try to keep the number of people present to a minimum. Unnecessary cousins, grandparents, or other relatives, unless they are directly involved as caretakers or are especially important to the children, should be excluded so that extraneous issues are not brought into the meeting. Finally, the practitioner should encourage the father and child to move slowly. Such reconciliations should be a step-by-step process. Moving slowly allows people to process the changes that are unfolding.

It is particularly important for the children in these situations not to assume blame for their parents' break-up or to be "triangulated" between the parents as these reunifications unfold. The mother and father should be clear at this meeting that their marital issues do not diminish the parenting responsibilities that each still has to the children. Children should be supported if they do not feel comfortable accepting a gift from the father. They should be encouraged to express their feelings, and the father should be taught how to listen to them nondefensively. Finally, an unintended consequence of a reunification between father and children may be that the mother feels ignored or unappreciated when they want to see the father again. The mother should be apprised of this common reaction in advance so that the experience is normalized for her.

Not all fathers will initially be interested in reconnecting with their children. It may be the child, mother, or possibly a grandparent who is making the initial overture. The father may need convincing that it is valuable to him to reconnect. If the father has absented himself because of the actions of the ex-spouse or children, the discussion will have to reassure him that the situation that led to his absenting himself has changed. If he has absented himself because of his own self-doubts, he will need a great deal of reassurance. (In cases where there has been a history of abuse, an independent evaluation of the father's competence to interact with the child should be undertaken prior to the contact.) If the child has refused to see the father, the reasons for the change in the child's desire to see the father will have to be explained. The father will have to feel he is important to the child as a *father* and is not being sought out as a source of child support, college tuition, or as a compatriot in a battle with the mother.

The importance of the mother's role in the reconnection cannot be overemphasized. She can facilitate or block the incipient relationship between the father and children. She must be involved in a manner that values and upholds the caregiving she has provided the children during the father's absence.

In addition to the concrete approaches suggested once visitation has begun, the time the father spends with the child should be structured. Men feel more comfortable with specific tasks than with vague guidelines about what to do with their children. Activities should initially be planned that will reinforce the father's parenting abilities.

Depending upon the willingness of the mother, she may help by informing the father regarding the types of activities the children enjoy. Whether the father needs help with parenting in general or with specific information about his children will depend upon the length of time that has expired since he has seen the children and his general knowledge and comfort level. This intervention will also attempt to draw a boundary around the parental subsystem for the benefit of the children, a Structural Family Therapy notion. In this way, the father will begin to redefine himself as a father.

Independent work with the father can also focus on family-of-origin issues, in which the father tries to identify patterns of abandonment and connection that have existed in prior generations (Bowen, 1976). Fathers tend to blame the "system" or their ex-spouses for their lack of contact rather than looking for familial patterns that may have an effect on their behavior. This externalizing behavior will make reconciliation and reconnection more difficult. By exploring these patterns and asking the father to think about his own family processes, he may be helped to differentiate from his own family of origin if he has not already. Whether he was forced out of the picture or stepped out on his own, this will help him put his own behavior and reactions in some broader familial context. Until that happens, he may continue to repeat behaviors that make connection problematic.

Specific interventions will vary by the case presented and must take into account the ethnic, racial, economic, and religious background of family members. The case studies previously described suggest the following interventions:

> **John**—John will need to be convinced of his importance to his son. Given his education, he would be a prime candidate for bibliotherapy (this book perhaps) as well as family-of-origin work. It is hypothesized that the importance of the father to the family was never learned in his own family. He also may have been raised in a family that regarded members not performing up to the highest standards as failures. And, perhaps, failures were supposed to absent themselves. In addition to dealing with these issues, he needs to be helped to accept himself. In accepting himself, he will be giving permission to those he loves to accept him while also sending the message that they do not have to be perfect themselves.

Sylvester—The work here is more systemic, more long-term, and less clear-cut. Without obtaining supervision of his visitations with his children, not much will change. Sylvester will need to take a long-term approach to his relationship with his children, as nothing will change quickly, despite the ruling of the court concerning visitation. He will need to accept having a neutral person supervise the time he and the children spend together until the children are psychologically able to be with him alone. If they believe he abused them, it may take years for them to feel safe with him. Sylvester should go so far as to incorporate the supervisor of visitation into his plans so that, from a Structural Family Therapy position, he and the supervisor (the adults) will have formed a supportive hierarchy of parenting. If he battles with the supervisor, he will be recreating a split in the parental hierarchy he is trying to establish. He will also need to guard against attacking Sharon, as that will only make the children feel more fragile.

Outcomes That Can Be Expected from the Interventions

These are relationships and family situations that have failed to be resolved. By their nature they are very complicated, and involve family members who are unaccustomed to communicating effectively. Success in resolving such long-standing and deep-rooted difficulties is hard to achieve. While Structural Family Therapy has been found to be successful in treating certain problems (see Minuchin, Rosman, and Baker, 1979), when it is applied to situations in which a parent and child have been out of touch, predictions about reunification are difficult to make.

Factors that would suggest favorable outcomes are: the age of the child, with older children increasing the likelihood of reunification; visitation by other children with the father; the occurrence of a significant family event that could offer an opportunity (or a lucky excuse) for contact and change; a commitment by the father or child to change either their desire for contact or their perception of the other party; a change in the mother's behavior if she has been a significant factor; or legal intervention that compels contact (Greif, 1997).

In essence, sound clinical work based on a Structural Family Therapy approach and a Bowen Family Systems approach that asks the father to examine his own past can offer opportunities for facilitating a reunification when other factors (such as a desire for reunification by the father and child, at least a minimal level of willingness for reunification by the mother, and a past history of father-child interaction that is not marked by abuse) are in place. Programs and rhetoric that are targeted at father involvement can build a culture for fathers in general that may influence this population of out-of-touch fathers.

Major Barriers to Involving Fathers in These Interventions and How We Can Reach Out

A major barrier to involving fathers is the fathers' perception that they are unimportant to their children. They are often the ones who are controlling contact and are refusing to visit, call, or write their children. One survey shows that men view themselves as less integral to the family than women (Families and Work Institute, 1995) and are not engaged and as accessible in the home as mothers (Pleck, 1996). Men tend to construct, with the help of women and society in general, a view of their contributions to the family as being primarily economic, although this perception is changing.

To a smaller degree, the mother's interference is perceived by the majority of fathers as the reason for the lack of contact. As mentioned, whatever intervention is attempted with these fathers will have to include her in a meaningful way. If the child begins to want more time with the father and the mother feels left out as a result, she will need support. The danger with any parenting program or media approach that systematically asks fathers to be more involved is that the importance of mothers will be given short shrift. If this happens, the family structure will be weakened and will ultimately hurt the child's sense of self.

CONCLUSION

This most difficult of populations has, for generations, troubled mental health practitioners, policymakers, educators, and others concerned with the welfare of children. Divorced and absent fathers have been a lightning rod for society's ills and are blamed for everything from problem behavior in their children and the economic instability of single mothers to the decline of many neighborhoods. Ample evidence exists to show that these charges are not always unfounded.

Bringing these fathers back into contact with their children is not always possible or warranted, particularly when there has been a history of abuse. Yet many fathers wish for greater inclusion than they have now and would provide their children enormous benefits. However, barriers do exist. The fathers often feel unwanted, insignificant, or prevented from greater involvement.

This chapter offers an understanding of how some of these tenuous relationships have evolved and suggests ways to mend them. We have heard from a number of fathers who are interested in a reconnection. The group of fathers that is more difficult to understand and reach are those who have dropped completely out of sight, who do not participate in surveys, and whose voices are not heard here. We also must find ways to reach them and keep this most important father-child connection alive.

REFERENCES

Amato, P. R. and Rezac, S. J. (1994). Contact with nonresident parents, interparental conflict, and children's behavior. *Journal of Family Issues, 15,* 191-207.

Arditti, J. A. and Prouty, A. M. (1999). Change, disengagement, and renewal: Relationship dynamics between young adults and their fathers after divorce. *Journal of Marriage and the Family, 25,* 61-81.

Bowen, M. (1976). Theory in the practice of psychotherapy. In P. J. Guerin (Ed.), *Family therapy: Theory and practice* (pp. 42-90). New York: Gardner Press.

Braver, S. L., Wolchik, S. A., Sandler, I. N., and Sheets, V. L. (1993). A social exchange model of nonresidential parent involvement. In C. E. Depner and J. H. Bray, (Eds.), *Nonresidential parenting: New vistas in family living* (pp. 87-108). Newbury Park, CA: Sage.

Czpanskiy, K. (1989). *Report of the Special Joint Committee on Gender Bias in the Courts.* Annapolis, MD: Administrative Office of the Courts.

DiBlasio, F. A. (1998). Decision-based forgiveness within intergenerational treatment. *Journal of Family Therapy, 20,* 75-92.

Doherty, W. J., Kouneski, E. F., and Erickson, M. F. (1998). Responsible fathering: An overview and conceptual framework. *Journal of Marriage and the Family, 60,* 277-292.

Families and Work Institute (1995). *Women: The new providers.* Whirlpool Foundation Study. Benton Harbor, MI: Whirlpool Foundation.

Furstenberg, F. F., Peterson, J. L., Nord, C., and Zill, N. (1983). The life course of children of divorce: Marital disruption and parental contact. *American Sociological Review, 48,* 665-668.

Gardner, R. (1987). *The parental alienation syndrome and the differentiation between fabricated and genuine child sex abuse.* Creskill, NJ: Creative Therapeutics.

Greif, G. L. (1995). When divorced fathers want no contact with their children. *Journal of Divorce and Remarriage, 23,* 75-84.

Greif, G. L. (1997). *Out of touch: When parents and children lose contact after divorce.* New York: Oxford University Press.

Ihinger-Tallman, M., Pasley, K., and Buehler, C. (1995). Developing a middle-range theory of father involvement postdivorce. In W. Marsiglio (Ed.), *Fatherhood: Contemporary theory, research, and social policy* (pp. 57-77). Thousand Oaks, CA: Sage.

Kerr, M. E. and Bowen, M. (1988). *Family evaluation.* New York: Norton.

King, V. (1994). Nonresident father involvement and child well-being. *Journal of Family Issues, 15,* 78-96.

Maccoby, R. H. and Mnookin, E. E. (1992). *Dividing the child: Social and legal dilemmas of custody.* Cambridge, MA: Harvard University Press.

Madden-Derdich, D. A. and Arditti, J. A. (1999). The ties that bind: Attachment between former spouses. *Family Relations, 48,* 243-249.

Minton, C. and Pasley, K. (1996). Fathers' parenting role identity and father involvement: A comparison of nondivorced and divorced, nonresident fathers. *Journal of Family Issues, 17,* 26-45.

Minuchin, S. (1974). *Families and family therapy.* Cambridge, MA: Harvard University Press.

Minuchin, S. and Fishman, C. (1981). *Family therapy techniques.* Cambridge, MA: Harvard University Press.

Minuchin, S., Rosman, B., and Baker, L. (1979). *Psychosomatic families: Anorexia nervosa in context.* Cambridge, MA: Harvard University Press.

Nichols, M. P. and Schwartz, R. C. (1998). *Family therapy: Concepts and methods* (Fourth edition). Boston: Allyn & Bacon.

Nord, C. W. and Zill, N. (1996). *Noncustodial parents' participation in their children's lives: Evidence from the Survey of Income and Program Participation. Volume II—Synthesis of the Literature.* Prepared for the Office of Human Services Policy, Washington, DC: U.S. Department of Health and Human Services.

Pleck, J. (1996, June). "Paternal involvement: Levels, sources, and consequences." Paper presented at the Co-Parenting Roundtable of the Fathers and Families Roundtable Series. Philadelphia, PA: National Center on Fathers and Families.

Sarbin, T. R. and Allen, V. L. (1968). Role theory. In G. Lindzey and E. Aronson, (Eds.), *The handbook of social psychology Volume 1* (Second edition, pp. 488-560). Reading, MA: Addison-Wesley.

Scoon-Rogers, L. (1996). U.S. Bureau of the Census, Personal Communication, July 17, 1996.

Seltzer, J. A. (1991). Relationships between fathers and children who live apart: The father's role after separation. *Journal of Marriage and the Family, 53,* 79-101.

Smock, P. J. and Manning, W. D. (1997). Nonresident parents' characteristics and child support. *Journal of Marriage and the Family, 59,* 798-808.

Snarey, J. (1993). *How fathers care for the next generation.* Cambridge, MA: Harvard University Press.

Tepp, A. V. (1983). Divorced fathers: Predictors of continued paternal involvement. *American Journal of Psychiatry, 140,* 1465-1469.

U.S. Bureau of the Census (1998). Household and family characteristics: March 1998. *Current Population Reports,* Series P20-515. Washington, DC: Government Printing Office.

Van Sell, M., Brief, A. P., and Shuler, R. S. (1981). Role conflict and ambiguity: Integration of the literature and directions for future research. *Human Relations, 34,* 43-71.

Chapter 4

Anger Management for Fathers

Charles C. Humphrey
Mark Toogood

After opening the doors to the Fathers' Resource Center in Minneapolis in 1992, founder and director Neil Tift discovered that many of the fathers who were being referred to him for training in parenting skills were ordered there by the courts. These men had been brought to the attention of the court because of incidents involving various degrees of abuse toward their children and/or the mothers of their children.

Tift was quick to realize that these men needed to develop skills to help them better manage their anger and enlisted the authors of this chapter to create a program to meet this need. The result was a psychoeducational, multicomponent program that follows a cognitive-behavioral model and which draws heavily on the works of Ellis (1993); Novaco (1975, 1976, 1977, 1978); Stosny (1995); McKay, Rogers, and McKay (1989); Tavris (1982); Gaylin (1989); and Charlesworth and Nathan (1985), among others.

Participants in the program attend sixteen weekly sessions. Each session lasts two and a half hours and focuses on one of the corresponding sixteen components of the curriculum outlined in "Dealing with Male Anger: A Model of Constructive Engagement" (Toogood and Humphrey, 1998). This curriculum is divided into a facilitator manual and an accompanying workbook from which homework assignments are made. Groups can vary in size, although eight to twelve members represents an optimal range.

THE PSYCHOLOGICAL AND SOCIAL FOUNDATIONS
OF ANGER MANAGEMENT

Anger is, perhaps, the most complex of all human emotions. It has also been one of the least studied. However, there is a growing body of literature on the subject. In building an anger management program for fathers, we began with an extensive review of the existing literature to develop a suitable working definition of anger and to broaden our understanding of its associated behaviors and any related explanatory concepts.

What Is Anger?

Anger has been defined in various ways depending on the theoretical perspective of the particular researcher or theorist. Tafrate (1995) has carefully delineated a number of theoretical approaches that have been used in studying anger. For the purposes of a program designed to help fathers effectively manage their anger, we considered definitions containing elements that are easily understood and that are related to the components we determined to be essential to a comprehensive program. We arrived at a definition of anger as *a heightened state of physiological and mental arousal in response to a violation, a threat, or an injustice, real or perceived, to one's self or one's interests.*

Expanding on this definition, we borrowed from the principles for understanding anger cited by McKay, Rogers, and McKay (1989). For example, we explain that anger is a natural emotional response to some things that happen to us. Although it may be difficult to discover what is behind anger, an anger response cues us to the fact that something is wrong. It is also a source of discovery. Respectful expression of anger can help us identify what the anger is about and the primary feelings behind it. It is a normal and positive response to those with whom we are angry and can be made part of an assertive communication style which, when applied, can raise self-esteem through open and direct expression and the assertion of personal boundaries. Anger, appropriately expressed, is a healthy release of energy that might otherwise be directed to its suppression. It can be viewed as a form of protection. Expressing anger for oneself and others openly, directly, and respectfully can preclude its being distorted in ways that force others away.

The Myths

Because the emotion of anger has been so misunderstood, many myths have arisen in an attempt to better understand its nature, origins, and the methods for managing it. A number of these myths have been dispelled or seriously challenged. Here are four noteworthy examples that, based on oft-cited research findings, continue to be held by many practitioners.

Anger Is Biochemical

A commonly held belief among those in the biomedical field is that anger is a biochemical phenomenon caused by hormones or limbic system activity. Testosterone in males and prolactin in women have been linked to aggressive and hostile behaviors (Kellner et al., 1984; Scaramella and Brown, 1978; Konner, 1962). Others have observed that norepinepherine contributes to feelings of anger (Friedman et al., 1960). In our definition of anger, the role of physiology in anger arousal is duly acknowledged. However, following Maranon (1924), Schacter (1971) produced a two-factor theory to more clearly understand the nature of anger. Abundant research supports his view that anger is the result not only of physiological processes, but requires a cognitive interpretation of those processes (Schacter and Singer, 1962; Schacter, 1971; Deschner, 1984).

Anger Is Instinctive

Freud believed that individuals are born with an innate aggressive instinct (Freud, 1962). Anthropologist Ardrey (1966) and ethologist Lorenz (1971) provided data and analyses that were persuasive in supporting this very prevalent belief. However, Leaky (1981) provided equally persuasive evidence to question this belief. The often noted "Seville Statement," issued as a result of the 1986 conference of distinguished psychologists, neurophysiologists, and ethologists, concluded that anger is "neither in our evolutionary legacy nor in our genes." (Kohn, 1988, p. 37). The "Seville Statement" has since been endorsed by both the American Psychological Association and the American Anthropological Association.

Frustration Is Followed by Anger

This is a paraphrase of the Dollard frustration-aggression hypothesis (Dollard et al., 1939). So much evidence has been accumulated to support this hypothesis that it is considered by many to be a law—one of the few that scientific psychology can claim. However, while extremely useful, it does require some qualification. In many cultures, frustration is actually followed by submission, dependence, or avoidance (Whitting, 1941; Bateson, 1941; Dentan, 1968). Even in our culture we see different responses. Some fathers, for example, respond to their children's acts of perceived disobedience with abusive behaviors. Others seek out parenting classes to more effectively modify the behaviors they perceive or interpret as disobedient.

It Helps to "Blow"

Orthodox Freudian psychoanalysts have followed the catharsis hypothesis in helping their clients reduce their anger and aggression. If the libidinal energy which fuels internal conflicts is blocked, they reason, it will result in a multitude of neurotic symptoms. Catharsis is seen as a way of removing some of this emotional energy and is believed, in the case of anger and aggression, to be achieved by angry words and the destruction of objects.

Subsequently, Neo-Freudian theories led to encounter groups, primal scream therapy, and the belief that it is important to just "let it all hang out." The research, however, has not borne this out (Feshbach, 1956; Straus, 1974; Ebbesen, Ducan, and Konecni, 1975; Tavris, 1982). Taken together, the results of these studies would indicate that expressing anger *in this way* can make us even angrier and help to solidify an attitude of general anger.

Distortions of Anger

There are constructive, positive, and healthy ways to express anger. Too often, however, the expression of anger is distorted in ways that can have results similar to "letting it all hang out." Decker (1994) and Tavris (1982) have described some of the ways in which anger can be distorted.

Blaming—"You did this"; name-calling; put-downs; not taking responsibility for oneself and one's feelings; getting on the other person's "case." The responses are usually defensive.

Sarcasm—Devious, ambiguous, and hostile joking at someone else's expense allows us to deny that we really meant what we said.

Vindictiveness—Actions taken so that we do not feel "one down." Getting even for real or imagined "wrongs" done to us.

Viciousness—"Going for the throat," "hitting below the belt," taking advantage of another person's vulnerability; betraying another person's trust; taking pleasure in causing pain in others; intentional cruelty.

Punitiveness—"Punishing" others for what they did to us; "teaching others a lesson" so they will not repeat the behavior we dislike.

Aggression—Pushiness; intrusiveness; bullying; being rude and abrasive; giving orders and commands; completely ignoring others or what others think, feel, and want; violating others' rights.

Sulking—Passively punishing others with a silence that is hostile, controlling, ominous, and threatening.

Manipulation—Controlling others indirectly; getting what we want without having to ask for it directly.

Scapegoating—Yelling or screaming at the kids, our partner, or our pets instead of figuring out where our anger is really coming from and directing it there; taking out our anger or our primary feelings on "targets" who do not deserve to be "dumped on."

Anger and Children

In their book, *When Anger Hurts,* McKay, Rogers, and McKay (1989) describe different fallacies or self-deceptions that can trigger anger toward children. Ellis refers to these as irrational beliefs or forms of "absolutistic, command-oriented thinking" (Ellis and Grieger, 1977, p. 5). The first of these is the "entitlement fallacy." Simply put, this is the belief that because we want something, we ought to have it. The truth is that children's behavior is invariably determined by their own needs.

The "fallacy of fairness" is that children should recognize the rights of others and acknowledge that it is only fair to put others' needs ahead of theirs. However, the father-child relationship is intrinsically unbalanced and unfair. It is unreasonable to expect fairness from children, particularly young children.

The belief that, as fathers, we can change our children's behavior by applying sufficient pressure is referred to as the "fallacy of change." Children are no different from adults in resenting and resisting pressure to change.

The "letting it out fallacy" is the belief that when a child hurts you, he or she should be punished. As McKay, Rogers, and McKay (1989) explain, this is a common and dangerous belief that can lead to over-reaction, physical aggression, and a sense of being out of control. As noted above, the "let it all hang out" approach to dealing with anger has been largely discredited.

The fathers who have come through our program almost universally follow the "spare the rod, spoil the child" principle, even when faced with the overwhelming amount of research data that clearly demon-strate how ineffective and often damaging the results of corporal pun-ishment can be.

The Anger Arousal Cycle

It is generally agreed that anger is a response to some form of stress (McKay, Rogers, and McKay, 1989; Novaco, 1976; Gaylin, 1989). In addition, we subscribe to Schacter's (1971) two-factor theory (dis-cussed previously). In other words, we believe that anger is a two-step process.

Anger arousal begins with the subjective experience that any form of stress provokes. But the two-factor theory states that this stress, while a necessary condition for anger arousal, is not a sufficient condi-tion. Also required is a cognitive component or what has been called an anger-triggering thought. This is based on the interpretation we give to the stress-inducing event. For example, your child refuses to clean his room or does it in a way that does not meet your standards. You might think, "What's wrong with him! He should clean his room and should do it in the way I told him to." This is an example of the "entitlement fallacy" described earlier. The core belief may be that your child is bad and deserving of punishment.

Stress leads to anger-triggering thoughts, which in turn lead to anger. The anger leads to other trigger thoughts, more anger, more trigger thoughts, and on and on. This feedback loop can be self-perpetuating and can often result in a constant state of anger.

Who Has an Anger Problem?

Tafrate (1995) has described a clinical approach to diagnosing anger using the *Diagnostic and Statistical Manual* (DSM-IV) (American Psychiatric Association, 1994) and other assessment methods. The practitioner should become familiar with his work.

However, in a number of settings, resources may not be available to conduct an elaborate and thorough anger assessment. We have found that one- or two-hour sessions with a skilled and knowledgeable interviewer can provide the necessary information required to make the determination that an individual has an anger problem. It is important to take into account any untreated condition such as chemical dependency or mental illness. This can be done by taking a history, including family of origin, and talking with the referral source.

Our view is that one has an anger problem if even subtle forms of anger cause the individual to engage in behaviors that are not in his or her best interest or that keep the individual from doing what is in his or her best interest. We also believe that a sure sign of an anger problem is the assigning of responsibility for one's anger to others (i.e., blaming). Other indicators include reports of police involvement in anger episodes, incidents of property being damaged or destroyed, break-up of relationships with others, trouble getting along with others in the workplace, frequent use of profanity, and distorted forms of expressing anger.

Belief Systems, Social Values, and Anger

According to Ellis and Grieger (1977), individuals develop a belief system that guides how they judge and evaluate situations, events, and other individuals. Although this system is unique to the individual, it involves certain beliefs that are held in common by the society at large. These are the beliefs that hold us together cooperatively. They are passed on to us by parents, teachers, and political and religious leaders. At the same time, these are not fixed and immutable. As social values change, so do individuals' beliefs.

Ellis also states that, although our beliefs are formed largely by the social environment, there is no universal norm and we make judgments according to arbitrary standards. However, the beliefs we hold are important factors in determining anger feelings and responses to any given situation. For example, if a father believes that his children should obey him at all times, he will become angry at those times when he perceives they are being disobedient and may hit them as a result.

The Importance of Anger Management for Fathers

For over thirty years, public awareness of child and spouse abuse and its impact on child development has grown considerably. It is known, for example, that fathers, including those not biologically related to the child or married to the mother, have been identified as perpetrators of abuse more than mothers (Lamb et al., 1985). Straus and colleagues (1980) cite data showing that violence by husbands toward their wives is associated with an increase in violence by both mothers and fathers toward their children.

Dutton (1995) found that abused wives frequently describe their husbands as having numerous "temper tantrums" and rageful episodes that seem out of proportion to the triggering event or situation. In our work with fathers, we still hear stories of abuse that horrify us, even though we have heard similar stories so many times before. We can only assume that there are many more that we do not hear. Consequently, we see, firsthand, a great need for programs like ours to help fathers deal more effectively with their anger.

THEORETICAL ASSUMPTIONS
OF CONSTRUCTIVE ENGAGEMENT

At the beginning of this chapter, our program was described as a psychoeducational, multicomponent program that follows a cognitive-behavioral approach. It rests on a number of assumptions we believe to be sound in designing an effective intervention strategy.

An assumption we make is that fathers, to effectively manage their anger, need to be informed of the root causes of anger, its impact on their children, and the cognitive and behavioral coping skills available to them. Consequently, our curriculum consists of preplanned educational sessions that can stand alone in accommodating open groups.

We also assume that a group approach is superior to a one-on-one approach. In a group, the individual father soon discovers that he is not alone in dealing with his anger problem and that others have problems that are as severe. By expressing himself freely, he finds reassurance that he is "not too bad." He also learns that rejection and ridicule are not necessarily a result of openness.

The assumption of a multicomponent strategy is that a combination of several techniques will yield superior results beyond any single approach. In this respect, we are followers of Raymond Novaco, a leader in the area of anger management. Combined approaches that include relaxation techniques, self-instructional training, and behavioral rehearsal have dominated the treatment literature on anger ever since his pioneering study on anger (Novaco, 1975). He refers to his multicomponent approach to anger management as stress inoculation. The procedure he follows involves three basic steps: cognitive preparation, skill acquisition and rehearsal, and application practice (Novaco, 1977).

The cognitive-behavioral approach is based on the hypothesis that a person's thoughts, interpretations, and self-statements about external events have a strong influence on emotional and behavioral functioning. The goal is to assist clients in identifying and challenging their irrational and distorted thinking patterns and to help them adopt more adaptive belief systems (Beck, 1976; Ellis, 1973). There are currently three dominant models: self-instructional training (Meichenbaum and Goodman, 1971), Beck's cognitive therapy (Beck, 1963), and rational-emotive behavior therapy (Ellis, 1962). Our model of constructive engagement draws heavily from each of these.

The self-instructional method is based on the premise that people's verbal self-statements or instructions influence their behavior. New instructions can be developed; these can interrupt old thinking and behavior patterns, and also direct new responses to problematic situations (Rhem and Rokke, 1988). Cognitive therapy assumes that, during upsetting events, individuals react with a stream of unplanned, automatic thoughts or cognitions. Some of these may be appropriate to the situation, while others are likely to be distorted and illogical. Beck (1971) believes that emotional disorders stem from such cognitive distortions and unrealistic appraisals of events.

Rational-emotive behavior therapy was developed by Albert Ellis in the 1950s. According to Ellis' (1962) A-B-C model, emotional disturbance (Point C) is the result of illogical and irrational thinking (Point B) about external events (Point A), and not the events themselves. Once irrational beliefs and thinking have been challenged and disputed, the client is assisted in developing alternative beliefs that are hypothesized to lead to healthier emotional functioning and more adaptive behavior.

CONSTRUCTIVE ENGAGEMENT (STRACK): A NEW APPROACH

STRACK is a convenient and easy mnemonic acronym that summarizes this strategy for helping fathers who are identified or who identify themselves as having an anger problem. It is also a reminder to participants in the program of the steps to follow when their anger has escalated to a point where they feel that they are going to lose control and become abusive or violent.

S = Stop

"Perhaps the single most effective strategy in controlling the escalation of anger is the 'time out' technique" (McKay, Rogers, and McKay, 1989, p. 134). It has been used successfully by many men who have participated in domestic abuse programs (Decker, 1994). This is an especially important strategy for fathers when there is the potential for abuse or violence directed toward their children or spouses. In essence, a time-out in father-child or father-spouse relationships is no different from a basketball coach who calls a time-out when his team is not following the game plan. Part of its effectiveness stems from the fact that this is a familiar and acceptable sports metaphor.

The goal is to slow down internal processes, let go of tension, and begin to think more clearly and realistically about the situation or event that triggered the anger, and to avoid feeling "out of control," which can result in abusive or violent behaviors. Fathers in our program are taught the steps involved in an effective time-out: sitting down when calm and talking with family members about the concept, coming to agreement on how to communicate the need to take a time-out, creating and using a time-out plan (rules and guidelines to follow, where he will go, what he will do, and how he will re-enter the situation), respectfully communicating his need for a time-out, taking responsibility for his own time-out, and making a commitment to return.

T = Take Responsibility

We almost always have some role in creating situations that result in our being angry. However, when we are in pain, our tendency is to determine who is to blame. According to McKay, Rogers, and McKay (1989), this impulse to assign blame lies at the root of chronic anger. When we decide that someone else is responsible for "making us angry," we feel that our anger is justified. Blaming focuses attention on damage, injury, defects, and weakness—on what is wrong—while obscuring solutions by locking us into the problem. We cannot blame and find solutions at the same time. It turns us into powerless victims. Taking responsibility, on the other hand, focuses on solutions and on strengths, resiliency, competence, creativity, and compassion. It is power.

There are other good reasons to take responsibility for our anger. First of all, the costs of anger are high. It can lead to ulcers, high blood pressure, and cardiovascular disease. Not only can anger lead to body damage, it can damage relationships. Angry people find themselves increasingly isolated. Those around them get fed up with the tension and hostility. Tavris (1982) observed that hostile Type A personalities vent their wrath at anyone who displeases them, thereby blocking off an important route to close friendships. A study by Hazaleus and Deffenbacher (1986) discovered that 45 percent of angry male subjects suffered a terminated or damaged relationship during the previous year.

R = Reframe

The basic cognitive-behavioral component of the program resides in this step. After an effective time-out, it becomes easier to reframe the situation by considering alternative ways of interpreting it through changing one's self-talk and becoming more positive in approaching a constructive engagement.

We have already shown that the cognitive-behavioral approach assumes that a person's thoughts, interpretations, and self-statements about external events have a strong influence on the development and escalation of anger. The goal for fathers in the program is to help them to identify and challenge their irrational and distorted thinking patterns and to help them adopt more adaptive belief systems. The concepts of self-instructional training, Beck's cognitive therapy, and Ellis' rational-emotive behavior therapy are all used in the program to train fathers on how to complete this step.

Reframing an anger-provoking situation during a time-out can best be accomplished if we understand where our anger comes from and what other feelings may be driving it. It is important to be aware of what we call "original wounds," "filters," and "hot buttons."

We define "original wound" as a fundamental violation or negation of the safety, value, and/or self-concept of the individual child or adult. Often rooted in shame-based family systems, the original wound gives us a certain "mental map" of the world. This mental map, or cognitive software, predisposes many of us to respond to perceptions of provocation with defensiveness, hostility, aggression, abuse, and even violence, rather than with constructive, nonviolent coping skills. We call the feelings associated with fundamental violations, "wounds." Three things about these wounds are important:

1. They are injuries to the sense of self and to self-esteem.
2. They consist of injuries to the attachment bond.
3. They constitute the most severe nontraumatic psychic pain.

Anger provides an immediate surge of energy and numbing of pain—a feeling of power—to replace the powerlessness of these wounds. So if anger works, we're not aware that we're feeling the wounds. It is the job of anger to numb pain, so we can attack those whom we perceive to be causing the pain.

We can begin building immunity to wounds by correcting the false image of the self that they entail (changing our self-talk). As these opposite statements are put into words, written down, and spoken aloud, the more powerful part of the brain dominates, at last starting to heal the wounds from which the feelings emanate.

We define "filters" as that set of assumptions we have about the way the world "really is," such that our view of things is, to some extent, predetermined. They include the mind-set of perceptions, interpretations, and judgments influencing how we communicate with others. Types of filters include perceptions of being rejected, shamed, abandoned, betrayed, victimized, humiliated, or degraded.

We define a "hot button" as any vulnerability or sensitivity which, when pushed, triggers a patterned response of rage or anger (especially when it is wired to an original wound).

A = Acknowledge

Before engaging a conflict constructively we need to ask certain questions (this should be part of a time-out, undertaken when physiological reactions have had a chance to subside): What was the person thinking and feeling? Did this person feel that I understood him or her? How would this individual describe me at that moment? What did my behavior seem like to this person? Did I feel understood? What might I have done to make myself better understood?

Upon returning to the situation the individual needs to exercise active listening skills. Such skills include paraphrasing, reflecting, asking for more information and clarification, and exhibiting active nonverbal listening skills (eye contact, not being distracted, positioning oneself toward the speaker). Active listening involves a number of skills that are accomplished only through careful practice.

C = Communicate

In constructively engaging another to resolve conflict before it escalates into destructive behaviors, it helps to identify one's particular style of communicating and to make changes as necessary. A predominant communication style will usually fall into one of four categories:

1. *Passive* (or nonassertive) communication involves the failure to stand up for our rights in a respectful and appropriate manner. It also involves standing up for our rights in a feeble or apologetic way. This

enables our rights to be violated in two ways: we disrespect ourselves when we ignore our preferences and needs; and we teach others that they can take advantage of us. Passive behavior pays off by allowing us to avoid potentially unpleasant conflicts with others. However, unpleasant consequences such as hurt feelings and lower self-esteem are likely to result. The nonverbal parts of passive communication include poor eye contact, low voice level, and scared-looking body posture.

2. *Aggressive* communication involves standing up for our rights at the expense of others. It is direct but dishonest because we are not expressing our true feelings when we are angry. Aggressive behavior violates the other's rights and may result in the loss of our rights. The purpose of aggressive communication is to dominate, control, humiliate, or put down the other rather than to simply express our honest feelings and thoughts. Like passive behavior, aggressive behavior leads to loss of self-respect and esteem. The nonverbal parts of aggressive communication include cutting others off, staring them down, yelling or raising voice levels, and threatening or intimidating body posture.

3. *Passive-aggressive* communication is an indirect way of showing anger. It violates others' rights without the huffing and puffing of aggressive behavior. Nevertheless, it is a type of aggression, and it is dishonest. The purpose of passive-aggressive behavior is to manipulate others by making them feel guilty or by passively resisting and avoiding whatever we do not want or like rather than expressing our honest feelings and thoughts. The nonverbal parts of passive-aggressive communication can resemble either assertive or passive behavior.

4. *Assertive* communication involves standing up for our legitimate personal rights without violating the rights of others. Assertive behavior is a direct, honest, and appropriate expression of our feelings, opinions, and beliefs. It involves respectfulness, good timing, and tactfulness. Assertion also includes empathy and consideration for the other person. This means that assertive communication involves listening to others and dialoguing with them. The nonverbal parts of assertive communication include good eye contact, matter-of-fact voice tone, open body posture, and an air of confidence and self-respect.

Silence

Silence may be a very important piece of information about the communication patterns between partners. In abusive relationships, silence may indicate fear. Because of abusive episodes, the partner who has been victimized may assume that if she talks to her partner, she will be abused. On the other hand, many men control their partners by being silent. Silence is a control mechanism that keeps the partner anxious and uncertain about a situation. Silence can also feel punishing, abusive, and withholding. Without verbal communication, a great deal of information can still be transmitted via nonverbal cues. Four of these nonverbal cues include:

1. *Context.* In abusive relationships, context has a significant impact on the "shared meaning" between partners. For example, in a relationship in which no abuse took place, the question, "What did you do today?" might seem innocent. However, the same question asked by a person who has been abusive might signify a totally different meaning. Perhaps in previous occasions the question, "What did you do today?" might have been followed by a litany of accusations and interrogatory statements. Physical or sexual abuse may have followed.
2. *Proximity.* Interpersonal distance in abusive relationships may be used as a tool to intimidate or threaten. If a person who is abusive approaches his partner and gets within inches of that person's body and/or face, this may be a way for the abuser to exert control and to intimidate the victim.
3. *Body Language.* Gestures, facial expressions, or body posture may convey threatening or intimidating messages. Clenching one's fists, raising one's hand, scowling, or narrowing one's eyes may be ways in which an abusive person uses body language to send messages of intimidation, threat, and control.
4. *Use of Voice.* Of course, one's voice inflections, tone, and volume can have a great deal to do with the content and intent of the verbal message. Sarcasm, rage, and belittling messages can be conveyed merely by a change in inflection, tone, or volume of the voice.

Anytime we use a statement beginning with "You . . ." (this includes statements such as "I think that you . . ." or "I feel that you . . .") then we are using some form of accusing or blaming. Accusing or blaming never leads to intimacy; this behavior is always destructive. All statements should start with "I."

Step One: "I feel _____." When you're in disagreement with someone, share your emotions, even though you feel vulnerable and afraid.

Step Two: "I want _____." State clearly what it is that you want, whether the other person can give it to you or not.

Step Three: "Will you _____?" or "Would you be willing to _____?"

Step Four: Remember that "No" doesn't mean rejection.

K = Keep Your Eye on the Prize

In learning how to try for a "win-win" result and to find solutions that promote everyone's safety, interests, and dignity, we stress the importance of following a "healing path." This is the commitment to oneself and others to pursue a path of reconciliation, forgiveness, and healing instead of a path of bitterness, anger, resentment, and revenge. This involves healing on different levels, including the physical, through exercise, good health, good eating, enough sleep, etc.; the spiritual, through reconnecting (or connecting) to a religious community or to a faith that inspires and sustains; the emotional, by sharing our hearts with others and by asking for and offering support; and the mental, by letting go of negative and angry thoughts.

It also involves developing a sense of compassion (Stosny, 1995). Anger and aggression are not genuine power, but merely destructive arousal states which we sometimes confuse with power. Genuine power entails a degree of control, self-awareness, and awareness of others that is impossible during anger arousal. When directed toward intimates, anger always results in some degree of shame, abandonment, anxiety, and depression. Compassion, on the other hand, provides the genuine emotional power of well-being. We can do something out of compassion, think about it ten years later and feel good about ourselves. And we can do something to a loved one out of anger, think about it ten years later and feel bad about ourselves. Compassion replaces an illusion of power with genuine power. Our innate capacity for self-compassion and compassion for others heals the hurt that gives rise to anger and aggression, while providing genuine personal power, security, well-being, and self-esteem.

Compassion does not mean giving in. Giving in or "going along to avoid an argument" virtually guarantees resentment. Resentment undermines and ruins relationships. Most of the time resolution without resentment is possible when a sincere effort is made to understand each other. We become the angriest (the most hurt), not when disappointed for not getting what we want, but when feeling misunderstood or disregarded or when disappointment is falsely interpreted to mean that we are unimportant or unlovable. With compassion, we never feel unimportant or disregarded or unlovable (although we may feel disappointed). This makes negotiation on all issues much easier. Compassion is absolutely necessary for resolution once feelings have been hurt. Understanding brings the parties in a dispute closer, while anger drives them further apart.

Compassion does not necessarily include generosity or magnanimity. It requires that we understand and regard the feelings of others as vital factors, but not the only factors, in decisions. With compassion we avoid the leading cause of failed relationships: power struggles. With compassion the goal is not to "win" a dispute, but to find a solution in which all parties feel regarded, important, and valuable.

EXPECTED OUTCOMES OF STRACK

Following completion of our program, we expect that the fathers we work with will practice the new skills they have been taught and model these skills for their children. Specifically, it is our expectation that they will move from blaming others for the events and situations that provoke their anger to taking personal responsibility for handling these in a respectful manner. Moreover, it is expected that they will use the problem-solving skills they have already demonstrated in other spheres of their lives.

We do not expect these men to eliminate their anger because, as we emphasize throughout the program, this is an impossible, if not unhealthy, goal. We hope that by following the principles they have been exposed to in the program, they will learn to better understand the root causes of their anger and the associated feelings that drive it, along with the behaviors that result from it. If they accomplish this, the expectation is that new and more positive, constructive behaviors will emerge.

We expect that, when they find themselves under stress and about to escalate, they will remind themselves of STRACK and begin to go through the steps. Finally, it is our hope and expectation that unhealthy attitudes will be replaced by attitudes of compassion and forgiveness for their own sake and for the sake of their children.

EVALUATION

Lacking sufficient funding, time, and resources, we have not been able to systematically analyze the data we have collected to evaluate the effectiveness of the program and must rely on the paucity of research findings relevant to the theoretical bases of our approach. Unfortunately, there is just a handful of outcome studies on the various approaches to treating anger, and in 60 percent of those, the subjects were college undergraduates who volunteered for treatment (Tafrate, 1995).

Using meta-analysis techniques, Tafrate (1995) found an overall effect size of .93 for this class of treatments (self-instructional training, Beck's cognitive therapy, and Ellis' rational emotive behavior therapy). In this same meta-analysis, the average effect size for multi-component approaches was 1.00. It did not say, however, exactly which combination of techniques is likely to be most effective.

At the end of our program, we have the fathers complete a questionnaire to provide us with feedback on the content of the program, the facilitators, and its effectiveness. We also ask for any comments on how we might improve the program. Although we are fully aware of the psychometric shortcomings of this kind of questionnaire, it can be reported that the comments have been uniformly positive, for example, "This class should be required in the schools. It sure would have made my life different"; "The only problem with this class is that it's not long enough"; "After two sessions, my kids noticed a difference. One even said 'You sure have been acting better lately. I like you this way.'"

One father who completed the program and went on to take the facilitator training course wrote an article describing his impressions (Carrick, 1998). This is part of what he had to say:

I have met with the group once a week, and my life has really taken on a new look. One thing I found is that you have to want to change in order to make it work. I dove right in and never looked back. I think a few guys didn't understand me. But when you find yourself in a circle with ten or so angry guys, and they're all half your age, you feel, "I'd better listen and take charge of myself. I still have time to change my life."

I feel excited about my life for the first time in twenty or so years. One thing I found in all my life of abuse, and much of the abuse I have not mentioned, is that the heart knows even when the mind can't comprehend. That's why I'm still here.

Humphrey (1999) addressed some other unexpected benefits of the program.

In one group there was a middle aged blind man, a CPA afflicted with cerebral palsy whose verbalizations were difficult to understand, a young Asian American who is both a gifted musician and brilliant computer expert as well as a devout atheist, a 52 year old boiler mechanic, a PhD in Peace Studies, a young black man who had been a drug dealer, a high school drop-out carpenter, and a 21-year-old whose primary interest involved "partying" with his friends. In a matter of weeks the black man, the Asian American and boiler mechanic began to socialize following each week's session—a comradeship I could not have anticipated in my wildest imaginings. In addition to developing new friendships deeper than any had known before, they kept each other accountable and provided mutual support in doing the work.

We believe in the effectiveness and validity of our approach to anger management. But, although this is an accurate and seemingly complete description of the program, it is so much more. Not mentioned is, perhaps, the most important, though intangible, component. That is the meeting of hearts and souls on a spiritual level unparalleled in my experience.

BARRIERS

There are a number of obstacles in doing the work we do. Perhaps the biggest is the failure of most fathers to recognize that they have an anger problem. Considering how men are socialized and the impact of the media's glorification of male violence, it is not unusual to hear fathers say that they do not have an anger problem. It is all part of the machismo. Also, for many fathers, anger has been one of the few emotions they have been allowed to express (real men don't cry, after all).

Most of the fathers who participate in our program are not able to pay for it themselves. Obtaining funding to meet costs while keeping fees low is very difficult. Those programs that are funded usually involve helping so-called "deadbeat dads" who are unable to meet their child support payments, and unable to find employment with sufficient compensation. This is not intended as a criticism of those programs. We obviously understand the importance of fathers meeting this responsibility and acknowledge the value of these programs in helping them to do that. Many such programs, however, ignore or do not address the underlying issues that account for these fathers being in this position. Included among these is anger—anger at what many of our fathers perceive as a legal, political, and social system that is inherently unfair.

Although far from being a representative sample, the fathers with whom we have worked are more than willing to support their children, but at the same time are denied access to them in custody and visitation decisions. One of our greatest challenges is persuading these fathers to apply the skills we teach when they are faced with the consequences of those decisions.

CONCLUSION

Some years ago when Neil Tift went searching for help in becoming a better father, he discovered that there were no programs or agencies in the Twin Cities of Minneapolis and St. Paul for fathers. Seeing this need and assuming there were others like him, he created the Fathers' Resource Center (FRC). In so doing, he became a driving force in the rapidly growing fathers' movement.

Through our own work, we have seen the great need for comprehensive fathering courses and, for now, how important it is to include an anger management component. A significant proportion of the fathers who came through our program were referred to anger management programs via the FRC's parent classes, support groups, and legal clinics when those in charge of these services observed excessive anger in many of the fathers they served.

At the same time, as we have seen, much research remains to be done to determine the effectiveness of the various approaches available to help fathers more positively and constructively cope with their anger. In the end, if fathers learn about their own anger, its causes and consequences, they will be able to help their children develop healthy ways to express this powerful emotion. It is our greatest hope that, eventually, programs like ours will no longer be needed.

BIBLIOGRAPHY

American Psychiatric Association (1994). *Diagnostic and statistical manual of mental disorders* (Fourth edition). Washington, DC: Author.

Ardrey, R. (1966). *The territorial imperative.* New York: Atheneum.

Averill, J. R. (1982). *Anger and aggression: An essay on emotion.* New York: Springer-Verlag.

Bateson, G. (1941). The frustration-aggression hypothesis and culture. *Psychological Review, 48,* 350-355.

Beck, A. T. (1963). Thinking and depression. *Archives of General Psychiatry, 9,* 324-333.

Beck, A. T. (1971). Cognition, affect, and psychopathology. *Archives of General Psychiatry, 24,* 495-500.

Beck, A. T. (1976). *Cognitive therapy and the emotional disorders.* New York: International Universities Press.

Benson, R. (1975). *The relaxation response.* New York: William Morrow.

Carrick, R. (1998). Never too old to change. *Father Times. A newsletter of the Fathers' Resource Center,* 14.

Charlesworth E. A. and Nathan, R. G. (1985). *Stress management: A comprehensive guide to wellness.* New York: Ballantine Books.

Conoley, C. W., Conoley, J. C., McConnel, J. A., and Kizney, C. E. (1983). The effect of the ABC's of rational emotive therapy and the empty chair technique of Gestalt therapy on anger reduction. *Psychotherapy: Theory, Research, and Practice, 20,* 112-117.

Decker, D. J. (1994). "The Pyramid Mental Health Center Anger Abuse Program: A comprehensive therapy and education group model to address and change men's controlling and abusive attitudes and behaviors." Minnetonka, MN: Pyramid Health Center.

Dentan, R. K. (1968). *The Semai—A nonviolent people of Malaya.* New York: Holt, Rinehart & Winston.

Deschner, J. P. (1984). *The hitting habit: Anger control for battering couples.* New York: Macmillan.

Dollard, J. R., Doob, L.W., Miller, N. E., and Mowrer, O. H. (1939). *Frustration and aggression*. New Haven: Yale University Press.

Dutton, D. (1995). *The batterer: A psychological profile*. New York: Basic Books.

D'Zurilla, T. J. (1988). Problem solving therapies. In K. Dobson (Ed.), *Handbook of cognitive behavioral therapies* (pp. 85-135). New York: Guilford.

D'Zurilla, T. J. and Goldfried, M. R. (1971). Problem solving and behavior modification. *Journal of Abnormal Psychology, 78,* 107-126.

Ebbesen, E., Ducan, B., and Konecni, V. (1975). The effects of content of verbal aggression on future verbal aggression: A field experiment. *Journal of Experimental Psychology, 11,* 192-204.

Ellis, A. (1962). *Reason and emotion in psychotherapy*. New York: Lyle Stuart.

Ellis, A. (1973). *Humanistic psychotherapy*. New York: McGraw-Hill.

Ellis, A. (1993). *Anger: How to live with and without it*. New York: Citadel Press.

Ellis, A. and Grieger, R. (1977). *Rational-emotive therapy: Handbook of theory and practice*. New York: Springer.

Feshbach, S. (1956). The catharsis hypothesis and some consequences of interaction with aggression and neutral play objects. *Journal of Personality, 24,* 449-462.

Freud, S. (1962). *The Ego and the Id* (translated by Joan Riviere). New York: W. W. Norton. (Original work published in 1923).

Friedman, M. S., St. George, S., Byers, S. O., and Rosenman, R. H. (1960). Excretion of catecholamines in men exhibiting a particular behavior pattern (A) associated with high incidence of clinical coronary heart disease. *Journal of Clinical Investigation, 39,* 758-764.

Gaylin, W. (1989). *The rage within: Anger in modern life*. New York: Penguin Books.

Goodenough, F. (1931). *Anger in young children*. Minneapolis, MN: University of Minnesota Press.

Hazaleus, S. and Deffenbacher, J. (1986). Relaxation and cognitive treatments of anger. *Journal of Consulting and Clinical Psychology, 3,* 37-58.

Humphrey, C. (1999). Confessions of an anger management counselor. *The Times for Fathers and Families. A Newsletter of the Resource Center for Fathers and Families, 10*. Reprinted by permission of Arnie Engelby, Director, Resource Center for Fathers and Families.

Jacobson, E. (1938). *Progressive muscle relaxation*. Chicago:University of Chicago Press.

Kellner, R. M. T., Buckman, M., Fava, G. A., and Masougiacomo, I. (1984). Prolactin, aggression and hostility: A discussion of recent studies. *Psychiatric Developments, 2,* 131-138.

Kohn, A. (1988). Make love not work: We keep hearing we are an aggressive, warlike species. Scientists keep telling us that we have a choice. *Psychology Today, 22*(1), 34-40.

Konner, M. (1962). *The tangled wing*. New York: Holt.

Lamb, M. E., Gaenbauer, T. J., Malkin, C. M., and Shultz, L.A. (1985). The effects of child maltreatment on security of infant-adult attachment. *Infant Behavior and Development, 8,* 35-45.

Leaky, R. (1981). *The making of mankind.* New York: E. P. Dutton.

Lemerise, E. A. and Dodge, K. A. (1993). The development of anger and hostile interactions. In M. Lewis and J. M. Haviland (Eds.), *Handbook of emotions* (pp. 537-546). New York: Guilford.

Lewis, M. (1993). The emergence of human emotions. In M. Lewis and J. M. Haviland (Eds.), *Handbook of emotions* (pp. 233-236). New York: Guilford.

Lorenz, K. (1971). *On aggression.* New York: Bantam Books.

Maranon, G. (1924). Contribution a l'etude de l'action emotive de l'adrenaline. *Revue Francaise d' Endocrinologie, 2,* 301-325.

Masters, J. C., Burish, T.G., Hollon, S. D., and Rimm, D. C. (1987). *Behavior therapy.* San Diego, CA: Harcourt Brace Jovanovich.

McKay, M., Rogers, P. D., and McKay, J. (1989). *When anger hurts.* Oakland, CA: New Harbinger Publications.

Mehr, J. (1980). *Human services: Concepts and intervention strategies.* Needham Heights, MA: Simon & Schuster.

Meichenbaum, D. H. and Goodman, J. (1971). Training impulsive children to talk to themselves. *Journal of Abnormal Psychology, 77,* 127-132.

Novaco, R. W. (1975). *Anger control: The development and evaluation of an experimental treatment.* Lexington, MA: D.C. Heath, Lexington Books.

Novaco, R. W. (1976). The functions and regulation of the arousal of anger. *American Journal of Psychology, 133,* 1124-1128.

Novaco, R. W. (1977). Stress inoculation: A cognitive therapy for anger and its application to a case of depression. *Journal of Counseling and Clinical Psychology, 45,* 600-608.

Novaco, R. W. (1978). Anger and coping with stress; Cognitive-behavioral interventions. In J. Foreyt and D. Rathjen, (Eds.), *Cognitive-behavior therapy* (pp. 135-173). New York: Plenum Press.

Radke-Yarrow, M. and Kochanska, G. (1990). Anger in young children. In N. L. Stein, B. Leventhal, and T. Trabasso (Eds.), *Psychological and biological approaches to emotion* (pp. 297-310). Hillsdale, NJ: Erlbaum.

Rhem, L. P. and Rokke, P. (1988). Self-management therapies. In K. Dobson (Ed.), *Handbook of cognitive behavioral therapies* (pp. 136-166). New York: Guilford.

Scaramella, T. H. and Brown, W.A. (1978). Serum testosterone and aggressiveness in hockey players. *Psychosomatic Medicine, 40,* 262-267.

Schacter, S. (1971). *Emotion, obesity, and crime.* New York: Academic Press.

Schacter, S. and Singer, J. (1962). Cognitive, social, and physiological determinants of emotional state. *Psychological Review, 69,* 379-399.

Spivack, G., Platt, J., and Shure, M. (1976). *The problem solving approach to adjustment.* San Francisco: Jossey-Bass.

Stosny, S. (1995). *Treatment manual of the Compassion Workshop.* Silver Spring, MD: Community Outreach Service.

Straus, M. A. (1974). Leveling, civility, and violence in the family. *Journal of Marriage and the Family, 36,* 13-29.

Straus, M. A., Gelles, R. J., and Steinmetz, S. K. (1980). *Behind closed doors: Violence in the American family.* New York: Doubleday/Anchor.

Tafrate, R. C. (1995). Evaluation of treatment strategies for adult anger disorders. In H. Kassinove (Ed.), *Anger disorders: Definition, diagnosis, and treatment* (pp. 109-129). Bristol, PA: Taylor & Francis.

Tavris, C. (1982). *Anger: The misunderstood emotion.* New York: Simon & Schuster.

Toogood, M. and Humphrey, C. (1998). "Dealing with male anger: A model of constructive engagement." Unpublished manuscript.

Whitting, J. W. M. (1941). *Becoming a Kwoma.* New Haven: Yale University Press.

Wolpe, J. (1958). *Psychotherapy by reciprocal inhibition.* Stanford, CA: Stanford University Press.

Woods, P. J. (1987). Reductions in type A behavior, anxiety, anger, and physical illness as related to changes in irrational beliefs: Results of a demonstration project in industry. *Journal of Rational Emotive Psychotherapy, 5,* 213-237.

SECTION II:
EDUCATIONAL INTERVENTIONS

Chapter 5

Parent Education
for Incarcerated Fathers

Glen Palm

When I first read about parenting programs for incarcerated fathers in the late 1980s (Giveans, 1988), I quickly dismissed the idea that fathers in prison would need or want parent education. Ten years later and after five years of teaching a parenting class in the state correctional facility in my community, I am convinced that this is an important group of fathers that we have discounted and neglected. When I first met with the staff at our local correctional facility and asked how many of the 800-plus men were fathers, they could only guess. They did not even keep records about this information. We have stripped incarcerated men of the social role of fatherhood. Perhaps recognition of prisoners as fathers gives them a human quality we do not want to acknowledge, much less nurture and support (Adalist-Estrin, 1995). Recent data suggest that there are currently over 500,000 incarcerated fathers (Child Welfare League of America [CWLA], 1999) and an even larger group of men who will spend some time incarcerated while they are fathers. The number of incarcerated fathers is larger than we would like to acknowledge, and the current social attitudes toward these men is that they are criminals first and foremost, in prison to be punished. Even though the social role of fatherhood has been taken away as part of their identity, and their ability to function as fathers is limited by incarceration (i.e., provider, caretaker, role model), there is a depth of caring and sense of responsibility about these men that emerges with some probing. One of the incarcerated fathers we worked with talked about fatherhood and what it meant to him, illustrating the powerful impact children can have on their fathers, even when physically separated by incarceration.

She is my baby. I love her, and that is gonna play a major role. The major role is the change in my life, not a bad life, but being more careful as an adult. *[Some of the changes you've made are?]* Stop drinking, stop cursing, go to church, try to achieve my GED. Other things I have been doing for my daughter and myself but if I had no daughter I probably wouldn't have, you know.

This chapter will weave together fragments of theory, research, and an evolving practice of parenting education with incarcerated fathers. The critical "data" and insights come from the 125-plus inmates who have shared their hopes about and struggles with being and becoming good fathers when most people have written them off as "bad dads." The first section will examine some of the research and theoretical frameworks that inform parenting education with incarcerated fathers. The remainder of the chapter will focus on practice, including needs of incarcerated fathers, program goals, recruitment and barriers, evaluation strategies, and finally a summary of core learnings to guide effective practice.

REVIEW OF RESEARCH

Lanier (1995) builds a strong case and describes an agenda for more research on incarcerated fathers. The literature on incarcerated fathers and programs for fathers is limited, yet fragments of research, theory, and practice can be constructed to build a rationale and guidelines for creating parenting programs. Much of the research and literature on families and incarceration understandably focuses on the children and effects on family life (Adalist-Estrin, 1994). Also, more attention is given to mothers in prison and the subsequent negative impacts of this situation on children (Hostetter and Jinnah, 1993).

How Many Incarcerated Fathers?

The number of fathers currently incarcerated has been an elusive figure. Reports of the actual number of men in prison at any given time do not reflect the total number of fathers, children, and families who may have experienced the stress of father incarceration over the past decade. There are currently 1.7 million people incarcerated and 3.8 million more are on parole or probation (CWLA, 1999). The number of fathers, families, and children who have experienced the trauma of incarceration is substantial and likely exceeds the frequently cited 500,000 fathers (U.S. Department of Justice, 1991). In addition, the prison population is projected to increase in the near future by as much as 50 percent (CWLA, 1999). This is a large and growing group of fathers and families in which parent education can play a critical role in the rehabilitation of the men and the maintenance of fragile family relationships.

Characteristics of Fathers in Prison

While the research on fathers in prison is limited, we are beginning to define some of the common characteristics of fathers who are incarcerated. In the Child Welfare League of America Web site (1999) the following profile has been reported. The typical inmate who is a parent grew up in a single-parent home, and one-third have had an immediate family member incarcerated. Many incarcerated fathers have experienced nonnuclear family care, with 14 percent having been raised by relatives and 17 percent having spent time in other settings. Fathers who are inmates reported a 30 percent rate of substance abuse among their parents and 12 percent reported physical or sexual abuse. Incarcerated fathers typically have a limited education and undeveloped employment skills and 90 percent had incomes below $25,000 at the time of their arrest.

A similar profile emerged in a study of 1,600 Minnesota male inmates in 1993 (Gilgun, 1994). Over half of the men (56 percent) reported that their fathers were absent and 26 percent had fathers who did not complete high school. The rate of physical and sexual abuse reported was two to three times higher than on the CWLA (1999) Web site report, with 37 percent reporting physical abuse and 26 percent reporting sexual abuse when they were growing up. The percentage of alcohol and marijuana use in their families when they were growing up is also higher—at 45 to 50 percent. The differences in these profiles may be related to the smaller population of incarcerated fathers in just one region of the country or how the questions were asked and interpreted.

I have worked with over 125 incarcerated fathers in one prison in Minnesota over the past five years and will provide some details about this group that have not been reported in the literature. The men who participated in my parenting classes represent a range of racial and ethnic backgrounds. About 50 percent of these men were African American, 30 percent white, 15 percent Mexican American, and the remaining 5 percent were Asian American and Native American. The ages of the fathers ranged from seventeen to forty-five years, with most of the men between eighteen and thirty years. The educational background varied from some high school to a few men who had completed some college courses. Many of the inmates in the parenting groups were working on obtaining their GEDs. About three-fourths of the men became fathers for the first time during their teen years and many had more than one child but with different mothers. The majority of the men spent some time without their fathers while growing up. The issue of physical abuse was discussed in great detail in parenting classes and the perceptions of what is abusive behavior toward children have been effected by personal experiences. During group discussions the men consistently identified three different levels of physical punishment: (1) spanking; (2) being "whopped" with a belt or other object; and (3) being beaten with fists and other objects. Disagreement existed about boundaries for abuse, but most inmates agreed that the third level is abusive while the other forms of discipline were seen as appropriate punishment. This description of physical punishment may explain the differing reports of abuse in the other studies. The standard definitions of abuse and family violence may be discounted by a group that experiences a high level of violence as normal. Attitudes about the use of physical punishment with children vary within a group of inmates. Some inmates are looking for alternatives to physical punishment while others see spanking with a hand and "whopping" as necessary tools to teach children respect and good behavior.

The family backgrounds described above reflect many risk factors that fathers appear to be passing on to their children. The need for intervention and support toward healthy family life and parenting practices is obvious. However, parenting education is only one piece of a program of rehabilitation. I work with fathers who often are involved in one or more of the following programs: vocational education, adult basic education, Reshape (a substance abuse program), anger management, and a critical thinking class. The men in the parenting classes clearly see these other programs as relevant to being good fathers. These programs support men in the pursuit of individual and vocational growth and development that is essential to fulfilling the responsibilities of fatherhood.

Programs for Incarcerated Fathers

Brenner (1999), in a recent review of the data on fathers in prison, notes the lack of evaluation research in fatherhood programs. Programs are being developed in several states and at individual institutions. As with most fatherhood programs developed over the past two decades (McBride and Palm, 1992), they are often grass-roots efforts with limited budgets. Although these programs make intuitive sense—this is a group of fathers who could obviously benefit from learning better communication and discipline skills—they have not been assessed for results on recidivism, child outcomes, future child support payments, or cost-effectiveness (Brenner, 1999). The number of programs that exist, the number of men who participate, and the content and format of programs are also not known at this time. There have been reports of parenting programs for incarcerated fathers since at least the mid-1980s (McCall, 1988; Bartell, 1988) and the number of parent education programs appears to be increasing. In 1989 there were over 100 prison-related family support programs in thirty-nine states (National Resource Center for Family Support Programs, 1992). Carter (1996) and Knitzer and Bernard (1997) also reported that the number of programs for fathers in correctional facilities is increasing.

Knitzer and Bernard (1997) outlined some of the newer initiatives for incarcerated fathers in reviewing programs for responsible fatherhood at the state level. Statewide initiatives for incarcerated fathers were described for seven states. These represent a variety of programs in which parenting may be a specific topic within the context of a larger program, for example, a life skills program (Illinois); a six- to eight-week video course on parenting (Missouri); a twelve-week, ninety-minute group parent education program for twelve to fifteen men (New Jersey); and a play group for incarcerated fathers and their young children that runs two hours a week for up to eight weeks (Vermont). There are other programs that are identified in a recent Family and Corrections Network Report (Mustin, 1999). Bowling (1999) describes the Minnesota Early Learning Design (MELD) for Young Dads program at a juvenile detention center that serves fifteen- to eighteen-year-old fathers. An outline for a "Long Distance Dads" program at a state correctional facility in Pennsylvania also recently appeared on the Internet (The Fathers Workshop, 1999). The Web site provides a topical overview of twelve sessions. I have also spoken with individuals from several other states (Utah, Florida, Indiana, Michigan, Wisconsin, and Minnesota) over the past couple of years about parenting programs for fathers in correctional facilities. Professionals working in this area are eager for more information and ideas for improving programs, yet few avenues for sharing information currently exist.

The variety of program designs and the lack of program evaluation data point to a real need for more research. The research needed at this point is still very basic. What programs do exist? What are the program formats that have evolved? How many fathers and families are being served by programs? What are the short-term outcomes that have been documented? Later in this chapter a section on evaluation addresses some specific approaches that may be helpful in guiding program development and beginning to build a research base about program outcomes. The new wave of programs for fathers should begin to generate more information on program designs and their effectiveness.

Rationale for Creating Parenting Programs for Incarcerated Fathers

Although at this point there is little direct evidence of program effectiveness, there are some convincing rationales for creating parenting programs for fathers. Hairston (1990) reviews research on recidivism and points out the important role of social support from family members in reducing rates of recidivism. Hairston also explores fatherhood as a motivating factor for avoiding future criminal activity. Palkovitz and Palm (1998) encountered several men who reported that becoming a father had changed their values and deterred them from self-centered and often self-destructive lifestyles. Parenting programs tap into strong generative desires to be a good parent and to change one's lifestyle for the sake of one's children. Without any connection to families, and without the support and educational influence of parenting programs, this critical motivational factor and the potential for being a caring parent may wither as men repress their sense of caring and internalize feelings of guilt, failure, and alienation surrounding their experience of fatherhood.

Another reason for supporting responsible fathering in men who are incarcerated is the well-being of the child. Brenner (1999) reported that benefits to children are not agreed upon. Some people believe that contact with incarcerated fathers is detrimental to children. Children of offenders are already at risk and are six times more likely than their peers to end up in prison (Jacobs, 1995). Will programs that encourage incarcerated fathers to take responsibility and maintain a relationship with their children put the child at a greater risk? This is a complex question that has no easy answer. Each family has unique characteristics that may influence whether increased father involvement, contact, and responsibility has a positive or negative impact. The male inmates that I encountered are also ambivalent about how much contact they want to have with their children while they are incarcerated. They worry about the questions children have about being in prison and if exposure to prison will have a negative impact on them. Still, most want to take responsibility for and keep in contact with their children. They want their children to know that they love them. They also want the chance to teach their children not to repeat the mistakes they have made. Unmarried fathers taking financial responsibility for children is also an issue that is part of our current welfare reform movement (Brenner, 1999). Although incarcerated fathers may receive a reprieve from child support payments while in prison, they will be expected to pay when they get out. It makes sense to prepare fathers for the roles of psychological parent and breadwinner so that they may have a positive influence when they reconnect with their children.

The rationale for creating parenting programs for incarcerated fathers is based on two important expected outcomes. The first is that fathers will be motivated to change and can become responsible parents. The second is that children will benefit from the financial contribution of a father and the development of a caring and supportive father-child relationship. We currently have no research evidence regarding which programs are most likely to produce these outcomes. However, we also have reason to believe that positive outcomes are possible, at least to some extent, in a majority of cases.

DESIGNING A PROGRAM
FOR INCARCERATED FATHERS

This section will focus on the design process for creating a parent education program in a correctional facility. The first step in the process involves the identification of the unique psychological and social needs of incarcerated fathers. The second step is the articulation of conceptual frameworks and program goals. Recruitment issues will be briefly addressed, and the program content and methods will also be described. Finally, an approach to program evaluation will be outlined, including some specific strategies and results.

Psychological and Social Needs
of Incarcerated Fathers

A first step in developing a program is *listening* to the needs and concerns of the group through a needs-assessment process. In this case, three focus groups with ten to twelve fathers, and follow-up interviews with twelve of these fathers, were conducted before starting a parenting program. Palm (1996) outlines some of the needs and issues of incarcerated fathers. Although fathers in prison have some overlapping interests with fathers in general, such as effective discipline, communication with young children, and understanding the changing role of fathers, incarcerated fathers must face several unique issues. The following list summarizes some of the issues and concerns that emerged from the focus groups and follow-up interviews.

1. *Finding ways to stay close to my child.* Men want to know more about how to "let children know that you care." Keeping in contact and "letting them know that I love them" was a common theme. Some men were discouraged by the barriers they faced, including limited

funds for phone calls, long distances that made visits impossible, and mothers acting as gatekeepers. Many men talked about writing letters and drawing pictures, and some were able to call on a regular basis.

2. *Answering a child's questions about prison.* Many fathers were unsure of how to respond to children's questions and what to tell them. One man commented:

> As much as I try and explain to him why I'm here, what this place is all about, sometimes I can't help thinking that maybe, I hope he doesn't get to thinking that it is all right. His mother kind of explains it as a time-out, similar to when she sends him to the corner on a time-out.

3. *Communicating with the child's mother.* This topic comes up in a variety of contexts, from worrying about mothers' caretaking ability to mothers who don't allow visitation or communication. One of the fears for many inmates is that they will be replaced by another male who will take on the role of father in their child's eyes. There is a great deal of emotional ambivalence about mothers—from frustration and anger to genuine caring. Managing a co-parenting relationship from behind bars is a challenge. Many men find it easier to communicate with the child's mother indirectly, through their own parents or siblings.

4. *Making the transition to work and family life when released.* Many men are concerned about how to best reconnect with their child when they are released from prison. "How to move into the relationship, and build it up again." This transition period will bring up feelings of abandonment and anger in children and the child's mother. These feelings are difficult for men to cope with when they are trying to reestablish a close and caring relationship and are expecting support and respect from their children and family.

5. *Coping with the loss of the ability to be a protector, nurturer, and role model.* Fathers worry about what may happen to their children in their absence. "I guess my major concern would be something major happening to them, like an illness . . . or things like that where I wouldn't be able to go and be with them at their time of need." Fathers may feel powerless in carrying out some of the traditional functions of fatherhood. They can acknowledge these limitations while finding new and creative ways to be a good father during incarceration.

Conceptual Frameworks Guiding Program Development

There are two conceptual frameworks that offer some important insights into developing programs for incarcerated fathers. The first framework is generative fathering (Palkovitz, 1992; Snarey, 1993; Dollahite, Hawkins, and Brotherson, 1997; Hawkins and Dollahite, 1997) and was described in the introduction of this book. This framework provides a closer look at the individual development of fathers and uses Erikson's concept of generativity as a way to chart adult growth and development in fathers. Microstructural theory, the second framework, focuses on understanding the social context from a microstructural perspective. These two frameworks complement each other by focusing on both the individual and the social context.

Generative Fathering

The generative fathering model articulated by Dollahite, Hawkins, and Brotherson (1997) allows incarcerated fathers to work toward good fathering even while behind bars. For example, one of the things that fathers do as part of a first session is to define a list of fifty or more things that they can do to be, or become, a good dad while in prison. The various tasks of generative fathering suggest some specific areas to develop through parent education (Palm, 1997). Fathers in prison may have some unique opportunities for reflection and can focus on both *ethical work* (committing to act for the good of the child) and *development work* (promoting and supporting growth in the child). However, it may not be as easy to address *relationship work* (building a healthy, loving relationship) and *stewardship work* (providing resources and opportunities for the child), although these may be worked on later when some of their personal issues/problems are resolved.

Generativity through fathering is not an automatic biological response in men. There are many young fathers who are still working on the developmental issues of identity and intimacy (Rhoden and Robinson, 1997). Palkovitz and Palm (1998) describe important changes that take place as men become fathers. Some of the men in this study were incarcerated and had become fathers at a very young age. They have intentions of being good fathers, but they face many barriers. Some of these are personal development issues, such as not knowing what values are important and how to pass them on. They also are uncertain about vocational interests and how to be providers for their children. They may be committed to remaining connected to their children but fail to see the importance of maintaining a respectful relationship with their children's mothers. There may be a generative spark in their hearts, but they do not know how to manage all of the demanding responsibilities of fathering. Fatherhood can be seen as part of a foundation for identity. However, programs that serve young fathers must also address the other cornerstones of identity, including vocational choices, value systems, and intimacy, including relationship skills and a sense of responsibility and commitment. When these issues are addressed, fathers are better able to achieve the full range of generative fathering opportunities.

Microstructural Theory

Microstructural theory addresses structural conditions in society, in this case prison culture and social attitudes about incarceration and how these structures affect the functioning and development of the people within them. According to microstructural theory (Risman, 1987), men in prison will adjust to the culture and expectations of the prison environment. The prison environment deemphasizes parenting. The creation of a parenting program introduces an important change, even if it is restricted to one time a week for two hours. The prison environment at its best promotes education and personal rehabilitation, but peer group pressures often constrain this potential for growth. It was fascinating to see how open men were in individual interviews, sharing deep feelings of love and concern for their children, and then to see behavior more typical of adolescents from the same men in the parenting class setting. I have also observed times when men withdrew to protect themselves from the vulnerability and pain of sharing feelings of sadness, anger, and confusion about their relationship with their children and their child's mother. The prison environment is not a safe place for exposing vulnerable feelings about parenting. Depression is another factor in the prison setting that should be acknowledged in working with fathers (Everhard, 1995). The setting by its nature can contribute to emotional highs and lows and exacerbate mental health problems. The introduction of a parenting class is one way to change the social environment and create a safe space to explore the meaning of fatherhood and the strong emotional feelings connected with being an incarcerated father.

The negative aura of prison continues to haunt men when they return to society and try to reconnect with their children. Some of the major barriers to reconnecting with children are: social attitudes towards incarceration; limited job opportunities; family (especially in-laws) attitudes; and the lack of support systems for men to address individual and fatherhood issues. The informal support systems for men vary. Some men have parents or relatives who bring their children to visit on a regular basis, while others have partners or families who break ties and bar contact between incarcerated fathers and their children. Parent education programs for men who leave the prison system are lacking, yet they are essential to support the family reconnection process in a hostile social environment. Men also need assistance in finding jobs and establishing their role as provider. The social beliefs about incarcerated men create an image of violent and bad men who should be kept away from vulnerable children, even their own biological children. These social beliefs and expectations can keep men separated from their children and unable to engage in responsible fathering. Microstructural theory reminds us that individual change must be supported by social change in environments.

Defining Program Goals

The parent education program was designed to address some of the needs that fathers described in the first set of focus groups. The reasons these fathers gave for attending parenting groups illustrate the important goals for parenting programs for fathers in prison:

- I want my child to still know me and respect me.
- How to keep an ongoing relationship with a child when you are distanced from him. How to keep it growing.
- When you got a baby together and she [the mother] doesn't want you to see the baby, how to handle that.
- How to get my point across to my kid over the phone, because that is all that I am is a voice over the phone.
- I just want to show them the right way and not to follow in my footsteps. I don't want my kids in here. It would hurt me to see my kids in the same place that I have been.

- We need to understand what we are missing out on, make it worth not coming back.
- I want to learn to see things like they see it. I don't want to whop them for nothing because I'm mad at something else.
- I want to learn to influence my child. I have learned a lot of things and grown up a lot . . . I just want him to know beyond any shadow of a doubt that his father loves him.

The range of responses suggests that the fathers in prison have a variety of needs and interests related to learning more about parenting. Becoming a better parent opens up a door to hope that one can be a better person and one's children can avoid the mistakes and pain from the lessons their father has learned the hard way.

Program Content and Methods

The program content has evolved over time based on the initial assessment of needs and interests combined with general knowledge and skills that are included in most parent education programs. The content is outlined in a summary of the twelve-week program presented in Table 5.1. All of the topics are important and the sequence is critical to building group trust and emphasizing the child and father-child relationship as the initial building blocks, then the father-mother relationship, family responsibilities, and community context can be addressed. The program content is adjusted to address specific issues that a particular group brings up. For example, a recent group asked about birth control and family planning and information was shared on this topic.

After the twelve-week program there is a follow-up session with each individual. This session provides an opportunity to debrief the class and bring some closure to the experience. It is also the time when some of the men read a children's book on audiotape to send to their children. Most fathers also send a personal message and often struggle with how to best tell their child that they care. In addition, participants complete class evaluations, have a brief interview with the parent educator, and receive a certificate for completing the class.

Table 5.1. Parenting Class Outline 1998-1999

1. *Introduction and Good Fathering in Prison.* The first session assesses interests in different topic areas and establishes some ground rules. Men discuss changes in the role of fathers and brainstorm a list of practical ways to be good fathers while in prison.
2. *Family Traditions and Lessons from Dad.* This session begins by reflecting on family rituals and traditions experienced while growing up and how to establish some routines and consistency for children. Men also discuss the lessons taught by their own fathers about relationships, parenting, and family responsibility.
3. *Children As Individuals and Typical Development.* Children are the focus in this session. What are temperamental characteristics of child and self? What do we know about child development? Why children learn and develop at different rates.
4. *Effective Communication with Children.* Emphasis is placed on two important skills, reflective listening and using "I" messages. These are practiced in the visiting room, telephone calls, and letter writing.
5. *Understanding Feelings in Children.* The focus is on understanding how feelings develop and are expressed at different ages. Fathers play an important role as coach/model in developing emotional intelligence by helping children learn how to identify emotions and habits for expressing emotions.
6. *Rethinking Discipline—Fathers As Teachers.* The group explores discipline techniques used by their own parents when they were children. The goals and effectiveness of discipline techniques are discussed, with some attention to changing boundaries for abusive behavior. Culture and community are also addressed as factors in discipline practice.
7. *Exploring a Toolbox of Discipline Techniques.* The introduction of discipline as teaching, not punishment, reveals a variety of tools that are used by parents. A game provides practice for implementing the best tools in different situations.
8. *Male Issues Around Anger and Control.* Male issues regarding anger and control are explored through the video *Bad Dads* (Shapiro and Reiswerg, 1996). Anger is examined through a better understanding of trigger events, body responses, thinking patterns, and habits.
9. *Developing a Respectful Relationship with Your Child's Mother.* Mothers are depicted as the "door" to a good relationship with children. A better understanding of mother as a person who deserves respect and attention, and communication skills that promote respectful relationships are emphasized.
10. *Raising Safe Children in a Dangerous World.* The session focuses on fathers as protectors of children and examines the risks that children face in the community outside the family. A safe and loving family environment free of domestic and child abuse is stressed as a father's primary responsibility.
11. *Reconnecting with Children.* The experience of reconnecting with children after release is the focus of this session. It is important to stress realistic reactions from children who carry both anger and fear about the separation from their fathers.
12. *Support Systems for Good Fathering.* A final session examines male reluctance to acknowledge the need for support. A list of possible resources is shared with a discussion of the need for both formal and informal support while reconnecting with family members.

The methods used in a typical session reflect a variety of ways to engage fathers in thinking, feeling, and reflecting about parenting. A typical group is composed of ten to fifteen fathers. Group discussion is the primary method for examining most issues. Small group exercises are frequently used to match men who have children of similar ages. Icebreakers are often used to get everyone involved at the beginning of a session. For example, in the session on respectful relationships with mothers, each man is asked to introduce his child's mother and one or two strengths or good qualities that she has as a mother. Video clips from parenting programs, TV documentaries, or movies are used as triggers for discussion or practice of specific skills. Stories serve a similar function and are read aloud by a volunteer from the group. Materials that reflect both the prison culture and different cultural groups are incorporated. Handouts that summarize major points or concepts and some written exercises are also presented. A card game format is used to explore the effectiveness of discipline methods in response to specific situations generated by the group. A variety of teaching methods helps to engage different types of learners and to keep the group sessions interesting and fun.

Recruitment and Barriers

Inmates are recruited by flyers that go out to different departments and teachers in the educational program. In a typical class there will be inmates who have been referred by teachers, their team, and other inmates who have taken the class. There may also be an inmate who is court-ordered to attend a parenting class as a provision for having contact with his child. Since the class has been offered twice a year for only fifteen to sixteen inmates in an institution with 800-plus inmates, it was not necessary to spend a great deal of time or effort on recruitment. However, the need exists for some screening to exclude individuals who may not be ready due to limited contact with their child, uncertainty about paternity, or a previous history of domestic violence.

Some unique barriers to services for fathers are related to the nature of prisons. One barrier I have encountered is the uncertainty about transfers. Men are never sure when they will be leaving the prison for another institution. Some minor conflicts occur with other programs that inmates attend. The relationship between the inmate and the child's mother may be another barrier that changes over time and may affect the motivation to continue involvement in the program. Another barrier is lack of resources to offer parent education to all the inmates who would like to participate.

Program Evaluation:
Strategies for Improving Programs

Program evaluation is a major issue raised in the literature on fathering programs. (McBride and Palm, 1992; Brenner, 1999). The literature on evaluation of parenting programs for fathers is limited to a few short-term outcome studies (see Fagan and Iglesias, 1999; McBride, 1990, 1991). In general, there is confusion about the meaning of evaluation in the context of parenting programs. The typical researcher sees evaluation as an outcome study that employs specific pre- and post-test measures and, if possible, a control group to document "real" program changes. This approach to evaluation requires major investments of time and money and may not be appropriate for most intervention programs. The typical practitioner is more concerned with how participants experience and evaluate the program and how to improve the program. This tension between research and practice reflects two different perspectives about evaluation (Palm, 1998).

McBride and Palm (1992) point out that the levels of evaluation model from Jacobs (1988) could be helpful in guiding practitioners toward best practices with fathers. The following is an exploration of the Jacobs model as it has been adapted to this program.

Level I: Preimplementation—Needs Assessment

At the preimplementation level, the major form of evaluation is needs assessment. This was initially accomplished through focus groups and individual interviews. The groups addressed some basic questions regarding inmates' views of fatherhood, needs for parent education, and specific issues faced by incarcerated fathers. The group also generates and selects content during an initial class session. The individual interviews provide information about family structures, beliefs about fatherhood, topical interests, and commitment to the class.

These different approaches to needs assessment are important ways to learn about the specific needs and issues of fathers.

Level II: Accountability—Accurate Description of Participants and Services Offered

Demographic information is gathered through the initial interview. The small size of the classes and the limited number of services that are offered make this task easy. This information allows the program to track some of the characteristics of the participants, such as age, family structure, number and ages of children, and the intensity of parent education services.

Level III: Program Clarification— Refining Program Goals and Methods

The program clarification level involves gathering information from a variety of sources and adjusting the program goals and format to fit the perceived needs of the participants. This has been accomplished in several different ways. A midterm evaluation occurs after the sixth session to ascertain whether the class is meeting the needs of the fathers and what has been most useful. A final evaluation questionnaire queries participants about their satisfaction with various aspects of the program, including content and format. A final interview also provides feedback about what has been most useful to fathers. The feedback from participants has been used to fine-tune the program. For example, feedback about some of the videotapes helped the parent educator to adjust how they were being used and to look for material that was more sensitive to social class and culture. Ninety-minute sessions seem to work well. Some men would like more than twelve sessions and a system for ongoing support after the class ends.

Level IV: Progress Toward Objectives

The question of program effectiveness has often been seen as the key part of any evaluation. It typically involves objective measures of program effects that can be generalized across programs. One important distinction about program impacts is long- and short-term impacts.

It takes considerable resources to measure program impacts over a long period of time while short-term outcomes can more easily be identified and assessed. Toward this end, the program described in this chapter has collected three different kinds of information from participants that may be helpful in determining short-term program impacts. The first is a pre- and post-test measure of parenting attitudes and behaviors assessed through five critical incidents (e.g., Your two-year-old is yelling for candy in the visiting room. What do you do?). Some of the positive changes noted here have been: less violent reactions to specific situations, more emphasis on listening, better understanding of children, and more realistic expectations.

A second source of short-term effects is a self-report rating of various impacts on fathers. The self-reports have reflected changes in four different areas.

1. *Listening to the child's feelings and thoughts:* "I learned how to let my child know I'll be there for him"; "Listen, listen, listen."
2. *Understanding the role of fatherhood:* "I learned what I mean to my children"; "I can be a good father while in prison"; "I learned to put a higher value on the role of fatherhood."
3. *Finding discipline alternatives:* "I learned different ways to doing things than my parents"; "Fathers are teachers—different ways to discipline"; "Discipline without laying hands on."
4. *Communicating with the child's mother:* "Don't block out Mom"; "I learned the child's mother's point of view on many topics"; "The child comes before your differences."

A final question on the written evaluation is, "How would you describe the program to another inmate?" Some examples of responses follow and provide a brief summary of fathers' impressions of program goals and impacts as might be expressed to another inmate.

I would tell them it is a very good program if you have children. You need the program in your life, for yourself, and you need it for your children.

It's worth taking the class; it opens up your mind to being a father. There's a lot of good things to learn from it.

It's a class that helps you understand three things . . . parenting, communications, and pride, and it's fun.

We have not undertaken a long-term impact study (Level V), which clearly is important. However, in this case it would be difficult because of the nature of the population and the limited resources of the program. It would also be useful to examine the child and family outcomes in addition to the short-term outcomes for the inmates.

CORE LEARNINGS:
LESSONS FROM THE FIELD

Core learnings are formulated as hypotheses drawn from practice and tested against published literature (National Center on Fathers and Families, 1995; Kane, Gadsden, and Armorer, 1997). These learnings begin from the insights of practitioners and are articulated to promote further discussion and research. The core learnings offered here build on the efforts of Kane, Gadsden, and Armorer (1997) to define and refine core learnings about fatherhood programs. They are presented as initial insights applied to programs for incarcerated fathers. They combine my program experiences and my interpretations of the current literature and are offered to practitioners as general principles to consider in developing effective program practices.

1. *The father-child bond is both deep and fragile.* The father-child bond inmates describe is based on a sense of caring and emerging responsibility. The actual father-child relationships that evolved range from fathers who have never seen their children to men who were involved caretakers before being incarcerated. Many incarcerated fathers understand the responsibility of fatherhood and want to be good fathers. The depth and importance of the father-child bond is displayed by many incarcerated fathers who describe fatherhood as a life-changing experience. As one father said, "Fatherhood has brought maturity, more value to life; kids come before you. It has brought me away from things, friends, drugs . . . my number one priority [now] is my family." For many, however, relationships with their children remain fragile.

The father-child bond is the starting point for a parenting program. Strengthening the connection or working toward a healthy reconnection is a primary goal. Fathers recognize the inherent value of their connection to their children, and have a sense of how fragile that bond can be. The program can help fathers to understand their responsibility for shaping a healthy connection and the positive influence this can have on children and on themselves.

2. *Family relationships are often complex and embedded in a variety of family structures, cultures, and community settings.* The complexity and tenuous nature of family relationships for incarcerated fathers is a critical factor to understand when designing a parenting program. An initial interview provides an opportunity to learn about current family structures and community settings. For instance, an initial interview might reveal that a father has three children with two different women, that he feels closest to his second and third children, and that their mother is supportive of his relationship with his first child. Sometimes incarcerated fathers have idealized images of their complex family systems and limited skills for managing a simple family structure, much less a family system that is very complex and often full of conflict. The goal in a parenting program is to help men to accept their responsibilities for their children and understand the challenges of creating healthy family systems for the child's sake.

A typical group in a parenting class brings together a variety of cultural backgrounds. This diversity reflects the high percentage of minorities who are incarcerated. The issue of culture is addressed in a direct manner whenever possible. In an early class session the topic of family traditions and rituals is discussed to provide a place to describe positive cultural practices and identity. Men from similar cultural backgrounds have a tendency to sit with one another. It has been helpful to bring popular videos that depict different cultural groups in positive ways. Literature is used in the same way. A poem written by an incarcerated father has been one of the most powerful handouts that has been used. Most parenting curricula are of limited use (Everhard, 1995) because they do not address cultural issues and the specific experiences of fathers in prison.

3. *Incarcerated fathers bring some strengths to parenting.* The lesson here is an extension of the universal principle from parent education and family support programs (Family Resource Coalition [FRC],

1996). All parents bring some strengths to the task of parenting and managing family life. Fathers in prison also bring strengths that need to be unveiled, pointed out, and affirmed. The key to identifying these strengths is to listen carefully to fathers talk about their children and families. For example, a father recently explained that he sends his son a check for ten dollars every month. This is a practice that shows a sense of responsibility and commitment to his child. Classes for incarcerated fathers can create a positive tone by focusing on how fathers can show caring and responsibility for children while in prison.

4. *The co-parenting relationship with the child's mother is often unstable and fraught with ambivalent or negative feelings.* The father's relationship with his children's mother is a key factor in addressing the realistic prospects for reconnecting with the children. Men express a wide range of feelings and are involved in a variety of family systems. There are many barriers to creating respectful relationships with mothers and healthy family systems for children. It is most helpful to men to focus on those areas where they do have some control and to minimize blaming mothers. Many men are uncertain how to resolve ambivalent feelings about love, sexual attraction, and a sense of commitment and may withdraw when they realize the child's mother is in a new relationship with another man. The focus on father's sense of commitment to the child and the importance of respect for and support of the mother for the child's sake helps to circumvent some of the negative and ambivalent feelings. The co-parent relationship is not easy to manage for young unmarried parents (Arendell, 1996) and the distance imposed by incarceration makes it even more difficult.

5. *Young fathers will face complex developmental issues.* The literature describes the developmental issues that young fathers face (e.g., Marsiglio, 1995; Rhoden and Robinson, 1997; Palkovitz and Palm, 1998). Many programs for young fathers emphasize vocational and job preparation as critical to helping young men take steps toward assuming the provider role (Levine and Pitt, 1995). A parenting program can also bring fathers to a new awareness of additional areas of development that are involved in responsible fatherhood. Young fathers in prison can focus on obtaining vocational and job skills, relationship and parenting skills, and responsibility for their own moral develop-

ment as models for their children. The pursuit of responsible father-hood can be a catalyst for development in these other areas.

6. *Incarceration provides a unique opportunity to explore father-hood as part of a search for meaning and different life choices.* Fatherhood provides a motivation for many men to change from a self-centered to other-centered focus (Snarey, 1993; Palkovitz and Palm, 1998). For men in prison, the experience of incarceration provides time and space to reconsider the meaning of life and the importance of life choices for their children. A majority of the 125-plus men who participated in the initial interviews cited fatherhood as a primary motivation to turn their lives around. Although fatherhood is clearly a powerful motivator, actual changes in behavior are not always so easy to accomplish. However, it appears that incarceration can be a critical period for examining the responsibilities of fatherhood and beginning to work toward generative fathering.

7. *Parent education should be coordinated with other services to support responsible fatherhood.* The principle of collaboration permeates parent education in many different contexts (Family Resource Coalition [FRC], 1996; Carter, 1996; Palm, 1999). Parent education clearly meets a need for fathers to affirm the importance of their role and the responsibilities that come with it. It also provides knowledge and skills that are useful in direct communication and interaction with children. However, the role of fatherhood needs additional support, both within the prison setting and during the transition to the outside world. Within the prison setting men can further their education and job skills. Many fathers participate in other rehabilitation programs, including substance abuse treatment and anger management. They also work for small wages. The role of provider might be enhanced and reinforced if fathers were given an incentive to work harder or longer hours to send money directly to their families. Programs that support transitions to the outside world are especially important since this is a time of both stress and opportunity.

CONCLUSION

Given the large numbers of incarcerated fathers in the United States and the strength of their generative desires, helping these men through parent education to find ways to be better fathers is an important goal. Parent education is a powerful intervention strategy for this particular population of fathers. The conceptual frameworks of generative fathering and microstructural theory provide a foundation for designing parent education programs, and specific information on the needs of incarcerated fathers, program goals, recruitment, content and methods, and approaches to program evaluation are offered to guide program design. The importance of this work for potential rehabilitation of incarcerated fathers and the growing population of fathers in prison demand that we put more energy and resources into creating effective intervention programs. The challenging nature of this work also demands skilled and experienced parent educators committed to working with this population.

REFERENCES

Adalist-Estrin, A. (1994). Family support and criminal justice. In S. L. Kagan and B. Weissbourd (Eds.), *Putting families first: America's family support movement and the challenge of change* (pp. 161-185). San Francisco: Jossey-Bass.

Adalist-Estrin, A. (1995). Incarcerated fathers. *Family and Corrections Network Report #8,* 1, 6, 8-10.

Arendell, T. (1996). *Co-parenting: A review of the literature.* Philadelphia, PA: University of Pennsylvania, National Center on Fathers and Families.

Bartell, F. (1988). The nurturing program at the Monroe County Jail. *Nurturing News, 10*(1), 45.

Bowling, G. (1999). The MELD for Young Dads program. *Family and Corrections Network Report #20,* 10-11.

Brenner, E. (1999). Fathers in prison: A review of the data. *Family and Corrections Network Report #20,* 3-7.

Carter, N. (1996). *See how we grow: A report on the status of parenting education in the U.S.* Philadelphia, PA: The Pew Charitable Trusts.

Child Welfare League of America (CWLA) (1999). *Children with incarcerated parents: A fact sheet.* <http://www.cwla.org/prison/facts99.html>.

Dollahite, D. C., Hawkins, A. J., and Brotherson, S. E. (1997). Fatherwork: A conceptual ethic of fathering as generative work. In A. J. Hawkins and D. C. Dollahite (Eds.), *Generative fathering: Beyond deficit perspectives* (pp. 17-35). Thousand Oaks, CA: Sage Publications.

Everhard, L. (1995). Notes on parenting programs for incarcerated fathers. *Family and Corrections Network Report #8,* 7, 10.

Fagan, J. and Iglesias, A. (1999). Father involvement program effects on fathers, father figures, and their Head Start children: A quasi-experimental study. *Early Childhood Research Quarterly, 14*(2), 243-269.

Family Resource Coalition (FRC) (1996). *Guidelines for family support practice.* Chicago, IL: Family Resource Coalition.

The Fathers Workshop (1999). *Long distance dads: Incarcerated fathers program.* <http://www.thefathersworkshop.org/lddads.html>.

Gilgun, J. (1994). *A survey of Minnesota prison inmates: Risk and protective factors in adolescence.* Minneapolis, MN: Minnesota Citizens' Council on Crime and Justice.

Giveans, D. (1988). The positive effects of child development classes on incarcerated fathers. *Nurturing News, 10*(1), 16-17.

Hairston, C. F. (1990). Family ties during imprisonment: Do they influence future criminal activity? *Federal Probation, 52*(1), 48-51.

Hawkins, A. and Dollahite, D. (Eds.) (1997). *Generative fathering: Beyond deficit perspectives.* Thousand Oaks, CA: Sage Publications.

Hostetter, E. and Jinnah, D. (1993). *Families of adult prisoners.* Prison Fellowship Ministries at <http://www.fcnetwork.org>.

Jacobs, A. (1995). *Protecting children and preserving families: A cooperative strategy for nurturing children of incarcerated parents.* New York: New York Women's Prison Association.

Jacobs, F. (1988). The five-tiered approach to evaluation: Content and implementation. In H. B. Weiss and F. H. Jacobs (Eds.), *Evaluating family programs* (pp. 37-68). Hawthorne, NY: Aldine deGruyter.

Kane, D., Gadsden, V., and Armorer, K. (1997). *The fathers and families core learnings: An update from the field.* Philadelphia, PA: University of Pennsylvania, National Center on Fathers and Families.

Knitzer, J. and Bernard, S. (1997). *Map and track: State initiatives to encourage responsible fatherhood.* New York: National Center on Children in Poverty.

Lanier, C. (1995). Incarcerated fathers: A research agenda. *Forum on Correction Research, 7*(2), 34-36.

Levine, J. and Pitt, E. (1995). *New expectations: Community strategies for responsible fatherhood.* New York: Families and Work Institute.

Marsiglio, W. (1995). Young nonresident biological fathers. *Marriage and Family Review, 20*(3/4), 325-348.

McBride, B. A. (1990). The effects of a parent education play group program on father involvement in childrearing. *Family Relations, 39*(3), 250-256.

McBride, B. A. (1991). Parental support and parental stress: An exploratory study. *Early Childhood Research Quarterly, 6*(2), 137-149.

McBride, B. A. and Palm, G. (1992). "Intervention programs for fathers: Outcome effects on paternal involvement." Paper presented at the 100th annual convention of the American Psychological Association, Washington, DC.

McCall, C. (1988). Nurturant parenting: How is it possible inside prison? *Nurturing Today, 10*(1), 8-9.

Mustin, J. (1999). Introduction. *Family and Corrections Network Report #20,* 1.

National Center on Fathers and Families (1995). *Core learnings.* Philadelphia, PA: University of Pennsylvania, National Center on Fathers and Families.

National Resource Center for Family Support Programs (1992). *Family support programs and incarcerated parents*. Chicago, IL: Family Resource Coalition.

Palkovitz, R. (1992). "Parenting as a generator of adult development: Conceptual issues and implications." Paper presented at the Theory and Research Methodology Workshop, National Council on Family Relations, Orlando, FL.

Palkovitz, R. and Palm, G. (1998). Fatherhood and faith in formation: The developmental effects of fathering on religiosity, morals and values. *The Journal of Men's Studies, 7*(1), 33-52.

Palm, G. (1996). "Understanding the parent education needs of incarcerated fathers." Paper presented at the National Council on Family Relations Conference, Kansas City, MO.

Palm, G. (1997). Promoting generative fathering through parent and family education. In A. J. Hawkins and D. C. Dollahite (Eds.), *Generative fathering: Beyond deficit perspectives* (pp. 167-182). Thousand Oaks, CA: Sage Publications.

Palm, G. (1998). *Developing a model of reflective practice for improving fathering programs*. Philadelphia, PA: University of Pennsylvania, National Center on Fathers and Families.

Palm, G. (1999). Learning from incarcerated fathers. *Family and Corrections Network Report #20,* 1-2.

Rhoden, J. L. and Robinson, B. E. (1997). Teen dads: A generative fathering perspective. In A. J. Hawkins and D. C. Dollahite (Eds.), *Generative fathering: Beyond deficit perspectives* (pp. 105-117). Thousand Oaks, CA: Sage Publications

Risman, B. (1987). Intimate relationships from a microstructural perspective: Men who mother. *Gender and Society, 1*(1), 6-32.

Shapiro, A. and Reiswerg, B. (Producers) (1996, June 16). *Bad Dads*. Santa Monica, CA: FOX Broadcasting Co.

Snarey, J. (1993). *How fathers care for the next generation: A four-decade study*. Cambridge, MA: Harvard University Press.

U.S. Department of Justice (1991). *Prisoners in 1990*. Washington, DC: U.S. Department of Justice, Bureau of Justice Statistics.

Chapter 6

Web-Based Education and Support for Fathers: Remote But Promising

Travis R. Grant
Alan J. Hawkins
David C. Dollahite

"Fatherwork" is the term employed by Dollahite, Hawkins, and Brotherson (1997) to describe the challenges men take on as they engage in generative fathering. As men strive to rise to the challenges of fathering, they often find themselves faced with unfamiliar challenges and in need of some guidance—on-the-job training, if you will. The Fatherwork framework, however, does not explicitly address where fathers might turn for support or training in their efforts. Turning to one's own father may not be the best option for many men, both because of strained relationships and because of the significant changes in the social context of fathering that have occurred in a generation. The opportunity for peers to mentor and provide the advice or help that fathers may need will vary both in quantity and quality. Men can turn to traditional family life education programs for answers to these problems, but generally they do not; participants in traditional parenting education are overwhelmingly female (Palm, 1997). The Internet may provide an additional resource to assist fathers with the challenges of parenting by providing a unique arena for men to learn, share, and discuss the work they do as fathers.

According to eStats (1999), an Internet statistical service, there were over 37 million adults who regularly used the Internet in 1998 in the United States.* This number is up 28 million from 1997. Further, eStats estimates that the average growth rate for the next five years will be 15 percent per year. That would mean a jump to 85 million users in the United States by the year 2002. Although some might consider these figures to be high, they are actually conservative when compared to other studies which project as many as 175 million users by the year 2002 (eStats, 1999).

The typical Internet user in 1998 was a thirty-eight-year-old male college graduate with an income of about $58,000 a year. He was also most likely to be a married, white-collar worker (eStats, 1999). (Table 6.1 provides more specific information on the statistical make-up of all Internet users.) Although statistics regarding parental status are not reported by eStats, an analysis of the 1998 *Graphic, Visualization, and Usability Center's 10th WWW User Survey's* data (GVU, 1999) showed that 30 percent of the men who use the Web have one or more children. This translates into roughly 7 million fathers in 1998 who were using the World Wide Web, a figure that will increase rapidly over the next several years.

Clearly, the Internet and the World Wide Web present exciting possibilities for reaching and supporting fathers and potential fathers. In this chapter, we explore some reasons why Web-based education may be a rich resource to help fathers. Next, we sample and review several professional Web sites that specifically focus on father education and support. The sites we selected for review are hardly exhaustive; rather, they represent a sample of the sites with reliable information and resources about responsible fathering in various circumstances. Then, in greater depth, we focus on an evaluation of one Web site (FatherWork), that has systematically attempted to assess its educational effectiveness.

---

*eStats defines a user as a person who uses the Web on a regular basis, not just people who have logged online only once. Thus, this is considered to be a highly conservative figure.

Table 6.1. Basic Demographic Information on World Wide Web Users

Age		Education	
18-24	13%	High School Only	8%
25-34	22%	Some College	25%
35-44	34%	College Completion	30%
45-54	20%	Some Graduate School	16%
55-64	7%	Graduate School Completed	21%
60+	4%	**Occupation**	
Gender		Educational	27%
Male	61%	Computer-related	25%
Female	39%	Professional	22%
Marital Status		Managerial	18%
Married	42%	Other	8%
Divorced/Widowed	20%		
Single	38%		
Income			
Under $30,000	12%		
$30,000-$39,999	13%		
$40,000-$49,999	14%		
$50,000-$74,999	30%		
$75,000-$99,999	11%		
$100,000+	20%		

Source: eStats, 1999.

WEB-BASED EDUCATION AND FATHERS

Beyond the sheer number of fathers on the Internet, there are at least four more reasons for father educators to make use of this technology:

1. People who are using the Web are looking for information.
2. The learning style of many men may fit well with Web-based learning opportunities.
3. The Web provides a private, individualized method of learning.

4. The Web also can reduce the isolation some men may feel as fathers and open up opportunities to share both concerns and excitement about their work as fathers.

The Web As an Information Resource

The main reason most people use the Web is to obtain information, although it can be used for many purposes, including entertainment, "chatting," and shopping. According to eStats, "No matter what source you look at, gathering news and information is the top reason for using the Internet" (eStats, 1999). GVU reports that 74 percent of users access the Web to obtain "personal information" (GVU, 1999). In addition, people who used the Web in 1997 were mostly using it for personal rather than business purposes (eStats, 1999).

These points hold two important implications for father educators. First, to paraphrase a line from a popular movie, "If you create it, they will come." Fathers are on the Web looking for information (Morahan-Martin, 1998) and can benefit from what educators have to share. Second, because millions of fathers on the Web are looking for personal information, it is critical to have accurate, informative Web sites for them about fathering. One of the major problems with the easy access of information on the Web is that the quality of information varies considerably. Thus, trained father educators need to provide the best information possible for fathers (Morris, Dollahite, and Hawkins, 1999).

The Web and Men's Learning Style

Recent studies have shown that computers can be effective learning resources for many men. Men are likely to have an assimilating style of learning (Philbin et al., 1995), which is defined as learning through logically organizing and analyzing information (thinking and obtaining). Men were also found to be the least likely to have divergent styles of learning (Philbin et al., 1995), which includes imaginative learning, brainstorming, and reflective observation (feeling and watching). The study also reported that men are somewhat likely to be either convergent or accommodating learners.

These styles of learning involve doing and thinking, and doing and feeling, respectively. Thus, men generally are interested first in obtaining information; interest in discussing and talking about what they learn is secondary (although important for some). Although the Web provides methods of interaction and communication about items of learning, it is primarily a source for obtaining information.

Furthermore, many men are attracted by the "cool" technology or high-tech.aspects of the Internet. In one study, Abouserie, Moss, and Barasi (1992) reported that first-year male medical students had greater preferences for using computer-assisted learning compared to female students. They also found that the men got better grades than women did in a physiology course that used computer-assisted learning. Perhaps, then, many men are more accepting of computer-based or Web-based learning than women.

The Web and Private, Individualized Learning

The private and unobtrusive nature of Web-based learning may provide added benefits for many men because they do not have to talk publicly about their reasons for seeking information, as is often expected in parent-education groups. Experience has taught many professionals that men typically do not get involved in traditional family-life education. Palm (1997) argues that fathers have different communication styles than mothers and are usually less comfortable in small, face-to-face, group settings. Levine and Pitt (1995) also state that men are often skeptical about and sometimes threatened by these kinds of groups. They found that one-on-one support seemed to work best for fathers.

With these considerations about men and traditional family-life education in mind, we propose that the Web is a tremendous potential resource for fathering education because it meets the qualifications of being private and individualized. Men can come to a fathering Web site with a specific question in mind, and often find the answer on their own. A father does not need to tell a group about his concern unless he chooses to visit a chat room, forum, or other method of interacting. He can work out the problem himself, at his own pace and on his own level.

The Web As a Communication Community

Although many men do not want to talk or interact with others about parenting, there are others who desire this kind of learning and problem solving. Walther (1996) argues that the nature of online communication may reduce some kinds of inhibitions that can make personal communication easier for many. Morahan-Martin (1998) found that men are more likely than women to report being more open, more themsleves, and more likely to make friends online. Our experience in chat rooms, online discussion boards, and e-mail lists for fathers has shown that when men choose to participate in these types of discussions they are typically satisfied with the connections and information that they receive. Many fathers have expressed appreciation for having a forum where they can talk and share their ideas about parenting. The Internet has provided them with a specific outlet where they can ask questions, vent frustrations, and share their ideas about parenting.

It is interesting that probably the most active communication community is at a Web site called Daddys Home,* which is designed for stay-at-home fathers. Perhaps many of these men are feeling a sense of isolation and have found the online discussion with other fathers a source of support and a valued means of communication and connection. And even for fathers who prefer not to interact and who enjoy the privacy of Web-based learning, the sense of community, albeit "virtual" in nature, may still be appreciated. Thus, the Internet can provide a resource for fathers who desire to connect in a communication community.

Limitations of Web-Based Education

It should be noted that men of higher socioeconomic status currently are more likely to use the Internet (see Table 6.1). Therefore, Web-based fathering education does not yet reach all fathers, especially those in disadvantaged and at-risk populations. However, with

---

* See Appendix A for the URL addresses of all sites discussed in this chapter.

the rapid expanse of the Internet and the increase in free Internet service providers (eStats, 1999), the day may come when having Internet access is as common as having a telephone or television (Smith, 1999). Because using the Internet requires certain skills and knowledge, fathers who are comfortable with these technologies will be the most likely to benefit from online programs. However, as the Internet becomes more commonplace it will be important that programs be available for fathers with Web skills from beginning to advanced.

OVERVIEW OF FATHERING EDUCATION SITES: WHAT IS OUT THERE?

The tremendous number and variety of Web sites for fathers makes difficult the task of providing an overview of the resources now available online. Elliott (1999) organized Web-based family-life education programs according to the "Framework for Life-Span Family Life Education" (Arcus, 1987) sponsored by the National Council on Family Relations (see <http://www.familytrack.com/resources.htm>), but did not attempt to differentiate between Web sites of greater or lesser quality. We want to highlight what we think are some of the better resources. To assist in identifying these high-quality sites, we modified Robert Hughes' (1994) framework for evaluating family-life education. This framework includes an evaluation of the *content* of the program (e.g., theory and research, context, and practice); *instructional process* of the program (e.g., teaching plans and presentation); and *implementation issues* (e.g., intended audience, easy access). We made some minor modifications to fit the unique aspects of Web-based educational programs and to focus more specifically on fathers. (A synopsis of this modified framework is presented in Appendix B.) We try to show the variety of resources available to help fathers, and highlight sites that meet many of the criteria specified in the modified Hughes framework. We also attend to some of the Web-site evaluation issues raised by Morris, Dollahite, and Hawkins (1999). Certainly, more quality sites could be mentioned, but we are limited here by space constraints.

Most of the sites that we reviewed for this chapter were developed as an extension to an already-existing program for fathers, while a few sites are programs that exist only on the Web. Extending an already-existing program to the Web makes the program available to a much larger audience. These sites tend to provide access to resources that can help fathers rather than provide extensive education online. For example, the National Center for Fathering (NCF) makes some materials originally produced for radio and magazines available on the Web. The National Fatherhood Initiative (NFI) also provides a reproduction of Wade Horn's "Fatherly Advice," a syndicated column. Both of these sites provide a reliable resource for fathering information. The authors of the sites provide the information in an appealing format, which is one of the evaluation criteria in Hughes' (1994) framework.

Both NCF and NFI provide a forum for fathers to discuss the many issues related to fathering. There are discussion groups in which users ask for advice, give advice, and communicate with others across the country and around the world. Some other examples of such discussion groups can also be found at Fathers' Forum and Father's World. These forums are an example of how sites can provide a variety of learning activities for fathers, another evaluation criterion in Hughes' (1994) framework. A nice feature of these sites is that they allow for optional, active participation in these discussion groups. If a father does not want to share in the discussion he can "lurk" and simply read what other fathers are talking about.

Many Web-based programs address specific fathering circumstances such as divorced fathers, new fathers, and fathers with special-needs children. Fathers' Forum is a program designed for first-time fathers who are looking for more information about pregnancy and about the first years of their children's life. The National Fathers Network is a resource for fathers of children with special needs. It provides stories, advice, and other important information for fathers in this challenging circumstance. Divorced Dads provides a collection of letters from fathers, mothers, and children of divorce. (Appendix A lists other sites that provide information specific to fathers in various circumstances.)

Father advocacy sites are also common. These sites provide a look at the many different contexts of fathers, from the single divorced father to the married father. The American Coalition for Fathers & Children (ACFC) is one example of a group that focuses on fathers from all backgrounds. Their Web site provides research and information on the importance of being involved as a father. This organization also advocates for divorced fathers seeking help. Another example of an organization similar to ACFC is the Fathers' Rights and Equality Exchange (FREE). Their focus is on advice for the divorced father seeking greater opportunities to be present and involved in his child's life. Although there are many good fathering sites, there is still a need for sites that meet the needs of fathers in other challenging circumstances. In addition, there are few sites that focus on education specific to fathers of different racial and ethnic backgrounds, and more efforts are needed to reach such groups.

There are also several sites that specifically provide research for the father educator. Two of these research-specific sites are the National Center on Fathers and Families and FatherNet. Both of these sites are university based and provide access to fathering research for educators, but they would likely appeal to many fathers as well.

Although most professional Web-based programs are extensions of already-existing father-support organizations, a few programs exist only on the Web. The previously mentioned Divorced Dads site is one example of such a program. Another example, Father's World, provides a discussion forum, a mailing list, and many articles written by dads about what life is like as a father. This is one example of how a site can be interactive and appealing to all types of fathers, with many colorful graphics, humorous stories, and valuable information. Another site, Four-Fold Fathering (developed by Travis R. Grant), provides some information on what fathers can do to promote their children's development. It also provides a collection of songs that are written about fathering, or for children by fathers. Four-Fold Fathering also provides personal essays and poetry.

FatherWork (developed by Alan J. Hawkins and David C. Dollahite) is perhaps the most extensive site dedicated to online fathering education and it does not exist outside the Internet. (The official and lengthy title of the Web site is, FatherWork: Stories, Ideas, and Activities to Encourage Generative Fathering. The term generative, of course, comes from Erik Erikson's [1950] theory of psychosocial development across the life span, specifically, the seventh stage of generativity versus self-absorption.) FatherWork consists of more than 300 (printed) pages of material, including a set of real-life narratives organized into learning modules on fathering in various challenging circumstances, at various times across the life span, and other important topics of interest or concern to fathers and practitioners who work with fathers. The site also includes hundreds of activities for strengthening the father-child relationship. A virtual workshop on the site allows Certified Family-Life Educators to receive preapproved continuing education credit for professional certification without having to leave their home or office. The site is an example of how online programs can be theory- and research-based (another criterion established by Hughes), because the stories and ideas on the site are explicitly linked to both a conceptual framework for understanding fathering (Dollahite and Hawkins, 1998; Dollahite, Hawkins, and Brotherson, 1997) and to findings from empirical studies and scholarly works by reputable scholars.

Our overview documents some of the resources for fathers (and practitioners who work with them) that are available on the Web. Our coverage is only a sample of quality sites; many more educational resources are currently available, and more will come online in the future. While the *quantity* of Web sites for fathers will surely increase, the *quality* and *impact* of this kind of remote intervention for fathers is questionable. How helpful can such resources actually be? Americans seem to have a blind faith in the value of information, and the more information the better. But if father educators are going to invest time in Web-based education, or recommend it to their students, they need greater confidence that it can actually help the men who make use of it. Accordingly, we present an evaluation of the FatherWork site as an initial attempt to evaluate the outcomes of Web-based intervention.

EVALUATING OUTCOMES:
A CASE STUDY

The Development of FatherWork

Although the FatherWork site has undergone numerous changes and additions since it went online in June 1996, its basic premise and purpose have been constant: to provide high-quality education for fathers based on sound scholarship through a medium that can reach millions. Another constant has been the desire to construct a site that would be useful both for the practitioner who works with fathers ("wholesale users") and for individual fathers ("retail users"). The primary educational method used on the site is the presentation of real-life stories or narratives which have an ability both to educate and motivate (Dollahite, Hawkins, and Brotherson, 1996). Over the years, we gathered narratives from fathers with a great deal of assistance from a large cadre of students at Brigham Young University. These students helped collect the narratives, integrated them with the under-girding conceptual framework of the site, connected them to solid scholarship on fathering, and organized them into different learning modules. Later, students helped add an extensive list of developmentally appropriate activities for fathers and children. They also helped develop numerous metaphors for good fathering. The hope was that this combination of educational elements would engage the father's head, heart, and hands to increase his sense of responsibility. (For an example of a FatherWork learning module and these different educational features, see Appendix C.) Initially, the technical challenges of Web-based education were substantial because the developers were not trained in computer science. For the most part, students helped to surmount the technical challenges as well as assisting with the content and design challenges. No professional Web developers were used, except for consultation.

Method of Evaluation

Program evaluation in any setting is a significant challenge facing family-life educators. However, program evaluation is important to the overall, long-term quality of any program and to the progress of the profession of family-life education. Unfortunately, evaluation is often given inadequate attention in program design (Darling, 1987; Hughes, 1994; Small, 1990). This difficulty is compounded for Web-based family-life education because participants interact remotely and usually anonymously, and they guide their own learning by deciding what and how much of the information they want to examine. Interaction between the Web-based educator and the Web-based learner is limited at best and nonexistent in most cases. However, Web-based family-life education should not be exempt from program evaluation simply because it is challenging.

From the beginning, in our own work with FatherWork, we have sought feedback from users on their experiences and on the value of the site toward their efforts to be better fathers (or father educators). We present here a summary of those efforts and what we have learned so far in the hope that it may be helpful to other educators and practitioners interested in Web-based education for fathers. Although the work we present here is only a first step in terms of Web site evaluation, we believe it demonstrates that there is some value to fathers in this kind of remote intervention or virtual learning. First, we outline our various methods of ongoing, on-line evaluation. Then we present what we have learned, organized by a series of five questions that are important to evaluating the effectiveness of this kind of educational intervention. We also suggest areas for attention and improvement.

Qualitative Evaluation Data

We provided two methods for individual users to give us qualitative comments about their reactions to FatherWork. First, users are invited to "sign" a virtual guestbook and write short comments about the site. These comments are posted for all subsequent users to read and they provide a potential source of feedback on what the users value (or do not value) about the educational site. Although some comments are not relevant to an evaluation of the educational content, process, and the learning that takes place, many are informative. In addition, we encourage users to e-mail us directly with comments about FatherWork, and we provide them constant, easy access to that function. Some users take advantage of this opportunity, which provides us with a variety of data with potential program evaluation uses. We receive qualitative feedback, both from practitioners who work with fathers and from fathers (and other individuals) who access the site for their own educational use.

Quantitative Evaluation Data

FatherWork has more than twenty-five separate educational modules covering a wide variety of topics on fathering. At the end of each module is a set of four evaluation questions to be completed on a voluntary basis by users. These questions attempt to assess different dimensions of learning related to our original educational objectives, including the extent to which the module:

1. gave them helpful ideas (cognitive dimension);
2. affected them emotionally (affective dimension);
3. motivated them to take action to be better fathers (behavioral dimension); and
4. provided them a stronger ethical commitment to generative fathering (moral dimension).

Responses are provided by clicking a button on a four-point scale. An eye-catching, graphic interface is used to encourage more users to complete the evaluation questions (see Appendix C). Unfortunately, we estimate less than 2 percent of users provide this feedback.

Evaluation Results

Question 1: To what extent is FatherWork used, who uses it, when, and what are they interested in?

A software program attached to the site monitors visits to the site and which modules received the most "hits." Since the first few months of operation during the summer of 1996, FatherWork has steadily increased the number of "user sessions," or visitors, per day, from about twenty to more than 100. One hundred users a day is not a lot compared to some high-volume sites. Nevertheless, compounded over a year, the number suggests how efficient Web-based educational programs can be compared to traditional, classroom-based family-life education. The average user explores five to eight educational modules during the visit.

Analysis of the qualitative data suggests that probably 75 to 80 percent of our users are men. Still, given that the majority of all Web users are men and that our site is specifically about fathering, we are encouraged that women interested in fathering are also drawn to FatherWork. Qualitative data also suggest that most of our users are fathers interested in getting some good ideas. However, another target audience for FatherWork is professionals working with fathers.

We have received dozens of requests and feedback notes from professionals who work with fathers in educational, clinical, and religious settings.

FatherWork users visit the site at various times of the day throughout the week, not just at night or on weekends. We have been interested to note that many users visit the site in the late afternoon on weekdays. Perhaps these are individuals with Internet access at their place of employment who visit the site on their afternoon break. This also suggests that visiting the site does not necessarily subtract from family prime time in the evenings and weekends.

The most popular educational modules are in the "Fathering Across the Life Span" section. "Fathering Teenagers" has been one of the more popular educational modules, followed by modules on infancy and the toddler years. We have received numerous notes from new fathers expressing appreciation for this resource. Lately, the "Fathering Activities" module, which lists hundreds of fun, educational, and enriching activities that fathers can do with children in various developmental stages, has become quite popular.

The Web page that defines the term "generative fathering" in the site's title receives many visits. Similarly, the Web page that contains the theoretical framework for FatherWork is frequently visited. This Web page is essentially a long, academic article. Whether visitors read the whole article is unknown, but we are encouraged that visitors are at least interested in the theoretical framework behind FatherWork and are not automatically repelled by anything that smacks of stuffy, academic ideas. Also, the page that describes the creators of FatherWork is frequently visited. The fact that these background Web pages are regularly visited suggests that users value knowing who and what are behind the site.

Question 2: Does the content of FatherWork give users interesting ideas?

The quantitative evaluation data gathered from the small proportion of users who responded to the feedback question related to users' cognitive reactions (N = 236 in September 1998) indicated that FatherWork provided users with good ideas to improve their fathering. (The specific question was: "Please tell us to what extent the stories and ideas . . . gave you ideas to strengthen your fathering.") On a scale of 0 to 3 (0 = Not at All; 1 = A Little; 2 = Some; 3 = A Lot), the mean evaluation rating was 2.3 (*SD*=.80).

In the qualitative data collected, comments such as the following were the most common feedback we received:

- (from a divorced mother) "This has been an informative experience. I have two sons, 7 and 12, who have a dad who is only 4 miles away, but he is not involved in their lives, even though they want him to be. Anyway, I have to teach them to be good fathers somehow, even though they will not have any male role models other than those we can find in church or sports. I will discuss the stuff I find here with them. Thanks!"
- "Thank you!! This site is tremendous!! Being a custodial father with 3 teen daughters is a challenge and I'll take any help I can get. This site is well put together and has excellent content."
- "As a counselor in both private practice and the provincial correctional system (for assaultive men) I find this site to be a wealth of information. . . . Thanks for a refreshing site."

Question 3: Does the content on FatherWork affect users emotionally?

Our use of real-life stories and experiences for educational modules on FatherWork was explicitly designed to provide a stronger emotional content, which we believe can add substantially to the staying power of the educational experience. The quantitative evaluation data gathered indicated that FatherWork affected users emotionally. (The specific question was: "Please tell us to what extent the stories and ideas . . . Affected you emotionally.") On a scale of 0 to 3, the mean evaluation rating was 2.5 (*SD*=.73).

The qualitative data also provided encouraging feedback, although direct comments about the emotional impact of FatherWork were not common:

- "Thank you for providing a resource for fathers and fatherhood. . . . I was deeply touched by the experiences shared and the resources provided to families in this site."
- "This touched my heart. There ought to be a warning though, something to the effect of, 'Don't read at work.' It's hard to talk on the phone with a lump in my throat."

Question 4: Does the content on FatherWork motivate users to greater action?

In addition to providing good educational material, we hoped the content of FatherWork would motivate fathers to action as well. The limited quantitative data related to motivation (N=231) indicated that FatherWork encouraged users to action. (The specific question was: "Please tell us to what extent the stories and ideas . . . motivated you to take greater action to be the kind of father you want to be or motivate other fathers.") On a scale of 0 to 3, the mean evaluation rating was 2.2 (SD=.85).

The qualitative data included many comments from fathers that could be interpreted as expressions of renewed motivation for the work of generative fathering:

- "Thank you for a great site—give us new 'to-be dads' a little slack and continue the advice, philosophy, theology, and basic mechanics of fatherhood. I know I need it."
- "This is a great site. With three kids (4, 2, 7 weeks) I need all the help I can get. I think it is more important than ever to be a good father."
- "I am a father of one 16-month-old girl (so far!) and halfway through Graduate School. . . . Heaven knows how hard it is to keep up with the demands of graduate education and be there for your children. Thanks for the great fathering ideas and tips . . ."
- "I spent a great deal of time reading all the wonderful stories . . . This is truly one of the most inspiring sites for fathers on the Internet."

Question 5: Does the content on FatherWork deepen users' sense of responsibility to be a good father or their commitment to generative fathering?

FatherWork content was explicitly designed with moral content to encourage a deeper commitment to responsible, generative fathering. The limited data related to deepening a sense of responsibility or commitment (N=227) indicated that "FatherWork" strengthened users' ethical orientation to generative fathering. (The specific question was: "Please tell us to what extent the stories and ideas . . . deepened your sense of responsibility and commitment to good fathering.") On a scale of 0 to 3, the mean evaluation rating was 2.4 (*SD*=.79).

Although there were not many comments in the qualitative data directly related to this question, many comments had a tone of increased sense of responsibility and commitment:

- "I am very happy to have found this site. . . . The philosophy of continual development by both child and father throughout their lives brings the scope of this great undertaking into perspective. Most 'experienced Dads' always say that parenting is a solid 20+ year commitment. You have demonstrated that it is and should be a life-long process."
- "As Father's Day approaches . . . I was looking for a gift I could give to my six sons who are fathers to help them with their fathering. My daughter. . . led me [to] FatherWork . . . and I e-mailed the site address to them. Thanks for saying it for me. I know that 'no other success in life can compensate for failure as a father' . . ."

Some Tentative Evaluation Conclusions and Recommendations

Conclusion 1

Data can be collected, but . . . . With effort, some evaluation data can be collected and can shed light on how users are reacting and how well educational objectives are being met. From the limited data collected, we found that: (1) users appreciated and benefited from Father-Work; (2) we were reaching both fathers and practitioners who work with fathers; and (3) we were providing helpful ideas to strengthen fathering, touching hearts, motivating to greater action, and deepening a sense of responsibility and commitment to generative fathering. However, this first lesson must be tempered by lessons two and three.

Conclusion 2

The data may not be representative. Very few users seem willing to pause to provide evaluation data, either qualitative or quantitative. Hence, the data may not accurately represent the thoughts and feelings of the whole population of FatherWork users. Of course, there was no incentive other than goodwill for users to provide such data.

Conclusion 3

The data are likely to be positively skewed. When feedback data were given, it was highly skewed to the positive side and very general. An occasional user who enjoyed the site would express his or her general appreciation, but it was rare for individuals to provide specific, constructive criticism (other than technical glitches).

It will be difficult for Web-based family-life educators to get the full range (positive to negative) and specificity of online feedback needed to help in the ongoing process of revising and improving programs. Accordingly, we make the following recommendations for evaluating Web-based programs for fathers:

Recommendation 1

Build on traditional educational experience. Web-based fathering programs will benefit if their designers have had some experience with the program in traditional (face-to-face) family-life education. Experience with the program in a traditional setting likely generates valuable feedback on how fathers react to various features of the program and what is more or less effective that will be difficult to obtain online.

Recommendation 2

Use traditional evaluation research methods. Effective program evaluation of Web-based family-life education may require more traditional research methods. That is, evaluators may need to recruit subjects periodically to use the Web site and then fill out survey questions and/or be interviewed in focus groups about their learning. An experimental or quasi-experimental design that compares users of a fathering Web site to nonusers over time would be particularly helpful.

Recommendation 3

Explore innovative Web-based methods. Our online evaluation efforts hardly exhaust the possibilities. Other innovative methods for gathering evaluation data online should be tried. For instance, it is technically possible to invite users to fill out an exit survey. That is, when they exit the site, a page with survey questions appears. Filling out the questions should be voluntary, but perhaps more users would pause to answer a few questions if they were presented in this way. Some type of virtual or tangible incentive to provide feedback could also be considered (e.g., links to other sites, gift certificates, T-shirts, free books, etc.).

Recommendation 4

Keep trying. Although we have found that online evaluation is difficult, it is possible to make some assessment of how well the site is achieving educational objectives and how educational offerings can be improved. Accordingly, we encourage other evaluators to make similar attempts to help further the current understanding of the effectiveness of online education for fathers. A combination of online and traditional evaluation research methods may be the most effective approach to obtaining needed feedback.

CONCLUSION

In this chapter, we have argued for the value of the World Wide Web in providing education and support to fathers and practitioners who work with them. The overwhelming number of fathers searching for helpful information on the Web and the good fit between Web-based education and many fathers' learning styles suggest promise for this kind of remote intervention. Numerous quality resources are currently available on the Web. Our experience in assessing the educational outcomes of the FatherWork Web site gives us initial encouragement that Web-based education and support can be one more medium used by family-life educators to help fathers.

APPENDIX A

Sample of Web-based Father Education and Support Programs

Site Name	Address (URL)
American Coalition for Fathers & Children	http://www.acfc.org/
Boot Camp for New Dads	http://www.newdads.com/
Daddys Home	http://www.daddyshome.com/
dads & daughters	http://www.dadsanddaughters.org/
Dads at a Distance	http://www.daads.com/
Divorced Dads	http://www.geocities.com/Heartland/Meadows/1259/
Divorced Father	http://www.divorcedfather.com/
The Fatherhood Coalition	http://www.fatherhoodcoalition.org/
Fathering Magazine	http://www.fathermag.com/
FatherNet	http://www.cyfc.umn.edu/Fathernet/
Fathers' Forum	http://www.fathersforum.com/
Fathers' Rights and Equality Exchange	http://www.dadsrights.org/
Father's World	http://www.fathersworld.com/
FatherWork	http://fatherwork.byu.edu/
Four-Fold Fathering	http://four-fold.homepage.com/
National Center for Fathering	http://www.fathers.com/
National Center on Fathers and Families	http://www.ncoff.gse.upenn.edu/
National Fatherhood Initiative	http://www.fatherhood.org/
National Fathers Network	http://www.fathersnetwork.org/
Single & Custodial Father's Network	http://www.single-fathers.org/
The Single Fathers' Lighthouse	http://www.av.qnet.com/~rlewis3/index.html
WWW Virtual Library: Fatherhood	http://www.vix.com/men/nofather/nodad.html

Note: Due to the rapid changes within the Internet, some of these addresses may no longer be available.

APPENDIX B

Framework for Evaluating Web-based Family-Life Education

Issue	Recommendation
1. Content: Theory and Research	A. Base on current research.
	B. Include references or lists of other materials.
	C. Provide a "framework" for the educational material.
2. Content: Context	A. Consider the different contexts of fathers (work, school, church, etc.), or be explicit about the focus on a specific context.
	B. Consider cultural and social class contexts.
	C. Consider macrolevel contexts (time, country, and economy).
3. Content: Practice	A. Offer something new and different from what is available through other Web sites.
	B. Build upon other existing programs but do not replicate them.
	C. Note limitations the program may have.
4. Instructional Process: Teaching Plans	A. Use a variety of learning activities for participants:
	i. Different types of learning (i.e., essays, jokes, or activities);
	ii. E-mail communities;
	iii. Discussion groups;
	iv. Different pedagogical approaches (i.e., rational-technical, interpretive, critical/emancipatory (see Morgaine, 1992).
	B. Present materials quickly and efficiently. Length may be considered an attempt to provide breadth and depth. However, most readers of the Web quickly skim a page for the information they are seeking. Thus, quick presentation is essential to reach the audience.

Appendix B *(continued)*

5. Instructional Process: Presentation

A. Use appropriate reading level for fathers. (Even though Web literacy suggests a relatively high reading ability, keep the material very readable.)

B. Provide examples for fathers from many cultural/ethnic backgrounds and family types.

C. Provide an aesthetically pleasing presentation that will grab the interest of fathers. (Remember that when developing Web-based family-life education it is easier for people to leave the site than it was to get there.)

D. Follow the best practices suggested by Palm (1997) and Morris et al. (1999), which are: working from a strengths perspective, building on motivations already inherent in fathers, and using an individual focus to engage fathers.

E. Download time should be quick so that on-line time minimally subtracts from family time.

6. Implementation Issues
Intended audience; Easy access

A. Provide information about who they intend to help, and to some extent who may not find the site helpful.

B. Provide some easy way to access all the information found on the site (i.e., search function, a site directory or map, or other indexing methods).

Adapted from Hughes, 1994.

APPENDIX C

Illustration of a FatherWork Learning Module

FATHERWORK

Fathering Noncustodial Children
(Divorced Dads)

The most important . . . work you and I will ever do will be within the walls of our own homes.

—Harold B. Lee

Noncustodial fathers start out with two strikes against them. The first strike is that even under the best of circumstances, many fathers struggle to be actively involved with their children. The second strike is that when divorce occurs, nearly 90 percent of fathers live apart from their children. Researchers stress the importance of fathers' continued involvement in their children's lives, regardless of the marital situation (Gerson, 1997; Doherty, 1997). Other research suggests that many men do want to remain committed to their children, even when not living with the mother and child (Rhoden and Robinson, 1997). Biller (1993) suggests that although there are many interacting influences that impact how each child will adjust to divorce, none is more important than having continuous positive involvement with the father, as well as the mother. These strong connections are beneficial both to the children as well as the father, and they help both to deal with the challenges of changing family circumstances.

An assumption of most parents is that they will have a relationship with their child that consists of spending time together in the ordinary ways, such as bed and meal times; that families interact with each other daily. By their frequency, these events become so ordinary that they rarely stand out as notable. The term "prosaic" refers to the common or ordinary, and in family life, there is much that is prosaic. However, when divorce disrupts family structure, it also substantially diminishes family processes, many of which are prosaic. How can fathers who don't live with their children "be there"? How can they be good fathers during specified times or intermittent intervals? How do they create the prosaics of family life from a distance and on their own? Below are some stories of how some fathers who don't live with their children try to deal with this challenge, to find the ordinary connections in an extraordinary situation.

Noncustodial fathers are faced with many challenges, the first of which is to be actively involved with their children's lives. Even under the best of circumstances this can be difficult. However, noncustodial fathers are now realizing that the most important things that can be done are the little ordinary things. In reality, it is the little things that are missing and need to be done.

In this example of ethical work, a child expressed appreciation for the little things that her father did to be a part of her life.

Since my parents' divorce, my two brothers and I have lived with my mom. We were all teenagers at the time and didn't want anything to do with my dad. There seemed to be a big generation gap between my dad and us kids. However, he never gave up on us. He would stop by to visit us every few days since he lived close by. He would call to talk to each one of us and he never hung up the phone without telling us that he loved us, even though we hardly ever returned the kindness. He used to call us and offer to let us use his car on the weekends just so he would have a chance to see us. We were ungrateful, but still he offered. We were all confused and hurt that our parents would get divorced for what seemed like no good reason. I know it has been a real struggle for my dad, especially with the cold reception he has received from all his children, but now that we're older and living lives of our own, I'm glad he didn't give up on us. I know he loves us and it's fun to have him be a part of our lives. Now when he calls, I've learned how much it means to him to have a good conversation with us. I think that growing up has made it easier to understand him and get along with him. I appreciate all he's done for us because if he hadn't tried to keep the relationship alive, it would have died.

Although many noncustodial fathers live thousands of miles away from their children, their relationship with them can grow. In this example of mentoring and ethical work, one father told how he has been able to be a positive influence on his children's lives.

I found the best way to have a positive impact on my children was to call them every Sunday morning. I called every morning to set up a pattern. I knew on Sunday, the children should be rested and under little stress. When I was on the phone I tried to be a counselor who listened instead of giving advice. Later I would write a letter and give advice. By writing one can read what they are saying to their children and often will decide to rewrite some of the phrases. This helps you eliminate emotions that often arise in discourse between parent and child.

Other fathers found creative ways to show their love to their children and that the children had an important place in their lives. In the end, it is these little things that the child picks up on that enhance the relationship. In this example of stewardship work, a father shows his dedication to his children.

I knew it was important for children to have parents who care, so I tried to let them know that. After the divorce, the first townhouse I bought had three bedrooms. I put the boys' names on one bedroom door and my daughter's name on another. They always knew their dad had not abandoned them and they had a place to live if needed.

Another father expressed his feelings of not being around for everyday happenings:

[It] was really hard right at first with the divorce because you go through a period of time where, as a father, you're so lonely in the first place, you want to overcompensate, you want to show the kids that you love them so much and that you care about them so much . . . you miss that relationship so much. When you go from having them every day, you know, the day-to-day things, as a father you miss tucking them into bed, saying their prayers, reading a book. It might just be coming home from work and asking them how their day at school was. It can be anything like that.

Even after a divorce, fathers who are involved with their children assist not only with their children's adjustment to the divorce, but also increase their own satisfaction with the transition into a new family arrangement (Pasley and Minton, 1997). In this example of relationship work, a father used creative ways to keep in touch with his children on a regular basis:

I bought the boys a computer and signed them up for an online service so that they had e-mail. This way they learn about computers and also have access to me anytime that they feel like. It's fun seeing them trying to spell things and having them write about what they do that I usually don't know about because they've forgotten that stuff by the time they see me again.

Parenting from a distance, no matter how great or small, has it's unique challenges. "Fathers can and do redefine themselves in ways that allow them to stay engaged and feel good about fathering [despite the] overwhelming obstacles brought about by marital transitions" (Pasley and Minton, 1997, p. 133).

Metaphor

Fathering Noncustodial Children

Just as a person listening to the radio must carefully tune in to a station to understand the information, so must noncustodial fathers consistently be in tune with their children's lives. Even though thousands of miles can separate him from his children he can still tune his heart and mind toward them; he should avoid changing stations to avoid the pain of not being with his children on a daily basis. These fathers must make sure that they always have their radio turned on and tuned in to their child's life. If they do, they can share in the beautiful moments of joy, as well as the heartache. However, if they are not tuned in now, they will realize that when they want to be heard and listened to, no one will be at the receiving end; rather, they will only hear static.

We would like to hear experiences about fathers who live apart from their children. Please *submit* a story.

FatherWork Feedback Form on *Fathering Noncustodial Children*
"How are we doing?"

(Click the *one* button that matches your response.) Please tell us to what extent the stories and ideas in this section:	A Lot	Some	A Little	Not at All	Not Sure
1. "Turned on a light" (Gave you ideas to strengthen you fathering or to help strengthen other fathers.)	O	O	O	O	⦿
2. "Touched your heart" (Affected you *emotionally*.)	O	O	O	O	⦿
3. "Pumped you up" (Motivated you to take greater action to be the kind of father you want to be or motivate other fathers.)	O	O	O	O	⦿
4. "Set your moral compass" (Deepened your sense of responsibility and commitment to good fathering.)	O	O	O	O	⦿

Source: FatherWork. <http//www.fatherwork.byu.edu/noncust.htm>.

REFERENCES

Abouserie, R., Moss, D., and Barasi, S. (1992). Cognitive style, gender, attitude toward computer-assisted learning and academic achievement. *Educational Studies, 18,* 151-160.

Arcus, M. (1987). A framework for life-span family life education. *Family Relations, 36,* 5-10.

Biller, H. B. (1993). *Fathers and families.* Westport, CT: Auburn House.

Darling, C. A. (1987). Family life education. In M. B. Sussman and S. K. Steinmetz (Eds.), *Handbook of marriage and the family* (pp. 815-833). New York: Plenum.

Doherty, W. J. (1997). The best of times and the worst of times: Fathering as a contested arena of academic discourse. In A. J. Hawkins and D. C. Dollahite (Eds.), *Generative fathering: Beyond deficit perspectives* (pp. 217-227). Thousand Oaks, CA: Sage.

Dollahite, D. C. and Hawkins, A. J. (1998). A conceptual ethic of generative fathering. *Journal of Men's Studies, 7*(1), 109-132.

Dollahite, D. C., Hawkins, A. J., and Brotherson, S. E. (1996). Narrative accounts, generative fathering, and family life education. *Marriage and Family Review, 24,* 349-368.

Dollahite, D. C., Hawkins, A. J., and Brotherson, S. E. (1997). "FatherWork": A conceptual ethic of fathering as generative work. In A. J. Hawkins and D. C. Dollahite (Eds.), *Generative fathering: Beyond deficit perspectives* (pp. 17-35). Thousand Oaks, CA: Sage.

Elliott, M. (1999). Classifying family life education on the World Wide Web. *Family Relations, 48,* 7-13.

Erikson, E. H. (1950). *Childhood and society.* New York: W. W. Norton.

eStats (1999). *eMarketer eStats* <http://www.emarketer.com/estats/welcome.html>.

Gerson, K. (1997). An institutional perspective on generative fathering: Creating social supports for parenting equality. In A. J. Hawkins and D. C. Dollahite (Eds.), *Generative fathering: Beyond deficit perspectives* (pp. 36-51). Thousand Oaks, CA: Sage.

GVU (1999). *Georgia Tech's Graphics, Visualization & Usability Center's 10th WWW User Survey* <http://www.gvu.gatech.edu/gvu/user_surveys/survey-1998-10/>.

Hughes, R. Jr. (1994). A framework for developing family life education programs. *Family Relations, 43,* 74-80.

Levine, J. A. and Pitt, E. W. (1995). *New expectations: Community strategies for responsible fatherhood.* New York: Families and Work Institute.

Morahan-Martin, J. (1998). Males, females, and the Internet. In J. Gackenbach (Ed.), *Psychology and the Internet* (pp. 169-197). San Diego, CA: Academic.

Morgaine, C. A. (1992). Alternative approaches for helping families change themselves. *Family Relations, 41,* 12-17.

Morris, S. N., Dollahite, D. C., and Hawkins, A. J. (1999). Virtual family life education: A qualitative study of father education on the World Wide Web. *Family Relations, 48,* 23-30.

Palm, G. F. (1997). Promoting generative fathering through parent and family education. In A. J. Hawkins and D. C. Dollahite (Eds.), *Generative fathering: Beyond deficit perspectives* (pp. 167-182). Thousand Oaks, CA: Sage.

Pasley, K. and Minton, C. (1997). Generative fathering after divorce and remarriage: Beyond the "disappearing dad." In A. J. Hawkins and D. C. Dollahite (Eds.), *Generative fathering: Beyond deficit perspectives* (pp. 118-133). Thousand Oaks, CA: Sage.

Philbin, M., Meier, E., Huffman, S., and Boverie, P. (1995). A survey of gender and learning styles. *Sex Roles, 32,* 485-494.

Rhoden, J. L. and Robinson, B. E. (1997). Teen dads: A generative fathering perspective versus the deficit myth. In A. J. Hawkins and D. C. Dollahite (Eds.), *Generative fathering: Beyond deficit perspectives* (pp. 105-117). Thousand Oaks, CA: Sage.

Small, S. A. (1990). Some issues regarding the evaluation of family life education programs. *Family Relations, 39,* 132-135.

Smith, C. A. (1999). Family life pathfinders on the new electronic frontier. *Family Relations, 48,* 31-34.

Walther, J. (1996). Computer-mediated communication: Impersonal, interpersonal, and hyperpersonal interaction. *Communication Research, 23,* 3-43.

Chapter 7

Father/Male Involvement in Early Childhood Programs: Training Staff to Work with Men

Brent A. McBride
Thomas R. Rane

The purpose of the project described in this chapter was to develop and empirically evaluate the impact of an intervention program designed to encourage and facilitate father/male involvement in state-funded pre-kindergarten programs for at-risk children. The focus of this particular intervention program was to identify best practices in the development and implementation of initiatives to increase father/male involvement in early childhood education programs. We attempted to contribute to the knowledge base required to successfully plan, implement, and evaluate specific initiatives to encourage father/male involvement. Our program assessment was based on one question: What is the impact of an indirect intervention program, designed to provide support services for staff members, on the participation rates of fathers/men in parent involvement activities?

SOCIAL AND ECONOMIC ISSUES FACED BY FATHERS

During the 1990s researchers, policymakers, and practitioners alike witnessed an explosion of interest in the concept of fatherhood. Evidence of this strong interest can be seen in the increased number of books, special issues of scholarly journals, and magazine articles that were published on this subject during the 1990s (e.g., Booth and

Crouter, 1998; Dienhart, 1998; Doherty, Kouneski, and Erickson, 1998; Levine, 1993; Hawkins and Dollahite, 1997; Lamb, 1997; Marsiglio, 1995; Snarey, 1993). Paralleling this increased interest in the roles of fathers has been a shift in societal expectations for fatherhood, calling for men to assume a more active role in raising their young children (Coltrane and Allan, 1994; Furstenberg, 1995). The popular media treatment of this idea has gone so far as to suggest that "America is in the midst of an unprecedented revolution in men's paternal role expectations—that popular attitudes about what fathers can and should do are changing in ways not dreamed of before" (LaRossa et al., 1991, p. 994).

While this shift in societal expectations for fathers has occurred, a renewed interest in the roles that family members play in their children's educational process has emerged as well. Currently in the United States, parents, educators, and policymakers are all asserting the value of positive home-school partnerships. In a national survey, 95 percent of public school parents indicated that it is very important to encourage families to take a more active role in educating their children (Elam, Rose, and Gallup, 1993). Studies of teacher opinions have consistently reflected positive views of active parental involvement and home-school partnerships as well (Epstein, 1992). Along with this emphasis has emerged a growing literature base suggesting that active parental involvement and home-school partnerships in elementary and early childhood settings can have a positive impact on child outcomes (see Connors and Epstein, 1995; and Powell, 1993 for reviews). In line with public sentiment and the supporting research base, new legislation (PL 103-227, signed by President Clinton in March 1994) outlines the National Education Goals as put forth by the U.S. Department of Education. Goal number eight states that by the year 2000 every school in the nation will have a program to promote partnerships that will increase parental involvement in facilitating the social, emotional, and academic growth of young children (National Education Goals Panel, 1994).

This emphasis on family/parent involvement is somewhat problematic given the nature of many families/children who could benefit most from such partnerships. Others have argued that low-income families face many problems (e.g., financial distress, psychological stress, etc.) that make parental involvement less likely to occur in school settings, and that little is known about which parental involvement strategies are most effective in meeting the needs of the diverse groups of families being served in elementary and early childhood programs (Reynolds, 1992; McLoyd, 1990; Comer, 1988; and Powell, 1993).

The involvement of fathers is an important, yet often overlooked target in the effort to increase home-school partnerships in elementary and early childhood programs. The notion that most children, particularly those from low-income and high-risk backgrounds, have little or no contact with a father or other adult male is a myth that permeates program development efforts. Recent research challenges this myth (see Lamb, 1997 for a review), which has had a significant negative impact on policies and practices designed to encourage home-school partnerships. The lack of initiatives designed to encourage father involvement in school and home settings evidences lost opportunities for administrators and teachers to acknowledge and build upon the strengths that many men bring to the parenting situation—strengths that can be utilized in the building of more effective home-school partnerships (Levine, 1993; McBride and Rane, 1997).

When men do assume more active roles in raising and educating their children, they may play a critical part in enhancing and facilitating their offsprings' growth and development (see Lamb, 1997 for a review). Recent data drawn from the National Center for Education Statistics' (NCES) 1996 National Household Education Survey also suggest that children do better in school when their fathers are involved in the educational process, regardless of whether their fathers live with them (NCES, 1998). Although the findings from this nationally representative NCES study are encouraging, they tell us very little about the ways in which men become involved in early childhood settings (the focus of this NCES data set is on elementary and secondary schools), and provide very little insight into those factors which encourage fathers to assume more active roles in their children's education. The creation of parent involvement and support programs designed specifically for fathers may be one way to encourage and better prepare men to assume a more active role in raising and educating their young children. These programs can also expand the range of support services early childhood programs are able to offer as they attempt to become more family-centered.

INTERVENING
TO ENCOURAGE FATHER INVOLVEMENT
IN EARLY CHILDHOOD PROGRAMS

The target site for implementation of the intervention program being described in this chapter is a large, prekindergarten "at-risk" program in Illinois. This program enrolls approximately 300 children, ages three and four, who come from economically disadvantaged backgrounds. These children have been identified as being at-risk for later school failure based on the poverty level status of their families, in combination with one or more other indicators of risk (e.g., teen parents, limited-education parents, foster parents, single-parent homes). Approximately 60 percent of the enrolled children are African American and 35 percent are Caucasian. The target prekindergarten program provides a variety of comprehensive services for enrolled children and their families (e.g., preschool classes, parent education and support programs, adult education classes, a family resource center and lending library, school social workers).

The treatment site program has received an exemplary rating from the Illinois State Board of Education (ISBE) beginning in its first year of operation in 1985, and continuing each year since. Although viewed as a model PreK program by the ISBE and other schools in the state, previous work at this site indicated there was room for growth and improvement in efforts at establishing effective home-school partnerships, and in supporting parents to effectively raise their children. Like most early childhood programs, the target PreK site had done little to develop initiatives to reach out to fathers of children enrolled in their program. Data collected with this program during the 1992-1993 school year indicated that male participation in parent involvement initiatives implemented by school personnel accounted for less than 5 percent of the total parental participation (Garinger and McBride, 1995; McBride, 1993). Based on interviews and informal feedback, it was concluded the low participation rate of fathers in this program was due to a lack of knowledge, skills, and opportunities on the part of staff members, as opposed to their lack of desire to involve fathers or to a lack of interest on the part of families being served.

A second state-funded prekindergarten at-risk program in Illinois was identified to serve as a control site to evaluate the intervention program. This PreK program funded by the ISBE is similar to the treatment site program in all aspects (e.g., funding base, criteria for enrollment, services provided to enrolled children and their families, staff training and backgrounds, families being served, etc.). The control program enrolls approximately 175 children ages three and four who come from economically disadvantaged backgrounds, and who have been identified as being at-risk for later school failure. The close proximity of the location of the treatment and control site programs (i.e., communities that share common boundaries) helped in facilitating the data collection process, as well as ensuring similar populations were being served by the treatment and control site programs.

Based on pilot work conducted for the current project, an "indirect" intervention program was developed and implemented at the treatment site program. As mentioned earlier, the purpose of this indirect intervention was to provide support services to teachers working in the target PreK program to allow them to develop the knowledge base that is required to successfully plan, implement, and evaluate specific initiatives to encourage father involvement in their program. This intervention program was implemented with staff members at the target site program for two academic years prior to the evaluation data being collected, and continued during the academic year in which data were collected. The nature and content of activities that were implemented as part of the indirect intervention covered a broad spectrum, including staff development training sessions, sponsorship of special "men and kids" events, consultation meetings with individual teachers on issues related to father involvement, outreach initiatives to families of enrolled children on issues related to father involvement, and facilitation of team meeting discussions on father involvement and parent involvement in general. In implementing the intervention program, members of the research and program development group worked with three teams of four classrooms each at the target site program. Teachers and their respective staff worked in these three teams of four classrooms on a regular basis for all aspects of programming at the treatment program site.

The focus and intensity of the activities implemented as part of this indirect intervention varied over the course of the three years based on the identified needs and interests of individual teachers and teams. For example, one team of teachers met on a regular basis with the program development group to discuss issues related to father involvement, explore strategies for reaching out to fathers (e.g., revising intake/enrollment forms to identify males present in the child's life, scheduling home visits when fathers might be present, etc.), and to plan and implement activities targeted specifically for father involvement in their classrooms (e.g., "Men and Kids" gym night, a section of the classroom newsletter targeted for fathers and significant male figures, a classroom volunteer training session for fathers, etc.). In contrast, another one of the teams struggled throughout the duration of the intervention program with the concept of father involvement in PreK programs and whether an emphasis on such efforts was warranted. The program development group found itself spending a great amount of time engaged in philosophical and conceptual discussions related to father involvement with teachers on this team. A goal of these individual and group discussions was to give teachers on this team a forum where they could work through any preconceived notions and biases they may have had toward father/male involvement. The focus of the intervention was flexible enough to meet the needs of the teachers at whatever comfort level and knowledge base in which they found themselves.

BASIC ASSUMPTIONS AND VALUES: FATHER INVOLVEMENT IN EARLY CHILDHOOD PROGRAMS

The program development group focused on four specific issues identified by McBride and Rane (1997) as being critical to the success of initiatives designed to encourage father involvement in early childhood programs. First, the intervention program was developed under the premise that not all staff members would be equally committed to the concept of father involvement. Such resistance must be acknowledged and incorporated into initiatives. The indirect intervention acknowledged that such resistance existed among some staff members, and included activities to allow these teachers the opportunity to address biases against such efforts. Second, the program development group spent a great deal of time working with the teams of teachers during the first year of the intervention in developing clearly articulated rationales for why their program and classrooms should be concerned with father involvement. As part of this process teachers were asked to explore why they think such efforts are important, and how these initiatives could enhance the services being provided to families. In developing such clearly articulated rationales, the program development group could ensure that each team of teachers was committing time and energy to these activities, not because father involvement is a "hot" topic, but because they saw the benefits of such efforts for the children, the families, and the school.

Third, the program development group worked with the teams of teachers to clearly specify who the targets of their initiatives would be. It was acknowledged by all teachers that most children enrolled in the treatment site program had some sort of consistent interaction with a male figure, in spite of the high proportion of single-parent homes represented. The teachers determined that focusing their efforts exclusively on biological fathers would exclude a large proportion of men who play significant roles in the lives of these children. Thus, all efforts implemented as part of this initiative targeted fathers of enrolled children, or the "significant" male figure for these children. Broadening the definition of father to include "father figures" allowed teachers to be more sensitive to support networks among low-income families represented in their program, as well as acknowledging the diversity in the structure of families being served by the program. Finally, the program development group worked hard with each team of teachers to emphasize that their program did not require the creation of totally new initiatives. Like most prekindergarten programs, the treatment site program already had in place a wide range of initiatives designed to encourage parent involvement, although they were targeted primarily at mothers. Throughout the duration of the intervention, each team of teachers was continuously encouraged to examine their efforts to facilitate parent involvement, and to explore how these initiatives could be adapted to better meet the needs of fathers/men, thus encouraging their involvement.

In addition to the four specific issues outlined above, the indirect intervention was developed and implemented in a way that reflected many of the basic assumptions of adult learning outlined by Knowles (1987). For example, *adults have a need to know why they should learn something; adults have a deep need to be self-directing; adults enter into a learning experience with a task-centered orientation to learning.* Structuring the intervention program on these basic assumptions of adult learning created a climate where the teachers could have a sense of "ownership" in the program, and facilitated their investment in the intervention process.

EVALUATION
OF THE INTERVENTION PROGRAM

All fourteen teachers at the treatment site program and all seven teachers at the control site program participated in data collection procedures to evaluate the intervention program. At the beginning of the academic year in which evaluation data were collected (the third year of the intervention program), teachers at both sites completed a packet of questionnaires which included items on demographic backgrounds as well as two attitudinal measures on parent and father involvement in early childhood settings. Demographic items in the questionnaires included the teacher's age, educational background, years in the profession, and number of parent involvement courses taken as an undergraduate and graduate.

The Attitudes Toward Father Involvement (ATFI) scale was used to assess teachers' attitudes toward father involvement in early childhood programs. The ATFI scale, a six-item measure developed specifically for this study, asked teachers to respond to statements along a 5-point Likert-type scale: 1 = strongly disagree; 2 = disagree; 3 = no opinion; 4 = agree; 5 = strongly agree. Sample items from this measure included: "Parent involvement and support programs should be targeted at mothers since they are primarily responsible for child-rearing tasks" and "Mothers are more likely to respond favorably to parent involvement initiatives implemented in early childhood programs than fathers." Positively and negatively worded items were included in the ATFI to prevent a response bias. Higher ATFI scores were indicative of teachers who held more favorable attitudes toward encouraging father/male involvement in early childhood programs. Items from the ATFI were embedded within the second measure used for the study. Internal consistency for the ATFI was relatively high, with a Cronbach alpha of .76.

An adapted version of the General Attitudes Toward Parent Involvement (GATPI) scale was used to assess teachers' attitudes toward parent involvement in early childhood programs (Garinger and McBride, 1995) . The adapted version of the GATPI asked teachers to respond to thirteen items along a 5-point Likert-type scale. Sample items from this measure included: "Parent involvement can help teachers be more effective with students" and "Teachers cannot take the time to involve parents in meaningful ways." Higher GATPI scores were indicative of teachers who held more favorable attitudes toward encouraging parental involvement. Positively and negatively worded items were included in the GATPI to prevent a response bias. Internal consistency on this measure was moderately high, with an alpha of .68.

During the academic year in which evaluation data were collected, detailed information was gathered which tracked the parent involvement activities and contacts teachers had at both treatment and control program sites. The tracking of this information is required by the ISBE, but not at the level of detail needed for the evaluation study. Based on pilot data collected for the current study, a data recording sheet was developed for use by teachers. Teachers would record information on this sheet for each contact they had with a parent and/or family member. The types of information recorded for each contact included the method of contact (i.e., phone, school visit, home visit, note, other), the nature/focus of the contact (i.e., developmental progress, behavior, health issues, materials request, volunteer request, administrative, classroom visit, learning and developmental activities, relationship building, parent support, and other), who initiated the contact (i.e., school, family/home), gender of contact when initiated from home (i.e., male, female, mixed), and gender of who was contacted (i.e., male, female). Data recorded on these sheets reflected the full range of parent involvement contacts teachers had (e.g., one-on-one parent-teacher conferences to family members attending a school open house event).

Evaluation data were collected during the third year of the intervention program. At the beginning of the academic year in which these data were collected, teachers at both treatment and control program sites were trained in how to use the data recording sheets. Once trained, teachers used the data recording sheets to track their parent involvement contacts instead of the contact logs normally required by the ISBE. A four-week period of time was used to allow teachers to become comfortable with the data recording sheets before actual evaluation data for the study were collected. During this time, research assistants visited each teacher on a weekly basis to review information recorded on their sheets, clarify ambiguous information recorded, identify potential problem areas, and answer any questions the teachers may have had. Once the four-week training and phase-in period was complete, evaluation data for the study were collected at both sites in thirteen consecutive two-week segments. Research assistants would visit each teacher at the end of each two-week period to review and collect the data recording sheets, clarify any ambiguous information, and answer any possible questions. At the end of the twenty-six-week data collection period, each teacher received a $250 stipend as partial compensation for the extra time required to assist in this data collection process.

OUTCOMES OF THE EVALUATION

Means and standard deviations were computed for each of the demographic measures, as well as scores on the Attitudes Toward Father Involvement scale and the General Attitudes Toward Parent Involvement measure (see Table 7.1). Due to the exploratory nature of the evaluation being reported, as well as the relatively small sample size (i.e., fourteen teachers at the treatment site program and seven at the control site program), p values of .10 or less were used to determine whether significant differences existed in all analyses conducted. Examination of scores on the GATPI and ATFI measures suggests that teachers at both the treatment and control site programs held fairly positive viewpoints of parent involvement in general, and father involvement in particular. Independent means t-tests revealed no significant differences between treatment and control program site teachers on any of the demographic variables, as well as scores on the ATFI and GATPI measures. These findings indicate that teachers at both sites had similar backgrounds in terms of their education and teaching experience, and that both groups held similar attitudes toward parent involvement in general and father involvement in particular.

Table 7.1. Means and Standard Deviations—Demographics and Attitudinal Measures

Variable	Treatment Site[a]		Control Site[b]	
	M	*SD*	*M*	*SD*
Teacher's Age	32.86	8.98	34.00	12.08
Teacher's Education[c]	2.64	.63	2.43	.79
Years in Profession	9.36	7.75	9.86	8.03
Parent Involvement Courses—Undergraduate	.93	.99	.86	.90
Parent Involvement Courses—Graduate	1.14	1.10	.57	.53
Attitudes Toward Father Involvement Scale	24.93	3.83	24.14	2.91
General Attitudes Toward Parent Involvement Scale	56.14	4.55	57.14	2.48

[a] $n = 14$

[b] $n = 7$

[c] 1 = high school diploma, 2 = BS, 3 = MS/MEd, 4 = EdS, 5 = PhD/EdD

Note: t-tests indicated no significant differences between groups ($p < .10$).

Information from the data recording sheets for each of the thirteen two-week periods was collapsed to provide a composite picture of the parent involvement contacts teachers had during this twenty-six-week period. Proportions of contacts were computed for each of the major coding categories (i.e., method of contact, nature/focus of contact, who initiated contact, who was contacted, gender of who initiated contact, and gender of who was contacted) to provide a descriptive picture of the parent involvement activities experienced by teachers. Proportional scores were used due to the unequal number of teachers in the treatment and control site programs, as well as the resulting difference in the total number of parent involvement contacts over the twenty-six-week period.

To examine the impact of the indirect intervention on the parent involvement contacts of teachers at the treatment site program, information from the data recording sheets regarding the gender of these contacts was examined (see Table 7.2). Independent means *t*-tests indicated that when family members initiated parent involvement contacts, a significantly higher proportion of these contacts were initiated

Table 7.2. Proportion of Parent Involvement Contacts by Gender

Contact Category	Treatment Site	Control Site	*t*
Gender of Initiation[a]			
Male	.12	.08	1.84*
Female	.77	.84	−2.19**
Mixed	.12	.07	1.42
Gender of Contacted			
Family Member			
Male	.23	.12	3.18***
Female	.76	.88	−3.25***

[a] Gender of Initiation category for those contacts initiated by family members/ home; mixed category reflects parent involvement contacts with mixed genders in attendance (e.g., mother and mother's boyfriend attend a parent-teacher conference).
　*$p < .10$.
　**$p < .05$.
　***$p < .01$.

by fathers/males at the treatment site program ($t = 1.84, p < .10$) than at the control site. Conversely, a higher proportion of the contacts initiated by family members at the control site program were by females ($t = -2.19, p < .05$). Although not reaching a level of significance, the findings also indicated that fathers/males were involved in the initiation of a higher proportion of parent involvement contacts at the treatment site program via mixed gender contacts than those at the control site program ($t = 1.42, p = .186$).

Significant differences also emerged when examining the gender of family members involved in parent involvement contacts. Results indicated that teachers at the treatment site program reported that a significantly higher proportion of their parent involvement contacts were with fathers/males ($t = 3.18, p < .01$) than those of the control site teachers. Conversely, teachers at the control site program reported a significantly higher proportion of their parent involvement contacts were with females ($t = -3.25, p < .01$) than those of treatment site teachers. These findings indicate that teachers at the treatment site program were experiencing greater levels of participation in parent involvement activities across the various categories with fathers/men than teachers at the control site program.

IMPLICATIONS AND LESSONS LEARNED
FOR "BEST PRACTICES"

Due to several limitations that are present in the design used to evaluate this initiative (e.g., use of a posttest-only treatment and control group design, lack of long-term follow-up, small sample size, narrowly focused outcome data, etc.), caution must be used in generalizing the results to other, similar intervention programs. In spite of these limitations, the results of this evaluation are encouraging for continued research and program development work in this area. Findings suggest that fathers/men at the treatment site program were participating in parent involvement activities at a significantly higher rate than reported at the control site program. In addition, parent involvement contacts that were initiated by the home were done so at a significantly higher rate by fathers/men affiliated with the treatment site program than those initiated by the home at the control site program. The indirect intervention program that was developed and evaluated provides a promising model of support services which may be instrumental in helping early childhood teachers identify ways to encourage and facilitate father/male involvement in their programs. This intervention program also provides an example of a strong, long-term university-school partnership designed to address a problem area that has been identified by the local community, as well as being a national concern. In addition, this university-school partnership model which targets its intervention efforts at service providers (i.e., teachers), as opposed to providing direct services to children and their families, presents a more cost-effective way of delivering a service. Findings from this evaluation provide support for continued research and program development efforts in this area.

In addition to the evaluative data that highlights the positive impact of the program developed, process data collected over the three years of implementing this indirect intervention provide insight into several issues which need to be addressed if similar programs are to be successful. Early childhood and parent educators can use these insights as starting points or as suggestions for best practices in their own efforts to encourage more father/male involvement in their programs.

Acknowledge Resistance

Early childhood educators must acknowledge that not everyone will be committed to the concept of parent involvement initiatives targeted at fathers/men. Yet, the apparent lack of father/male involvement and "responsible" fathering behaviors is often cited as a major reason for young children being classified as at-risk for later school failure. Many people will question why resources should be targeted at these fathers/men when they are viewed as the primary cause of the problems facing children. Our experience has shown that resistance will come from teachers, school administrators, community leaders, mothers, and men themselves. In spite of the generally positive ATFI scores, resistance to the intervention initiatives was expressed by some teachers at the treatment site, indicating a possible social desirability factor in their responses on this measure. Program developers must recognize that such resistance may occur in spite of teachers' reports that they are in favor of father/male involvement.

Formulate a Clear Rationale

Early childhood educators will need to build a strong rationale for developing father/male outreach initiatives. Educators need to be specific in their reasons for developing parent involvement initiatives targeted at fathers/men. Prior to developing specific initiatives, educators must ask themselves why they think such efforts are important, and how the initiatives could enhance the services being provided to children and families. There are clear benefits to encouraging father/male involvement. These benefits must be the focus of the rationale for reaching out to men. Focusing on father/male involvement simply because it is currently a "hot" societal issue increases the likelihood that such efforts will wane when the next big issue emerges.

Clearly Specify Targets

Educators also need to be specific about the targets of their efforts to encourage father/male involvement. Research data have indicated that many children growing up in low-income and single-parent homes have regular and consistent interactions with a father and/or male role figure, although not necessarily their biological father. Focusing efforts exclusively on biological fathers will exclude a large proportion of men who play significant roles in the lives of these children. The key for educators will be to identify which men in the lives of children can be effectively targeted for outreach efforts.

Do Not Reinvent the Wheel

Many early childhood programs already include comprehensive parent involvement components, although they tend to be targeted primarily at mothers. When developing initiatives for father/male involvement, program leaders should first evaluate the parent involvement components already in place, and explore how they may be adapted to reach out to men in order to meet their unique needs. For example, if a program currently has in place a training session to prepare volunteers (primarily mothers/women) for working in classrooms, they should consider creating a parallel session for fathers/men.

Provide Training and Support Services

Most early childhood educators have received little, if any, formal education or training in the area of parent involvement. This is especially true in the area of father/male involvement. If such efforts are to be successful, teachers will need to be provided with staff development and in-service training experiences that give them a knowledge base from which to design and implement specific initiatives to encourage father/male involvement in their programs.

Help Women Become Facilitators

Although it would be desirable to have a male staff member provide leadership for such initiatives, this is often not possible since the majority of professionals in the field are females. Of course women can provide effective leadership in these outreach efforts, but to be successful they must be sensitive to differences in the ways men and women approach parenting and interact with young children. Men bring a unique set of strengths and needs to the parenting realm (McBride, 1990). The ways in which they have been socialized while growing up has contributed to differences in their communication styles, thought processes, expression of feelings, and so on compared to women (Konen, 1992). These differences need to be understood in the context of program services designed to facilitate and encourage father/male involvement in early childhood programs. As Palm and Johnson (1992) have argued, it is not the intention that acknowledgment of these differences will be used to reinforce negative sex-role stereotypes, but that denying differences in parenting styles limits the ability of programs to identify and address men's unique needs. Female leaders of outreach efforts to fathers/men must acknowledge these differences and build upon the strengths men bring to the table while at the same time being sensitive to men's needs.

Involve Mothers in Developing Initiatives

From the very beginning, mothers need to be involved in the development of initiatives designed to encourage father/male involvement. They need to be made aware of why resources are being put into developing these activities, and how they and their children will benefit. Mothers tend to be the gatekeepers for access to their children, especially with noncustodial fathers and significant male role figures. Eliciting the support and involvement of mothers in developing such initiatives can provide access to fathers/men, and help ensure the success of these programs.

Continue to Meet Mothers' Needs

As educators develop initiatives to encourage father/male involvement, they must not do so at the expense of efforts targeted at mothers. Acknowledging the unique strengths and needs of fathers/ men underscores the point that mothers also have unique contributions to make to their children's progress and success in school settings. While establishing initiatives to reach out to men, ongoing consistent efforts to involve mothers must be maintained.

Create a Climate for Father/Male Involvement

The key to success for these efforts lies in building a father-/male-friendly environment which facilitates a culture of male involvement in the program (e.g., creating an information bulletin board specifically for fathers/men, having a clearly identified adult male restroom in what is typically a female- and child-dominated environment). Creating a climate of male involvement is a long-term process. In building such a climate, men will begin to feel a sense of acceptance in terms of their participation and the importance of the roles they can play within the program, and also an expectation on the part of the program that men should assume more active roles.

Proceed Slowly

Efforts to build a culture of father/male involvement are much more likely to succeed if educators begin working with men in their comfort zone. Do not expect too much too soon. Start slowly and build upon successes. Initially, activities such as repairing or constructing playground equipment, demonstrating a professional skill, or participating in a sports-oriented activity will be much more comfortable for many men than singing songs or reading stories to a group of children.

CONCLUSION

Clearly, this is not intended as an exhaustive list of best practices related to the successful development and implementation of specific initiatives to increase father/male involvement in early childhood programs. Furthermore, there will likely be considerable overlap in discussions of these issues by early childhood administrators and staff. Nonetheless, based on recent research, and our own experiences in developing and evaluating the intervention program described in this chapter, the best practices presented here form a helpful framework for beginning the important task of developing and implementing initiatives to increase father/male involvement in early childhood education settings.

REFERENCES

Booth, A. and Crouter, A. C. (1998). *Men in families: When do they get involved? What does it take?* Hillsdale, NJ: Lawrence Erlbaum Associates.

Coltrane, S. and Allan, K. (1994). "New" fathers and old stereotypes: Representations of masculinity in 1980s television advertising. *Masculinities, 2*, 1-25.

Comer, J. P. (1988). Educating poor minority children. *Scientific American, 259*(1), 42-48.

Connors, L. J. and Epstein, J. L. (1995). Parent and school partnerships. In M. Bornstein (Ed.), *Handbook of parenting: Applied and practical parenting* (pp. 437-458). Mahwah, NJ: Lawrence Erlbaum Associates.

Dienhart, A. (1998). *Reshaping fatherhood: The social construction of shared parenting.* Thousand Oaks, CA: Sage.

Doherty, W. J., Kouneski, E. F., and Erickson, M. F. (1998). Responsible fathering: An overview and conceptual framework. *Journal of Marriage and the Family, 60*(2), 277-292.

Elam, S. M., Rose, L. C., and Gallup, A. M. (1993). The 25th annual Phi Delta Kappa/Gallup Poll of the public's attitudes toward the public schools. *Phi Delta Kappan, 75*(2), 137-152.

Epstein, J. L. (1992). School and Family Partnerships. In M. C. Allen (Ed.), *Encyclopedia of educational research* (Sixth edition, pp. 1139-1151). New York: Macmillan.

Furstenberg, F. F. Jr. (1995). Fathering in the inner city: Paternal participation and public policy. In W. Marsiglio (Ed.), *Fatherhood: Contemporary theory, research, and social policy* (pp. 41-56). Thousand Oaks, CA: Sage.

Garinger, J. and McBride, B. A. (1995). Successful parental involvement strategies in prekindergarten at-risk programs: An exploratory study. *The School-Community Journal, 5*(1), 59-77.

Hawkins, A. J. and Dollahite, D. C. (1997). *Generative fathering: Beyond deficit perspectives.* Thousand Oaks, CA: Sage.

Knowles, M. S. (1987). Adult learning. In R. L.Craig (Ed.), *Training and development handbook: A guide to human resource development* (pp. 168-179). New York: McGraw-Hill.

Konen, D. (1992). Women facilitators. In Minnesota Fathering Alliance (Eds.), *Working with fathers: Methods and perspectives* (pp. 113-128). Stillwater, MN: Nu Ink Press.

Lamb, M.E. (Ed.) (1997). *The role of the father in child development* (Third edition). New York: Wiley.

LaRossa, R., Gordon, R. J., Wilson, A., Bauran, A., and Jaret, C. (1991). The fluctuating image of the 20th century American father. *Journal of Marriage and the Family, 53*(4), 987-997.

Levine, J. A. (1993). Involving fathers in Head Start: A framework for public policy and program development. *Families in Society, 74*(1), 4-19.

Marsiglio, W. (Ed.) (1995). *Fatherhood: Contemporary theory, research, and social policy.* Thousand Oaks, CA: Sage.

McBride, B. A. (1990). The effects of a parent education/play group program on father involvement in childrearing. *Family Relations, 39,* 250-256.

McBride, B. A. (1993). "Parental involvement in prekindergarten at-risk programs: How do the players perceive the game?" Final report submitted to the Spencer Foundation Small Grants program.

McBride, B. A. and Rane, T. R. (1997). Father/male involvement in early childhood programs: Issues and challenges. *Early Childhood Education Journal, 25*(1), 11-15.

McLoyd, V. C. (1990). The impact of economic hardship on black families and children: Psychological stress, parenting, and socioemotional development. *Child Development, 61*(2), 311-346.

National Center for Education Statistics (NCES) (1998). *Students do better when their fathers are involved at school.* Online: <http://www.nces.ed.gov/pubs98/98121.html>.

National Education Goals Panel (1994). *The National Education Goals report: Building a nation of learners.* Washington, DC: U.S. Government Printing Office.

Palm, G. and Johnson, L. (1992). Planning programs: What do fathers want? In the Minnesota Fathering Alliance (Eds.), *Working with fathers: Methods and perspectives* (pp. 59-78). Stillwater, MN: Nu Ink Press.

Powell, D. R. (1993). Supporting parent-child relationships in the early years: Lessons learned and yet to be learned. In T. H. Brubaker (Ed.), *Family relations: Challenges for the future* (pp. 79-97). Newbury Park: Sage.

Reynolds, A. J. (1992). Comparing measures of parental involvement and their effects on academic achievement. *Early Childhood Research Quarterly, 7*(3), 441-462.

Snarey, J. (1993). *How fathers care for the next generation: A four-decade study.* Cambridge: Harvard University Press.

Chapter 8

Turning the Hearts of Fathers: Faith-Based Approaches to Promoting Responsible Fatherhood

Wade F. Horn

> Children's children are the crown of old men, and the glory of children is their father.

Proverbs 17:6

At the conclusion of the Old Testament scriptures comes this stern warning: "I will send you the prophet Elijah before that great and dreadful day of the Lord comes. He will turn the hearts of the fathers to their children, and the hearts of the children to their fathers; or else I will come and strike the land with a curse" (Malachi 4:5-6, KJV). Given the specificity of this biblical admonition and the current scope of fatherlessness, it would be surprising if faith-based organizations were not actively involved in fatherhood support, promotion, and skill-building interventions. In fact, many are. Indeed, faith-based ministries are touching the lives of hundreds of thousands, if not millions, of men. In terms of reach, no secular intervention on behalf of the institution of fatherhood comes even close (Dollahite, 1998).

Much of this activity, however, has been centered in evangelical Protestant churches, or, on smaller scales, within individual churches, especially within the African-American community. Surprisingly, mainline Protestants, Jews, and, to a lesser extent, Roman

Catholics, have been slower to implement fatherhood promotion, support, and skill-building activities. This does not mean these faith traditions have nothing to say about fatherhood. Of course they do. But mainline Protestants, Jews, and Catholics, at least in the United States, have been more accommodating than evangelical churches to recent shifts in family organization that have occurred within the larger culture, including the growing absence of fathers (Wilcox, 1997). Hence, these faith traditions have lagged behind evangelical Protestant denominations in articulating a clear vision of the family and fatherhood (Browning, 1995).

It is also important to acknowledge that although not every faith tradition or denomination has implemented a special fatherhood outreach, support, or skills-building ministry, most, if not all, faith-traditions incorporate, at least to some degree, responsible fathering messages into their regular worship activities. Indeed, both the Church of Jesus Christ of Latter-Day Saints (Mormon) and the Southern Baptist Convention have recently adopted formal statements on the family, including messages about the importance of responsible fatherhood. Hence, even in the absence of specific ministries and activities for fathers, many men are exposed to responsible fatherhood messages through regular sermons and personal scripture study. While accepting that such activities can—and do—have a profoundly positive impact on the behavior of men and fathers, the focus of this chapter is on those "extracurricular" fatherhood activities specifically designed to address today's crisis of fatherlessness and to promote more involved, caring, and responsible fathering.

This chapter begins with a discussion of the basic assumptions and values underlying faith-based approaches to fatherhood promotion, moves on to a description of specific programmatic initiatives being undertaken by various faith-based organizations, and concludes with a discussion of the major barriers and challenges facing faith-based approaches to fatherhood interventions. Although other religions represented within the United States have, on occasion, implemented fatherhood-promotion activities, such as the Nation of Islam's 1995 Million Man March, this review is limited to a discussion of fatherhood-promotion activities within the Judeo-Christian faith tradition, since this is the faith tradition with which the vast majority of religiously affiliated men in the United States identify.[*]

BASIC ASSUMPTIONS

The first, and most basic, assumption underlying faith-based approaches to fatherhood promotion is that a vital, initial step to becoming a good father is to become a man of God. In a recent interview, Max Lucado, pulpit minister of the 2,000-member Oak Hills Church of Christ in San Antonio, Texas, and best-selling author of books on the family and fatherhood, put it this way: "What prevents a father from being just like Jesus is not having a spiritual Father himself. . . . If I want to be a good father, I go to my heavenly Father and He tells me how to be a good father. Prayer is the first, intermediate and last step in regard to our children" (Nappa, 1999, p. 41).

The reason for establishing a relationship with God first is that faith-based approaches to fatherhood promotion assume that knowledge of God's relationship with His children provides the model for how human fathers should relate to their children. Although humans are not expected to be perfect, human fathers are expected to strive to mirror with their own children the perfect love that God has for His children. As such, a father cannot merely be loving, he must *be* love (Stanton, 1999).

But scripture contains more than just abstract ideals about fatherhood; it also provides concrete lessons as to what a good father is and does. According to scripture, good fathers should, for example, love their children (Genesis 37:4), instruct and guide them (Ephesians 6:4; Proverbs 22:6; 1 Thessalonians 2:11), rebuke and punish them when necessary (Deuteronomy 21:18-21; Proverbs 3:11-12), nourish them (Isaiah 1:2), and provide for their needs (Matthew 7:8-11). Thus, the biblical script for fatherhood is one that combines love with discipline, and compassion with justice.

---

[*]A recent analysis of the active religious affiliation (i.e., attending more than once a year) of American fathers, using the National Survey of Families and Households, found that 37 percent were unaffiliated, 23 percent were mainline Protestants, 19 percent were Catholics, 14 percent were evangelical Protestants, 2 percent were Jewish, and 5 percent were other, principally Mormons (Wilcox, 1999).

For Christians, God also models fatherhood through His relationship with His own son, Jesus Christ, and through Christ's own behavior and teachings. When, for example, God introduces Jesus to others, He does so with great affection, saying, "This is my beloved Son, in whom I am well pleased" (Matthew 3:17, KJV). He also expresses his deep love and affection directly to Jesus himself, saying, "Thou art my beloved Son, in whom I am well pleased" (Mark 1:11, KJV). So too, then, are fathers directed to bless their children with encouragement and support, as well as direction and spiritual strength (Wilcox, 1999).

Fathers are also expected to reach out constantly to their children with great tenderness and gentleness, as Christ did throughout His ministry (see Mark 10:14, for example). And, though sometimes disappointed, fathers are never to abandon their children. Instead, as shown through Jesus' parable of the prodigal son, fathers must always stand at the ready to accept their children back when they have strayed.

Thus, faith-based approaches to fatherhood promotion are based on the belief that men do not have to invent a fatherhood script, for that script is already available to them through the example of God's perfect love for His children, and, for Christians, through His relationship with, and teachings of, Jesus Christ (Stanton, 1999).

Faith-based approaches also assume that fathers should rear their children so that they too will come to know God. In Proverbs 22:6, fathers are instructed to "[t]rain up a child in the way he should go; and when he is old, he will not depart from it" (KJV). A similar urging is made in Ephesians 6:4, when the writer states, "Fathers, do not exasperate your children; instead bring them up in the training and instruction of the Lord" (NIV). Thus, it is not enough that children are taught to know and obey one's earthly father. They must also come to know and obey their Heavenly Father. It is the father's job to ensure that this happens.

A third major assumption underlying fatherhood-promotion activities within a Judeo-Christian tradition is that the proper context for fatherhood is within holy matrimony. According to scripture, when God created man and woman, He also created marriage (Genesis 2:18-24) as a permanent (Matthew 19:6) and intimate (Matthew 19:5) bond, through which one produces godly offspring

(Malachi 2:14, 15). Thus, the most important work a father will ever do—indeed, it is God's charge to him—is to righteously raise his children along with his wife within the holy covenant of marriage. This does not mean that faith-based fatherhood interventions do not provide support, outreach, encouragement, and skill building to divorced or unwed fathers. Many do. But faith-based approaches are more explicit than most secular fatherhood interventions in their recognition of married fatherhood as the ideal.

Finally, faith-based approaches assume that being a good father to one's own children is not sufficient. To be a man of God also means tending to fatherless children. Deuteronomy is particularly replete with admonitions to defend the cause of the fatherless (Deuteronomy 10:17-18), ensure that the fatherless are provided with sufficient nourishment (Deuteronomy 14:28-29, 24:19, 26:12), and provide the fatherless with justice (Deuteronomy 24:17). Indeed, the highest calling for humans is to take care of the fatherless, for [a] father to the fatherless . . . is God in his holy dwelling (Psalm 68:5, NIV).

Thus, the Judeo-Christian tradition contains within it a moral imperative to love one's children as God loves us, to become a father only within the context of holy matrimony, to take care of and mentor the fatherless, and to help both one's own children and fatherless children develop a personal relationship with God. Although the specific activities of various faith-based fatherhood interventions may differ, each is built around these core assumptions and ideas.

EVANGELICAL PROTESTANT APPROACHES TO FATHERHOOD INTERVENTIONS

Within evangelical Protestant communities of faith, the family is accorded great importance (Hunter, 1987), both because the family is seen as an embodiment of God's love for His people, and because of their concern that the traditional, two-parent family is under attack by today's popular culture (Wilcox, 1997). Thus, evangelical approaches to fatherhood interventions frequently have both an internal, or individual, father focus and an external, or societal, focus.

In promoting fatherhood, most evangelical churches combine the historic notions of father as head of the household and strict disciplinarian with the more modern view that fathers should be deeply involved in the lives of their children and emotionally open and expressive with their wives and children (Wilcox, 1997). As such, conservative Protestants have largely incorporated a therapeutic focus emphasizing the importance of feelings, relationships, and self-esteem into their fatherhood script (Wilcox, 1999). This is evidenced by the writings of such popular authors within evangelical circles as Stu Weber, author of *Tender Warrior: God's Intention for Man* (1993), and Robert Lewis, author of *Raising a Modern Day Knight: A Father's Role in Guiding His Son to Authentic Manhood* (1997). Hence, fathers within this faith tradition are typically urged to spend time with their children, empathize with their feelings, and praise them frequently, while at the same time dispensing consistent and just discipline.

What follows is an illustrative, but not exhaustive, overview of national men's ministries within evangelical Protestantism incorporating a major focus on fatherhood promotion. Some common themes found within this faith tradition include an emphasis on first developing a personal relationship with God; the use of gatherings of men, in large and small groups, both to impart information concerning what it means to be a responsible father and to hold one another accountable for living up to these ideals; and the production of written, audio, and visual materials to aid in the teaching of a fatherhood ideal (for a fuller description of these and other faith-based approaches to fatherhood promotion see Eberly, 1999).

Promise Keepers (PK)

The largest and most visible men's ministry emphasizing the role of men as fathers is Promise Keepers. Founded in 1990 by former University of Colorado head football coach Bill McCartney and his friend Dave Wardell, Promise Keepers is based on the premise that the failure of large numbers of men to live up to their family and social obligations is a failure of faith. Hence, by bringing men into closer communion with God, they will be inspired to take responsibility for their actions, be faithful to their families, and keep their word, even when doing so is costly or difficult (McCartney, 1999).

The first meeting of Promise Keepers was held in 1990 when seventy-two men gathered to fast and pray. A year later, in 1991, 4,200 men attended the first Promise Keepers Men's Conference at the Coors Event Center in Boulder, Colorado. The movement quickly grew from there, as tens of thousands of men began coming together at events held in athletic stadiums all across America. On October 4, 1997, PK's mass gathering phase culminated when upward of a million men—roughly 1 percent of all men in the United States—came together to repent and pray in Washington, DC, at a rally titled "Stand in the Gap: A Sacred Assembly of Men." Overall, as many as 3 million men have gathered at Promise Keepers events to pray, seek reconciliation, take stock of their own moral and spiritual inventory, and dedicate themselves to being better men, husbands, and fathers.

At the foundation of Promise Keepers are "Seven Promises" focusing on spiritual development; pursuing accountability fellowship relationships with other men; maintaining sexual, moral, and ethical purity; building a strong family; supporting one's church; racial reconciliation; and sharing one's faith with others. Through the making—and more important, the keeping—of these seven promises, PK seeks to help fathers nurture, discipline, protect, and provide for their families, stay committed to their wives and children during times of difficulty, and learn to balance the responsibilities of home and work.

In addition to stadium events, PK also offers pastors instructional tools and study guides for their use in challenging men in their congregations to grow in their faith and keep their promises to their wives and children. Promise Keepers also organizes community service projects and publishes a variety of printed materials, including *New Man* magazine and a number of books and worship tapes.

At the 1997 "Stand in the Gap" gathering, founder Bill McCartney announced that participation in future stadium rallies would be free, rather than charging the typical $60 admission fee. This change in strategy resulted in a financial crisis, culminating in PK's dramatic layoff of its entire staff in April of 1998, although much of PK's staff were eventually rehired. Promise Keepers has since announced that while it will continue to organize some stadium events, it is scaling back the size of these events and focusing more on local church gatherings. Part of this change in focus seems to be the result of a desire to effect more permanent and lasting change in the behavior of men who do become Promise Keepers. For more information on

Promise Keepers, the reader is referred to Janssen and Weeden (1994) as well as PK's Web site <www.promisekeepers.org>.

Dad: The Family Shepherd (DFS)

Established in 1984, Dad: The Family Shepherd is a men's ministry based in Little Rock, Arkansas. The purpose of DFS is to equip the local church to motivate and teach men to reflect biblical values in their relationships with their wives, their children, and at work. DFS is concerned that although the family is the most important unit in society, it is often the most attacked. DFS seeks to counter these attacks by helping men become more effective spiritual leaders in their homes.

DFS targets Christian fathers of all ages, socioeconomic levels, and races. Its primary mode of intervention is conferences involving groups of men, usually in a church or retreat setting. A series of nine videotapes is used at these conferences, covering such topics as positively influencing future generations; loving beyond normal limits and putting love into action; discovering the essential nature of biblical manhood; achieving unity and harmony with one's spouse; loving one's wife physically, emotionally, and spiritually; balancing life's priorities and managing resources; making one's children feel secure in your love; and building up children's confidence and equipping them for life.

As a follow-up to the conferences, men are organized into "E-Teams," the purpose of which is to encourage and hold one another accountable to biblical principles relating to being a godly man, husband, and father. Indeed, DFS proposes that getting men involved in small groups is critical in helping them exercise more intentional family leadership and realize the unique role they play in the development of their children.

As of 2000, 95,000 men have attended DFS conferences and approximately 75 percent of these men have joined an E-team (personal communication, DFS, September 6, 2000). The reach of DFS may soon become even more extensive because the Assemblies of God Church, with nearly 1.5 million members in the United States, has recently formed a partnership with DFS to introduce this ministry to members of its congregation. For more information on DFS, the reader is referred to Simmons (1991) or DFS's Web site <www.dtfs.org>.

Dad's University (Dad's U)

Dad's University is a division within Family University. A learning center without walls, Family University's mission is to strengthen relationships in American families. Family University consists of six colleges, focusing on fathers, mothers, child development, single parenting, step-parenting, and grandparenting. Churches, businesses, and other organizations, as well as individuals who enroll in these various colleges, receive quarterly shipments of curriculum material consisting of videocassettes, audiotapes, books, workbooks, and other teaching materials.

Dad's University seeks to educate fathers about the important role they play in their child's development and to teach them how to exercise intentional leadership in their families. According to Dad's U founder and president Paul Lewis, the goal is to help men discover that the joy they receive from a healthy relationship with their children is more important than any other accomplishment in their lives.

Seminars, frequently held in corporate as well as church settings, is Dad's University's primary method of reaching fathers. Dad's U also encourages local churches to establish themselves as an Extension Campus Church, in return for which they receive family skills training, localized editions of its quarterly magazine *Smart Families,* a Family University Campus Pastor as a consultant, and materials to establish a Family Resource Center Library. Dad's U also has developed a parenting curriculum, published by Zondervan Press, which is currently being marketed to 350,000 churches and other religious organizations. It is estimated by founder Paul Lewis, that Dad's U currently reaches nearly 40,000 men. For more information on Dad's U, see *The Five Key Habits of Smart Dads* (1994) by Paul Lewis or visit their Web site <www.familyuniversity.com>.

North American Missions Board (NAMB)— Men's Missions

Formerly known as the Southern Baptist Brotherhood Commission, the goal of the men's missions of the NAMB is for men to become involved in community and world evangelism efforts. In promoting mission work, it is expected that men will develop a greater sense of purpose and commitment to their families, their churches, and the world—believing that if you mobilize a man, you mobilize a family.

One of NAMB's strategies for reaching fathers is through a curriculum, published by LifeWay Christian Resources of Nashville, Tennessee, called Legacy Builders, the purpose of which is to (1) educate men on the importance of their role as a father, (2) outline for men the characteristics of a godly man, (3) challenge men to develop these qualities in their own lives, and (4) encourage men to develop and implement a godly legacy for their families. It is estimated that the Legacy Builders curriculum has been used by more than 20,000 men in small groups and retreats (personal communication, Jim Burton, September 6, 2000). For more information on Legacy Builders, the reader is referred to Burton (1996) or NAMB's Web site <www.namb.net>.

Great Dads

Great Dads was formed in 1996 by Robert Hamrin. The vision of the organization is to see fathers across America turn their hearts to their children and thereby enrich children's lives, bring joy to fathers, and renew American society. Great Dads seminars focus on six basic principles of being a "great dad": providing unconditional love and affection; spending time with one's children; communicating constantly and creatively; being a partner with Mom; instilling moral and spiritual values; and establishing a fathering legacy.

At the end of each seminar, men are encouraged to sign a commitment card to their children, which reads: "You are a unique gift from God and a very special treasure in my life. I am thrilled that you are my child. So it is with great joy that I commit myself to be a Great Dad to you—always loving you, encouraging, and caring for you—with the guidance and grace of God." As of March 1999, almost 2,000 men have participated in the Great Dads seminars, nearly all of whom signed commitment cards to their children (personal communication, Robert Hamrin, March 1999). For more information on Great Dads seminars, see *Straight from a Dad's Heart* by Robert Hamrin (1993) or visit their Web site <www.greatdads.org>.

THE CATHOLIC CHURCH
AND FATHERHOOD INTERVENTIONS

Given the Catholic Church's historic emphasis on the importance of marriage and the family, it is somewhat surprising that the Church has been relatively slow to confront the crisis of fatherlessness. Despite the vigorous efforts of Pope John Paul II to confront family break-down, the Catholic Church in the United States has taken a largely accomodationist approach toward changes in the family (Wilcox, 1999). Consequently, men attending Catholic churches are far less likely than their evangelical Protestant counterparts to encounter a homily or ministry aimed at providing them with inspiration and direc-tion in terms of their role as fathers.

There are two exceptions to this generalization. First, grounded in the fundamental Catholic teaching that marriage is a sacrament and a living sign of God's love for the world, the Catholic Church has been in the forefront of interventions to better prepare couples for marriage, enrich marriages after they occur, and provide outreach to troubled marriages (Pilla, 1999). Within these marriage ministries, the impor-tance of fathers being involved with and emotionally expressive to-ward their wives and children is frequently emphasized.

The second exception is a new ministry titled St. Joseph's Covenant Keepers (SJCK). Established in 1994 by Steve Wood as a division of the Family Life Center International, the heart of St. Joseph's Covenant Keepers is getting fathers in touch with God the Father. SJCK then encourages fathers to follow the example of St. Joseph, Jesus' earthly father. Because God chose St. Joseph to be the "Guardian of the Redeemer," he is believed to be the ultimate model of a godly husband and father. In order to follow this model, fathers are encouraged to make eight commitments: affirm Christ's Lordship; follow St. Joseph's example in their own lives; stay committed to their wives until death; spend time with, educate, and discipline their children; protect and provide for their families; and follow the Catholic Church's teachings on marriage, family, and human sexuality.

St. Joseph's Covenant Keepers' primary methods for reaching fa-thers includes conferences, printed material, a bimonthly news-letter, radio broadcasts, and audio and videotapes. SJCK targets both residen-tial and nonresidential fathers so long as they are willing to uphold the eight commitments (Wood, 1995). As of August 1999, it is estimated that SJCK has reached over 31,000 fathers (Steve Wood, personal communication). For more information on SJCK, the reader is referred to Wood (1997a; 1997b) or its Web site <www.dads.org>.

MAINLINE PROTESTANT DENOMINATIONS
AND FATHERHOOD INTERVENTIONS

Mainline Protestantism has been the slowest of the major faith traditions in America to develop fatherhood-specific interventions. Rather than focusing on the crisis of fatherlessness, most mainline Protestant seminaries and university-related divinity schools have preferred instead to concentrate on such topics as women's rights, abortion, homosexuality, and economic justice (Browning, 1999). Mainline Protestant churches have given little emphasis to fatherhood or direction to fathers. Indeed, an informal survey undertaken by Diane Knippers of The Institute on Religion and Democracy found that not a single denomination official contacted was able to point to a church teaching document that defined or discussed a theological understanding of fatherhood (Knippers, 1999).

Nevertheless, there are stirrings within some mainline Protestant churches indicating that at least some denominations may be beginning to address the fatherhood issue. This is good news, for with a combined membership of over 50 million Americans, mainline Protestantism represents an excellent opportunity for reaching men and fathers.

United Methodist Church

In 1996, the United Methodist Church established the General Commission on United Methodist Men with the mission of raising the spiritual awareness, commitment, and growth of men across the church. One of its programs is Heartland Expeditions, a weekend retreat experience for men. In these retreats, men are assigned to teams of three to five with as much range in age, race, and socioeconomic background as possible. Each team is then led through a succession of exercises designed to help them experience the impact of fatherhood, rather than merely learning information about it (Malone, 1999). The purpose of these expeditions is to help men heal past hurts from their fathers, build relationships with other men, realize the important role they play in their children's lives, and make a commitment to serve their families with greater fervor. After the retreats, men are encouraged to participate in small Bible, prayer, and accountability groups. The ultimate goal is to help men become better connected with their families, other men, and the church. For more information on the men's ministries of the United Methodist Church, visit the United Methodist Men's Web site <www.ummen.org>.

Presbyterian Church (USA)

A new men's ministry, called Presbyterian Men, has recently been launched within the Presbyterian Church (USA). The mission of Presbyterian Men is to lead men into a vital relationship with Jesus Christ and to assist them in their spiritual, personal, and community development. A quarterly newsletter is its primary means of reaching men and fathers.

Reflecting the generally accomodationist tact of mainline Protestant denominations, the little focus this ministry has on fatherhood is largely restricted to providing support for divorced men and single fathers. Nevertheless, the Presbyterian Church (USA) has recently reported an increase in men's prayer, Bible study, and fellowship groups in local congregations, with some taking the initiative to affiliate with Presbyterian Men or Promise Keepers (Knippers, 1999). Thus, at least at the local congregational level, individual Presbyterian churches may be taking more seriously the need to provide guidance, inspiration, and direction to men and fathers. For more information on Presbyterian Men, the reader is referred to the Web site of the Presbyterian Church, USA <www.pcusa.org>.

SMALLER FAITH-BASED FATHERHOOD INTERVENTIONS

In addition to national men's and fatherhood ministries, there are also a myriad of examples of local churches, especially within the African-American faith community, developing their own ministries to men and fathers. For example, Pastor DeForest "Buster" Soaries of the First Baptist Church in Somerset, New Jersey, has established an extensive array of men's services, with a particular focus on fatherhood. Activities include quarterly breakfasts with guest speakers, an annual men's retreat, outreach activities to neighborhood boys, a mentoring program, recruitment of men to work in the church's various ministries, involvement in Promise Keepers, and a men's Bible study. Their approach involves bringing all types of fathers—married fathers, single fathers, unwed fathers, and divorced fathers—together in fellowship, rather than segregating them, with the assumption that the church needs to deal holistically with the diversity of fatherhood issues in its congregation (Soaries, 1999).

Similarly, the First Evangelical Free Church in Rockford, Illinois, has developed a program called POPS to assist men in becoming better fathers, husbands, and disciples of Christ. Other examples of individual churches implementing ministries for fatherhood include the Calvary Baptist Church in Lancaster, Pennsylvania, the New Covenant Presbyterian Church in Philadelphia, and the Zion Prospect Baptist Church in Yorktown, Virginia.

A number of fatherhood interventions operate outside of a specific church or denomination, which nevertheless incorporate a faith-based message into their services, and which often provide outreach to very high-risk fathers, such as inner city, low-income fathers. For example, Charles Ballard's Institute for Responsible Fatherhood and Family Revitalization <www.responsiblefatherhood.org>, first established in 1982 in Cleveland, Ohio, encourages men to develop a personal faith as part of its work providing outreach to low-income, and mostly noncustodial, dads. Similarly, Father Matters, a program for fathers based in Renton, Washington, and founded in 1998 by Reverend H. David Jones, seeks to serve individuals who are hurting over their relationship, or lack of relationship, with their own fathers through seminars in churches, schools, and prisons.

Other examples of this approach include the Los Angeles-based Brotherhood Organization of a New Destiny (B.O.N.D.) and NYM Ministries. B.O.N.D. (<www.bondinfo.org>) is dedicated to rebuilding the family by rebuilding the man. B.O.N.D. participants, which include both African-American men and women, are taught self-reliance, self-control, and moral values, achieved through group meetings, workshops, individual and family counseling, mentoring programs, bimonthly newsletters, and radio and television broadcasts. Founded in the mid-1960s by Clair and Clara Schnupp, NYM Ministries (<www.nymministries.org>) works primarily, although not exclusively, with Native Americans. NYM Ministries provides individual and family counseling, conducts workshops on family life, fathering, and sexual abuse, and publishes a variety of materials including a bimonthly newsletter and a weekly study series complete with Bible study, commentary, illustrations, and family activity suggestions.

BARRIERS AND CHALLENGES AHEAD

One of the most important challenges facing faith-based approaches to fatherhood intervention is advocating a strong fatherhood script while at the same time not offending the sensibilities or prerogatives of modern women. Promise Keepers, in particular, has faced severe criticism from some feminist groups who complain that it is promoting male domination both in the home and in the greater society. Such suspicions were reinforced when, in June of 1998, the South Baptist Convention, the nation's largest Protestant denomination, adopted an amendment to its "Faith and Message" statement which stated, among other things, that a wife should "submit" to her husband's "servant-leadership" and "serve as his helper in managing their household and nurturing the next generation."

To some extent this issue is a matter of misunderstanding surrounding the use of the term "servant-leadership." As understood within Christianity, the concept of the "servant-leadership" is one that instructs men to be humble and model themselves after the sacrifice of Christ for the Church (see Ephesians 5:20-33). Indeed, it was this self-subordinating servant role that Christian men are supposed to play which, according to Don Browning of the University of Chicago, differentiated the early Christian male from the more egoistic position of men in the surrounding Greco-Roman world (Browning, 1999).

Hence, the true servant-leader is not in it for himself. Rather, his role is to sacrifice himself for his wife and children as Christ sacrificed himself for the Church. Thus, when the apostle Paul wrote in his letter to the Ephesians, "For the husband is the head of the wife as Christ is the head of the church" (Ephesians 5:23, NIV), he did not mean this as an excuse for domestic tyranny, but as a reminder that the husband's role is to be the "chief servant" within the household (Browning, 1989).

In an attempt to reassure those who view the term servant-leader with suspicion, University of Chicago professor Don Browning and his colleagues have recently advanced the notion of "equal-regard marriages." Modeled after the commandments that "[y]ou shall love your neighbor as yourself" (Matthew 19:19, KJV) and to "[submit] to one another in the fear of God" (Ephesians 5:21, KJV), equal-regard marriages entail husband and wife treating each other as persons, working for the good of the other, allowing each other to have full access to the privileges and responsibilities of both public and private life, taking equal responsibility for parenting, and working out their respective divisions of labor in mutual obligation. This model encourages couples to arrange their respective responsibilities and privileges with a sense of flexibility, mutual regard, and attention to individual abilities and inclinations (Browning et al., 1997). The Church of Jesus Christ of Latter-Day Saints, for example, incorporates this equal-regard concept in their Proclamation to the World on the Family, in which fathers and mothers are "obligated to help one another as equal partners" (Center for Studies of the Family, 1995).

Judging from the empirical literature, the actual behavior of religiously affiliated men is closer to Browning's equal-regard marriages than to strict patriarchal marriages. Indeed, there is little evidence that religious couples in the United States, including evangelicals, approach marriage differently than do nonreligious couples. For example, Melinda Lundquist and Christian Smith of the University of North Carolina found no differences in the way evangelicals and other married couples dealt with family finances, child rearing, and work decisions (Lundquist and Smith, 1998). Other research has found no differences in the patterns of male household labor between evangelical men and other Americans, nor is there any evidence that evangelical men are more likely to physically abuse their wives (Ellison, Bartkowski, and Anderson, 1999; Wilcox and Bartkowski, 2000).

Thus, contrary to the suspicion of some that faith-based fatherhood interventions, and especially evangelical interventions, might encourage a return to a strict patriarchal marriage model, the available evidence suggests that religiously affiliated men, including evangelicals, are actually no different than nonreligious males in the way they behave within marriage. In fact, research has rather consistently found that church attendance, religious devotion, or both, are positively related to various indicators of marital quality and success, including happiness and satisfaction, adjustment, and duration (Dudley and Kosinski, 1990; Hansen, 1987), and, if anything, the frequency of attending religious services is inversely related to the likelihood of perpetrating domestic violence (Ellison, Bartkowski, and Anderson, 1999). For faith-based fatherhood promotion interventions to gain more legitimacy in the secular culture, these research findings will need to receive more attention.

Another challenge for faith-based interventions is to overcome the perception by some that religiously oriented fathers are more cold and distant in their relationships with their children than are nonreligiously affiliated fathers. This perception is reinforced because evangelical Protestant groups are more likely to embrace traditional gender roles and strict disciplinary child-rearing codes.

Often overlooked, however, is the fact that faith-based interventions also encourage active, involved, and emotionally expressive fathering (Dollahite, Marks, and Olson, 1998). Hence, while adhering to a traditional view of men as "head of the family" and emphasizing the need for fathers to be strict disciplinarians, the fatherhood script advanced by faith-based interventions has largely embraced the broader culture's "softer" father ideal (Wilcox, 1997). In fact, several recent studies have found that even after controlling for income, education, and race, religious fathers, including evangelicals, mainline Protestants, and Catholics, are more likely than nonreligious fathers to be involved with their children in one-on-one and group activities, and to praise and hug their children. Further, they are less likely to yell at them (Wilcox, 1999). Thus, according to Brookings scholar W. Bradford Wilcox, the *real* new fathers—those who are highly involved in the lives of the children and expressive toward them—may, in fact, be religious fathers, including evangelical fathers, despite the fact that religious fathers are more likely to profess adherence to more traditional gender-role attitudes (Wilcox, 1999).

A third challenge to faith-based approaches to fatherhood promotion is to demonstrate that their interventions result in lasting and positive behavioral change. The truth is we do not know whether attendance at faith-based rallies, weekend retreats, and accountability groups leads men to become better fathers or whether the impact of these interventions ceases when the participants reenter the threshold of their own home. Empirical studies addressing this question, although needed, simply have not yet been published.

Nevertheless, there are a number of reasons to believe that faith-based approaches are capable of achieving some degree of lasting behavioral change. First, many men do find faith-based interventions both inspirational and motivational. Many fathers find these interventions so attractive, they become repeat attendees at rallies, retreats, and other gatherings. With repetition, there is an increased likelihood that behavior change will occur.

Second, faith-based interventions combine messages about meaning, transcendence, and personal salvation with concrete information about effective fathering skills. As reviewed earlier in this chapter, religiously affiliated fathers are, on average, more involved, emotionally expressive, and supportive of their children than are nonreligiously affiliated fathers (Wilcox, 1999). This suggests that faith-based activities are capable of providing men who identify with and regularly attend religious activities with the motivation and skills to be an involved father.

Third, faith-based interventions frequently follow up attendance at one-time events with participation in ongoing, smaller accountability groups. It is likely that participation in an accountability group provides men with a network of social support and encouragement for positive father involvement, as well as social pressure to refrain from disengaged or abusive fathering. Given what we know about the positive influence of social support networks on behavior, participation in these smaller, ongoing activities may, in fact, be the most important factor leading to actual behavior change.

It is possible, of course, that fathers who are attracted to faith-based interventions are men who are already involved and responsible fathers. If so, faith-based approaches may be mostly "preaching to the choir," and not very effective at reaching men who are wayward, distant, or even abusive fathers. On the other hand, the promise of faith-based interventions lies in their power not only to teach skills, but to change hearts. Faith can be, and frequently is, a powerful motivator for personal change. The question for faith-based fatherhood interventions is: How successful are they in actually reaching, and exerting a positive influence on, disconnected, uninvolved, and irresponsible fathers?

My hunch is that there is a good deal of "preaching to the choir" going on. But sometimes even the choir needs preaching to. And there are certainly enough testimonials to suggest that some men are, in fact, transformed by faith-based fatherhood interventions from disconnected, uninvolved, and irresponsible fathers into loving, involved, and committed dads. Still, much more research needs to be done to determine the degree to which faith-based interventions produce positive improvements in fathering behavior and, if so, how they do it.

A fourth challenge for faith-based interventions is demonstrating positive impacts on the well-being of children. As I have argued elsewhere (Horn, 1999), it is not enough for a fatherhood intervention to show positive impact on the lives and behavior of fathers. Rather, the most important goal of any fatherhood intervention must be whether or not it results in improvements in the well-being of children.

To my knowledge, no single study has directly examined this question for faith-based interventions. However, what we do know is that children who grow up connected to faith and engaged in religious activities are less likely to experience academic failure, become pregnant as teenagers, abuse alcohol, or use illegal drugs (Top and Chadwick, 1998; Ellison, Bartkowski, and Segal, 1996). Given that one of the assumptions underlying faith-based approaches to fatherhood interventions is the necessity to bring up one's children to know God, it is reasonable to assume that children of participants in faith-based programs will have a greater propensity to become engaged in religious activities. If so, it is reasonable to hypothesize a positive impact of faith-based interventions not only on the behavior of the father, but on his children as well.

A final challenge for faith-based interventions is finding ways to collaborate effectively with more secular fatherhood promotion activities. At first blush, this would appear rather easily done. Both, after all, are concerned with increasing the skills and involvement of fathers. But there is something additional in faith-based interventions that is largely absent from secular approaches: The placing of fatherhood within a broader, more transcendent, and specifically spiritual context. This is not to say that secular approaches do not agree that fatherhood has a spiritual component. But many working within secular intervention approaches will, no doubt, be uncomfortable with the placement of fatherhood within a specific theological framework. On the other hand, asking faith-based fatherhood interventions to, in effect, "tone down" their theological underpinnings in the name of collaboration would, I'm sure, be viewed by many faith-based interventions as akin to asking them to give up their soul.

Nevertheless, faith-based and secular interventions should strive toward more effective collaboration. An important first step would seem to be for secular and faith-based fatherhood programs to develop a greater appreciation for each other's work. This might best be accomplished through aggressive outreach and information sharing in order to achieve a better understanding of each other's goals, methods, and beliefs. It might be especially helpful, in this regard, for each to attend the other's programs. Once a level of trust and understanding is developed, mutual referral-making might then be a logical next step.

THE PROMISE
OF FAITH-BASED APPROACHES

The great promise of faith-based interventions is its reach. There are more than 300,000 churches in the United States, attended by 60 percent of the population in any given month (Gallup, 1999). Millions of men are connected to a community of faith in some way. There is no secular organizational network that has the same degree of contact with as many men as do churches and synagogues.

But the reach of faith-based approaches is not limited to, nor even mostly about, numbers of men. Rather, the real promise of faith-based approaches to fatherhood promotion lies in their "internal reach"—the ability to reach deep into the hearts of fathers and fundamentally transform their lives.

Given this extraordinary reach—both external and internal—of communities of faith in the United States, what is surprising is not that some communities of faith have implemented targeted fatherhood interventions, but that so many others have not. For some, the reluctance to develop specific fatherhood interventions may be due to a fear of being perceived as being connected to the highly publicized, and in some quarters controversial, Promise Keepers.* Others may desire to maintain a focus on broader issues of social justice, rather than concentrating on programs for individual men and their families. Still others may simply be unaware of the harsh realities of fatherlessness and its attendant consequences for the well-being of children. Also, there are those who undoubtedly believe that through regular religious service and personal scriptural study, men are already being instructed in responsible fatherhood without the need for any special programs or ministries.

Whatever the reason for the failure of some communities of faith to aggressively confront today's crisis of fatherlessness, what is clear is that faith-based fatherhood interventions have an extraordinary capacity to attract men. Millions of men have attended Promise Keepers rallies. Tens of thousands of others have been involved with Dad: The Family Shepherd, Dad's U, and Legacy Builders. No secular interventions have come even close to attracting the numbers of participants that routinely attend faith-based seminars, workshops, rallies, and retreats. The obvious question is: Why?

I believe the reason lies in the ability of faith-based fatherhood interventions to inspire and provide meaning to men in ways that secular approaches cannot; for only faith-based approaches can provide men with a more transcendent understanding of why they ought to be good fathers. Most men long for personal meaning and significance. They want their lives to count for something; they want their lives to matter. Faith-based fatherhood interventions answer this most basic of yearnings by saying to men that they matter to God. And when men come to believe that they matter to God, their work as earthly fathers is given a transcendence that no social scientist or secular fatherhood enthusiast can ever hope to provide. Indeed, what faith-based interventions say to men is this: when you are an involved, loving father to your children, you give your children a glimpse of the Heavenly Father's love, and in so doing, you provide both you and your children with a cosmic connection that transcends earthly experience. What could matter more than that?

---

*Indeed, the General Assembly of the Presbyterian Church USA (PCUSA) recently voted by a margin of more than 3-2 *not* to commend Promise Keepers for its Christian witness to Presbyterian men despite testimony from Rick Porter of the Presbytery of southern New England, who estimated that ten times as many PCUSA men are involved in Promise Keepers as they are in Presbyterian Men.

APPENDIX

Sample of Web-based Father Education and Support Programs

Site Name	Address (URL)
Brotherhood Organization of a New Destiny (B.O.N.D.)	http://www.bondinfo.org/
Dad: The Family Shepherd (DFS)	http://www.dtfs.org/
Dad's University (Dad's U)	http://www.familyuniversity.com/
Great Dads	http://www.greatdads.org/
Institute for Responsible Fatherhood and Family Revitalization	http://www.responsiblefatherhood.org/
North American Missions Board (NAMB)	http://www.namb.net/
NYM Ministries	http://www.nymministries.org/
Presbyterian Men, Presbyterian Church (USA)	http://www.pcusa.org/
Promise Keepers	http://www.promisekeepers.org/
St. Joseph's Covenant Keepers (SJCK)	http://www.dads.org/
United Methodist Men	http://www.ummen.org/

Note: Due to the rapid changes within the Internet, some of these addresses may no longer be available.

REFERENCES

Browning, D. S. (1989). *A fundamental practical theology: Descriptive and strategic proposals*. Minneapolis: Fortress Press.

Browning, D. S. (1995). Religion and family ethics: A new strategy for the church. In N. T. Ammerman and W. C. Roof (Eds.), *Work, family, and religion in contemporary society* (pp. 157-176). New York: Rutledge.

Browning, D. S. (1999). Fatherhood as a point of convergence beyond old categories. In D. Eberly (Ed.), *The faith factor in American fatherhood: What America's faith communities can do to restore fatherhood* (pp. 191-202). Lanham, MD: Lexington Books.

Browning, D. S., McLemore, B. M., Couture, P., Lyon, B., and Franklin, R. (1997). *From culture wars to common ground: Religion and the American family debate.* Louisville, KY: Westminster John Knox Press.

Burton, J. (1996). *Legacy builders.* Lafayette, LA: Vital Issues Press.

Center for Studies of the Family. (1995). The family: A proclamation to the world. Read by President Gordon B. Hinckley (Church of Jesus Christ of Latter-Day Saints) at the General Relief Society Meeting, September 25, 1995, in Salt Lake City, Utah. Quoted in *Fostering family strength in a changing world.* Provo, UT: Brigham Young University.

Dollahite, D. C. (1998). Fathering, faith, and spirituality. *The Journal of Men's Studies, 7,* 3-15.

Dollahite, D. C., Marks, L. D., and Olson, M. M. (1998). Faithful fathering in trying times: Religious beliefs and practices of Latter-day Saint fathers of children with special needs. *The Journal of Men's Studies, 7,* 71-93.

Dudley, M. G. and Kosinski, F. A. (1990). Religiosity and marital satisfaction: A research note. *Review of Religious Research, 32,* 78-86.

Eberly, D. (Ed.) (1999). *The faith factor in American fatherhood: What America's faith communities can do to restore fatherhood.* Lanham, MD: Lexington Books.

Ellison, C. G., Bartkowski, J. P., and Anderson, K. L. (1999). Are there religious variations in domestic violence? *Journal of Family Issues, 20,* 87-113.

Ellison, C. G, Bartkowski, J. P., and Segal, M. L. (1996). Conservative Protestantism and the parental use of corporal punishment. *Social Forces, 74,* 1003-1029.

Gallup, G. Jr. (1999). What Americans believe about fatherhood and the role of religion. In D. Eberly (Ed.), *The faith factor in American fatherhood: What America's faith communities can do to restore fatherhood* (pp. 39-58). Lanham, MD: Lexington Books.

Hamrin, R. (1993). *Straight from a dad's heart.* Nashville, TN: Thomas Nelson Publishers.

Hansen, G. L. (1987). The effect of religiosity on factors predicting marital adjustment. *Social Psychology Quarterly, 50,* 264-269.

Horn, W. F. (1999). Did you say movement? In W. F. Horn, D. Blankenhorn, and M. B. Pearlstein (Eds.), *The fatherhood movement: A call to action* (pp. 1-16). Lanham, MD: Lexington Books.

Hunter, J. D. (1987). *Evangelicalism: The coming generation.* Chicago: University of Chicago Press.

Janssen, A. and Weeden, L. K. (1994). *The Seven Promises of a Promise Keeper.* Colorado Springs: Focus on the Family Publishing.

Knippers, D. (1999). Fatherhood in the mainline Protestant tradition. In D. Eberly (Ed.), *The faith factor in American fatherhood: What America's faith communities can do to restore fatherhood* (pp. 113-128). Lanham, MD: Lexington Books.

Lewis, P. (1994). *The five key habits of smart dads.* Grand Rapids, MI: Zondervan Publishing House.

Lewis, R. (1997). *Raising a modern day knight: A father's role in guiding his son to authentic manhood.* Colorado Springs, CO: Focus on the Family.

Lundquist, M. and Smith, C. (1998). "The triumph of ambivalence: American Evangelicals on sex-roles and marital decision-making." Paper presented at the annual meeting of the Scientific Study of Religion, Montreal, Canada.

Malone, L. (1999). One denomination's efforts. In D. Eberly (Ed.), *The faith factor in American fatherhood: What America's faith communities can do to restore fatherhood* (pp. 267-279). Lanham, MD: Lexington Books.

McCartney, B. (1999). Men as Promise Makers and Keepers. In D. Eberly (Ed.), *The faith factor in American fatherhood: What America's faith communities can do to restore fatherhood* (pp. 241-249). Lanham, MD: Lexington Books.

Nappa, M. (1999). In the grip of fatherhood: A dad-to-dad conversation with Max Lucado. *New Man,* May/June, 40-42.

Pilla, A. M. (1999). Fatherhood in the Roman Catholic tradition. In D. Eberly (Ed.), *The faith factor in American fatherhood: What America's faith communities can do to restore fatherhood* (pp. 91-96). Lanham, MD: Lexington Books.

Simmons, D. (1991). *Dad: The family counselor.* Colorado Springs, CO: Victor Books.

Soaries, D. (1999). One pastor's personal struggle. In D. Eberly (Ed.), *The faith factor in American fatherhood: What America's faith communities can do to restore fatherhood* (pp. 281-289). Lanham, MD: Lexington Books.

Stanton, S. (1999). The core of the universe. In W. F. Horn, D. Blankenhorn, and M.B. Pearlstein (Eds.), *The fatherhood movement: A call to action* (pp. 147-160). Lanham, MD: Lexington Books.

Top, B. L. and Chadwick, B. A. (1998). *Rearing righteous youth of Zion: Great news, good news, not-so-good news.* Salt Lake City, UT: Bookcraft.

Weber, S. (1993). *Tender Warrior: God's intention for man.* Sisters, OR: Multnomah.

Wilcox, W. B. (1997). "Religion and fatherhood: Exploring the links between religious affiliation, gender role attitudes and paternal practices." Working paper 13, Sociology Department of Princeton University, Princeton, NJ: Princeton University, Sociology Department.

Wilcox, W. B. (1999). Emerging attitudes about gender roles and fatherhood. In D. Eberly (Ed.), *The faith factor in American fatherhood: What America's faith communities can do to restore fatherhood* (pp. 219-239). Lanham, MD: Lexington Books.

Wilcox, W. B. and Bartkowski, J. P. (2000). *The conservative Protestant family: Traditional rhetoric, progressive practice.* In E. J. Dionne, Jr. and J. J. Dilulio Jr. (Eds.), *What's God got to do with the American experiment? Essays on religion and politics.* (pp. 32-37). Washington, DC: The Brookings Institution.

Wood, S. (1995). *Eight commitments for successful fathering.* Port Charlotte, FL: Family Life Center Publications.

Wood, S. (1997a). *Christian fatherhood.* Port Charlotte, FL: Family Life Center Publications.

Wood, S. (1997b). *Executive summary: St. Joseph's Covenant Keepers.* Port Charlotte, FL: Family Life Center Publications.

Chapter 9

Legal Support
for the Father-Child Relationship
in Disunited Families

Anne P. Mitchell

INTRODUCTION

Our legal system is, at its heart, an adversarial system—one designed to pit one party against the other, person against person, and
thus, in the family law arena, parent against parent.

However, for the most part, a family that has become disunited, or
is about to become so, needs support and guidance. They do not need
to have the flames of disharmony fanned by the adversarial process.

Nowhere is this more poignantly apparent than in the case of the
involved, hands-on father who upon divorce or separation suddenly
finds himself relegated to the role of occasional "visitor" in his children's lives. At a time when his children need him the most, he is
ripped out of their lives, and powerless to find his way back in.

In my many years of practice as a fathers' rights attorney, I have
seen it literally thousands of times: the newly single father first hope-
ful, then incredulous, and finally beaten and resigned, going to court
time and again only to find his every effort to maintain a meaningful
relationship with his children belittled, frustrated, or flatly denied by
the very court he trusted to protect that relationship. Worse yet is the
toll that this whole process takes on his children, who now find themselves caught in the cross fire of these family court skirmishes.

In 1996, there were more than 19 million children living apart from
their fathers (Saluter and Lugaila, 1998). We know now that children

who are raised without access to their fathers are far more likely to be involved in such destructive behaviors as truancy, alcoholism, drug abuse, and juvenile crime. As David Blankenhorn notes in his book, *Fatherless America,* "[p]ut simply, we have too many boys with guns primarily because we have too few fathers" (1995, p. 31). And of course, it is not just boys who are so deeply affected by the absence of their fathers; teen girls raised in father-absent circumstances are twice as likely to give birth to their own father-absent children (Garfinkel and McLanahan, 1986). Sadly, according to the Federal Bureau of Census, nearly one-half (42 percent) of the fathers of those 19 million children have no time-share privileges—they do not have access to their children (Federal Bureau of Census, 1995).

As noted previously, many fathers who want to be involved in the lives of their children, and who turn to the legal system for assistance, find instead that our adversarial court system only serves to further estrange them from their children. As Maccoby and Mnookin (1992) reveal, fathers who go to court to gain time with their children consistently get far less custody and time-share than they ask for.

Fortunately, several legal tools may serve as alternatives to the traditional courtroom battle, including options that can facilitate healing of the family system while promoting a consistent, involved relationship between father and child. In this chapter, you will learn what these tools are and how they can be used to assist the single father in maintaining his relationship with his children, as well as how to handle the special situations in which a father is accused of abusing his child, or in which the child has been kidnapped by the other parent.

KNOW THE RULES

Perhaps one of the most important duties of the father advocate is to make sure that the client understands which things are worth challenging and which things are not. There is nothing more frustrating for a client than to find out that he has just spent the last year, and several thousand dollars, fighting an issue for which the conclusion was foregone, rather than focusing his efforts on something to which he could have actually made a difference.

Many matters in family law are governed by rules that are not subject to debate. Generally, resisting the outcomes dictated by these rules will only serve to cost the client a great deal, both emotionally and financially, while gaining nothing. In fact, it may backfire, as the court is likely to get annoyed with having its already strained resources tied up in hearing a matter for which there is no legitimate rebuttal. Although most of these rules are related to support and finances, they may still influence, and impact, the issue of custody or time-share.

Wage Assignments

It is now the law in all fifty states that a wage assignment (garnishment) order will be issued by the court in all cases involving child support. It is possible to negotiate with the other side so that the order is not actually served on the payor's employer, and thus will not take effect, so long as the payor is never late with, or misses, a payment. However, if the father has ever been even a day late, or a dollar short, the odds of such a concession are slim.

Child Support, "Add-Ons," and Time-share

In nearly all states, child support is considered to cover the basics, such as food, shelter, and clothing. The court can, and often will, include several types of "add-ons," meaning things which the payor must pay in addition to child support. Typical add-ons include the cost of child care, health insurance, and uninsured medical expenses. The cost of child care and uninsured medical expenses will often be split between the parties when the custodial parent is working.

Also, although it is true that, in theory, the issues of child support and time-share are separate, and one cannot be withheld for failure to come through with the other, the reality is that the court will not be sympathetic to a father who is asking for increased time with his children if he is failing to pay child support. If the advocate is working with a father who is in this situation, he or she should help him to get started paying his child support before, or at the same time as, they initiate the request for increased time-share.

On a related note, a mother often will fight a request to increase a father's time-share because she believes that it will cause her child support to decrease. One very successful method for dealing with this, where the father can afford it, is to offer to keep child support set at the old amount if the mother agrees to the increased time-share. This has the effect of immediately removing her primary motivation for denying the increase in time-share, and child support can always be revisited at a later date.

Attorneys Fees

Most states have provisions that specifically authorize the court to order one party to pay another's attorneys fees. The two factors most often considered, in order of emphasis, are (1) who earns more money, and (2) which party, if any, has brought the case before the court unreasonably. If a father earns substantially more than the mother, it is likely that he will have to pay at least a portion of her attorney's fees.

Taxes

Current Federal law, and many state laws, are such that whoever has primary physical custody gets the tax deductions for the children. Period. It does not matter how much support is contributed to the cost of raising the child. However, the custodial parent may agree to sign one or more of the deductions over to the noncustodial parent. This is not ordered by the court very often, but it is frequently negotiated between the parties or their attorneys.

*   *   *

Helping a single father to be aware of those things which would be a waste of time and energy to challenge allows him to marshall his resources and focus his energy on the things which really matter: his children and his relationship with them.

LEGAL TOOLS TO USE
IN CUSTODY AND TIME-SHARE ISSUES

Father advocates have several options at their disposal when assisting a noncustodial father in becoming (re)involved, or more involved, in the lives of their children. Although the laws of each state and jurisdiction may vary, the following are generally available in some form, in every locale, although the local terminology may differ: hearings, restraining orders, supervised time-share, mediation, arbitration, Special Masters, co-parent counseling, parent-child counseling, psychological evaluation, and negotiated agreements.

A father who is initiating the legal action may have greater flexibility in choosing among these options. However, even a father who is the responding party should be able to avail himself of many of these legal tools. The parties may, by themselves, or through their attorneys, agree to use any of these options. If an agreement cannot be reached, the father's attorney should lodge a request with the court, asking that the court order the parties to utilize the option requested.

Hearings

The picture which springs to the minds of most when envisioning the involvement of the court system in a custody or time-share matter is that of the proverbial "day in court." In order to bring an issue in front of the judge, one of the parties must file a "motion"— a request that the court order whatever relief it is that the party is seeking. The other party then has an opportunity to respond to the motion in writing, and, eventually, the two will appear at a hearing before the judge, who will address the issues and rule on the motion.

This is usually the least desirable course of action for a single father, in part because issues of family dynamics are not generally well served by being subjected to the adversarial process, and in part because there is still a prevailing bias against single fathers in most courts. However, there are a few instances when a hearing before the court is the only feasible option, such as when the mother is in contempt of a court order, or when a truly urgent situation exists, such as one in which a child's safety is in jeopardy.

Restraining Orders

A restraining order is a particular type of court order that may result from a hearing. Most people are familiar with the type of restraining order that restrains one person from contacting or going near another person. However, a restraining order can be issued against nearly any activity, provided that it is an appropriate subject for the court to address. So, for example, a parent may be restrained from taking a child out of the area during the other parent's parenting time, from badmouthing the other parent in front of the child, or from other behaviors calculated to interfere with the other parent's time-share or alienate the child from the other parent.

Unfortunately, some restraining orders, even if granted, do not lend themselves to ready enforcement (the one against badmouthing the other parent in front of the child is one such example). The general rule is that courts are more likely to grant restraining orders for more egregious activities and for requests that are more practical to enforce. In cases where orders are granted which would, nonetheless, be impractical to enforce, it is important that the father be counseled as to how and when to best attempt to have the order enforced.

Supervised Time-share

For purposes of this chapter, the terms "time-share" or "parenting time" are used instead of the term "visitation." A father's relationship with his child is that of a parent, not of a visitor. Language is a very powerful tool, and by reducing a father to "visitor," it makes it too easy for fathers themselves, as well as others, to devalue their importance in the lives of their children.

Supervised time-share occurs when a parent is only permitted to see his or her children in the presence of a chaperon. Usually an order for supervised time-share is made because the mother or another family member has alleged abuse, excessive drinking, or other inappropriate behaviors on the part of the father, toward or around the children.

Most fathers who find themselves on the receiving end of a request or order for supervised time-share are understandably upset. Supervised time-share means that the father is not allowed to go anywhere or do anything with his child without somebody right there, monitoring every word and action. It can be awkward and insulting, at best, and paralyzing to the father-child relationship, at worst.

However, supervised time-share can also be a useful tool for the single father—particularly one who has been wrongfully accused of abuse or other wrongdoing. The father's advocate should opt for the use of a professional time-share supervisor, who will usually have a background in therapy, social work, or child development, rather than a friend or family member. The time-share supervisor should submit a report regularly to the court and the attorneys, indicating what occurred during each time-share, and including observations as to the nature of any father-child interactions. Such reports can help to disprove false allegations, or to demonstrate that a previous problem has been rectified. I have had cases that have been turned completely around based on the reports of the time-share supervisor.

Supervised time-share should not be allowed to go on indefinitely, unless absolutely necessary, and the father's advocate should make a motion to end the supervised time-share once the time-share reports demonstrate that a need for such supervision no longer exists.

Mediation

Many states now offer mediation for custody and time-share issues through their family court system; in some states, such as California, mediation is mandatory. Even in states that do not provide mediation, a request that the parents go to mediation for issues of time-share and custody will often be honored.

In mediation, the two parents meet with a third party (the mediator), whose job it is to help the parents to reach an agreement regarding custody or time-share. Mediation is typically conducted by Marriage, Family, and Child Counselors (MFCCs), Licensed Clinical Social Workers (LCSWs), and sometimes by attorneys.

Mediation is usually, although not always, confidential, and the mediator will not report to the court or anyone else what went on during the mediation sessions. This allows the parents to attempt to reach a meaningful agreement without fear of recrimination if they fail to reach such an agreement. A few family law systems, such as those found in certain counties in California, provide for family court mediators to make recommendations to the court based on what went on during the mediation; in such a case the mediation between the parents is obviously not entirely confidential.

A father who is requesting to alter the custody or time-share arrangement may request that the court order the parents to mediation. If the father is on the receiving end of such a motion, he may still request that the parties go to mediation before resorting to having the court rule on the issues raised.

Arbitration

Arbitration is similar to mediation, except that, unlike mediation, the person conducting an arbitration is empowered to make a decision as to the outcome of the issues. Arbitration may be binding (the parties must live with whatever outcome the arbiter dictates), or nonbinding (the parties still have the option of taking the issue to court). Generally speaking, both parties must agree to arbitration or the court cannot order it, as to do so without an agreement would be an impermissible delegation of judicial authority. It is useful to note that nearly all family law issues, including issues of support, finances, and property, as well as those of custody and time-share, readily lend themselves to resolution through arbitration.

Special Masters

Some states have provisions that allow for the appointment of a "Special Master." The Special Master is typically either a mental health professional or an attorney who is appointed to, in essence, micromanage the case; it is not unlike having your own private judge. Because the Special Master has quasi-judicial powers, and can make orders which carry the full weight and authority of the court, the parties must agree to the appointment of the Special Master, or, as with arbitration, the court cannot order it. Special Masters are particularly useful in cases in which there is a history of protracted and ongoing litigation over the day-to-day aspects of time-share.

Even in states that do not formally recognize the concept of the Special Master, the father's advocate should be able to introduce the concept in a request to the court, requesting the appointment of a therapist whose duties are consistent with those of a Special Master.*

---

*One can obtain more information about the Special Master program, and descriptions of those duties, from the Special Master Program, Superior Court of Santa Clara County, 170 Park Center Plaza, San Jose, California 95113.

Coparent Counseling

One of the most useful and underutilized tools in the legal advocate's store is the ability of the court to order counseling for various combinations of family members. Carol Marks, MFCC, of Saratoga, California, and I have developed a model for coparent counseling, which is a very effective means of achieving a working coparenting relationship, even where other methods (particularly those that are adversarial in nature) may have failed. We have used it successfully to reintegrate estranged fathers into the lives of their children, to remedy situations in which one parent is interfering with the other parent's relationship with the children, and even to forestall and avoid false allegations of abuse.

The primary goals of coparent counseling are to help the parents to dissipate some of the anger and hostility that may lay between them, build a better base of communication, learn to respect each other as parents, and cooperate as coparents for the sake of their children. In addition, many parents find that this sort of counseling gives them a place where it is safe and acceptable for them to communicate with each other, for the sake of the children, without the outside influence of the children, new spouses, and other family members.

Parent-Child Counseling

In cases where the father-child relationship has suffered due to a prolonged absence of the father, allegations of abuse, or other factors, or in cases where it is alleged that the child is fearful of the father, is alienated from the father, or simply "doesn't want to see" their father, an application should be made to the court requesting that the court order the child to participate in counseling with the father.

Some fathers may, at first, be resistant to parent-child counseling. However, sometimes this may be the best and, particularly in cases where there have been allegations of abuse, perhaps even the only way that a father will be able to see his child. Another advantage of parent-child counseling is that the therapist will be in a position to evaluate the parent-child relationship, and to let the court know if the relationship is not so problematic as some may allege. Finally, in the cases of both coparent and father-child counseling, the very fact that the father is requesting that the court order such counseling will demonstrate to the court that the father is very serious about doing whatever it takes to make his relationship with his children work.

Psychological Evaluation

Sometimes, no matter how hard one tries, mediation, negotiation, and even counseling do not work. One parent seems absolutely determined to control the situation, and to act as a gatekeeper to the other parent's relationship with the children, or even to cut him or her entirely out of the children's lives. In such cases, the advocate may wish to request that the court order a psychological evaluation of both parents, and, depending on the situation, of the children. Indeed, in some states, such as California, the court will routinely order such an evaluation where all other efforts to reach an agreement have failed.

The goal of a psychological evaluation is to allow the evaluator, almost always a PhD psychologist, to gain an accurate and detailed picture of each parent's personality, character traits, and parenting styles and abilities. If the evaluator also meets with the children, it will be to gain insights into how the children are faring under the current time-share arrangements, and to determine whether they would benefit from a change in those arrangements. The evaluator will then make a recommendation as to time-share and custody, based on all of this information.

In states where the court routinely orders custody and time-share evaluations, the court will almost always make an order consistent with what the evaluator recommends. For that reason, the father's advocate should be sure that the father will stand up to such close scrutiny, and also should be familiar with the candidates for evaluator, to ensure that whoever performs the evaluation is neutral regarding paternal- versus maternal-based custody and time-share.

Negotiated Agreements

The last, but by no means least effective, tool that the father and his advocate have at their disposal is the negotiated agreement. As the name suggests, this is an agreement that is negotiated between the parents or their attorneys. Once such an agreement is reached, it is reduced to a formal writing, signed by both parents and any attorneys, and then submitted to the court for the judge's signature. Once it is signed by the judge, it has the full authority of the court, and is as enforceable as any other court order.

The advantage of a negotiated agreement is that, because both parties are involved in crafting the final outcome, they are both more likely to be satisfied with that outcome. It is always better for the two parents to determine under what rules they are going to operate and coparent, rather than leaving it up to some third party. When parents leave such decisions up to somebody else, such as a judge, it usually is the case that nobody is happy with the results. Further, when both parties have been involved in determining how time-share and custody will be structured, each is more likely to comply with the resulting arrangements. Finally, a negotiated agreement is always less costly than an intervention by the court, not just in terms of financial cost, but in terms of emotional tolls as well, both to the parents and to the children.

One nice feature of negotiated agreements is that the parties can agree to almost anything they want to; so long as they both agree to it, the court will sign it. I once had a client who, after a long and bitter struggle with his ex-wife over certain time-share issues, reached an agreement with her that a particular issue, whenever it would arise, would be resolved by a coin-toss if they could not otherwise reach an agreement! I would not recommend this as a standard method of dispute resolution, but the point is that these two parents did agree to this, after years with no resolution through the court system, and so it was written into their agreement and signed by the judge.

PLAN A COURSE OF ACTION AND DO NOT LOSE SIGHT OF THE ULTIMATE GOAL

It is important to determine what the single father ultimately wishes to accomplish. Usually he wants to increase the amount of time that he is able to spend with his children. This can almost always be done, but it takes time, and patience. Increases in time-share will usually happen gradually, over the course of a carefully planned and methodically executed course of action.

For example, assume a divorced father has not seen his children in several months. He now wishes to see his children three weekends a month, from Friday after school until Monday morning. The standard time-share in your county is every other weekend, from Saturday morning through Sunday night. Under these circumstances, it is extremely unlikely that anyone is going to agree immediately to the time-share that the father is seeking. However, the other parent or the court may be willing to agree to a time-share of one full day, every other weekend, to start. This may not seem like much to the father. However, once having secured that one day every other week as a court order he has now gone from having nothing, to having an enforceable court order for regular time-share. Thus he has already vastly improved his position.

If the father maintains this time-share for a few months, he will then be in a much better position to revisit the issue. He will be able to demonstrate how consistent he has been with this new time-share and to ask that the time-share be increased to two days, with an overnight, every other week. Next, he may be able to increase the time-share to Friday evenings through Monday mornings.

Generally, the court will almost always want to see some consistency in maintaining a lesser time-share before granting more sweeping blocks of time, and will be inclined to increase time-share by intervals, not in one fell swoop. The key is to determine where the father wants to end up relative to time-share, and then to map out how he can most effectively get there, utilizing one or more of the legal tools detailed in this chapter. Although the father may, at first, feel that this sort of strategy will take too long to implement, it is most often the case that the desired outcome will be attained much more quickly than would be the case in trying to prevail in an adversarial court battle. Custody and time-share cases can last for months, even years. They are also very expensive, and the outcome is not guaranteed. And finally, in a worst case scenario, after having exhausted all of the above options first, the father has still reserved the right to put the matter to trial, if necessary.

SPECIAL LEGAL ISSUES
FACED BY SINGLE FATHERS

False Allegations of Abuse

False allegations of abuse of a child, particularly of sexual abuse, are an increasingly common weapon in the divorce and custody arsenal. A false allegation is the perfect weapon. It is simple, fast, and guaranteed to achieve the desired result—the complete removal of the targeted parent from the child's and the accusing parent's life, along with a moral vindication or victory for the accusing parent.

The parent targeted with a false allegation is truly a victim in every sense of the word. But the accused parent is not the only victim of the false allegation. For all the pain and devastation which is heaped upon the accused parent, at least as much is often visited upon the children, as they are required to submit to endless medical examinations and psychological poking and prodding.

For these reasons, it is extremely important that the father's advocate counsel the client about the risks of false allegations of abuse. While nobody is immune, there are certain indicia that can signal the increased likelihood of a false allegation. One sign is a mother who attempts to exercise complete control over the children and their relationship with their father, and this effort to control becomes more pronounced the more the father resists, or whenever the court rejects her efforts to exercise such control. The father may also be a prime candidate for a false allegation if the child's mother was herself abused as a child, believes that she was abused, or is in therapy for being a "survivor of abuse."

Many fathers are unable to believe that the woman they were once involved with, the woman who "knows that they would never do such a thing," would make such an allegation. They need to believe it, and it is the father's advocate's job to help them to understand that it is critical to do whatever they can to forestall such an allegation, as, once leveled, a false allegation of abuse is very difficult to defend and disprove. The following is a brief list of measures that fathers can take to minimize the chances that a false allegation will be brought against them, or, if one is, that it will be considered true:

- Never allow his child to sleep with him.
- Never shower or bathe with his child.
- Avoid being naked around his child, and the child being unnecessarily naked around him.
- Arrange time-share with his child such that he is never alone with his child, particularly if he is in or anticipates a custody dispute. In other words, always have a witness around.

• If his children are of an age where they need assistance with bathing or going to the bathroom, and particularly if they are female, whenever possible have a woman assist them.

The above precautions may seem extremely restrictive, and indeed they are. Unfortunately, in the current climate where false allegations abound, they are also extremely necessary.

If, despite the above, a father is falsely accused of abusing the child, it is critical that the father's legal advocate take the matter very seriously and make every effort to quash the allegation as quickly and as thoroughly as possible. If the advocate is not familiar with defending a false allegation of abuse, he or she should contact somebody in the local legal community who is. It is not an understatement to say that fathers facing a false allegation risk losing their children forever, and they need and deserve the best representation and advocacy possible.

In addition, it is very important that a father who is falsely accused find a local support system. Most parents who experience a false allegation feel bewildered, alone, and unsure of what to do. They may feel as if they are the only person in the world ever to have faced such a problem, and they may wonder what they could possibly have done to deserve such a horrible fate. Contact a noncustodial parents' rights organization to find out about meetings, counseling services, and other resources. Three such organizations are:

Victims of Child Abuse Legislation (V.O.C.A.L.)
1030 G Street
Sacramento, CA 95814
800-745-8778

The Accused
c/o Clancy, Weisinger & Associates
1600 S. Main Street #185
Walnut Creek, CA 94596
510-930-7000

The Fathers' Rights & Equality Exchange
3140 de la Cruz Boulevard #200
Santa Clara, CA 95054
500-FOR-DADS

Finally, legal advocates should be familiar with any remedies that may be available for fathers once the allegation is disproven. Although it is very difficult to prove that the accusation was known to be unfounded when it was made, many states do have penalties for intentionally making such false allegations. In some states, the repeated use of false allegations can be grounds for a change of custody.

Parental Kidnapping

One of the most frightening events that parents can experience is having their child seem to vanish into thin air. According to the United States Justice Department, every year more than 350,000 children are abducted by their own parents.

"Parental kidnapping" is the taking of a child by one parent, depriving the other parent of lawful time-share with the child. It is important to understand that parental abduction can be performed by either parent, mother or father, custodial or noncustodial. If the custodial parent takes the child away in a manner which deprives the other parent of his or her court-ordered parenting time with the child, that is still parental kidnapping, even though the abducting parent may have been granted primary physical custody.

As with the false allegation of abuse, an ounce of prevention is worth a pound of cure. Parents who kidnap their children may go underground or even to another country, and once gone, finding the children, let alone retrieving them, can be a nearly impossible task.

Getting the Father Prepared

Every parent, whether he or she fears parental abduction or not, should have a valid, current order from the court which spells out the time-share arrangements they have with their children. Having a valid, detailed court order for time-share is the single most important thing that a parent can do to help prevent parental kidnapping.

The time-share order should be highly specific; if a court order reads only "reasonable visitation" or "time-share as the parties may agree to between themselves," then it will be very difficult to get the order enforced, let alone to prove parental abduction. For example, if a father tries to get the police to enforce an order that says only "reasonable visitation," it is difficult to prove that the order has been violated. If, on the other hand, the order provides for time-share on "the first and third weekend of every month," and it is the third weekend of the month and the child is nowhere to be found, that is a clear violation of the order.

In addition to having a detailed time-share order, the father should assemble two sets of the following:

- Several recent color photographs of all children and parents
- A list of any scars or unusual physical characteristics of both the mother and child
- Two sets of each child's fingerprints
- A list of all passport numbers, dates of issue, and the countries that issued them
- A list of all driver's license numbers and the issuing state (both the mother's, and those of any children who are licensed to drive)
- A list of all automobile registrations, serial numbers, makes, models, and descriptions
- A list of all credit cards, bank accounts, and Social Security numbers
- A list of all the names and numbers of all negotiable instruments such as stocks and bonds, brokerage accounts, and stock brokers
- A list of all retirement accounts
- A list of any other tangible assets that are easily converted into cash, such as jewelry, collections, and expensive equipment
- The names, addresses, and telephone numbers of the mother's family members and close friends

The father may already have in his possession much of this information, as many of the items outlined above will have been acquired during the marriage. The father's legal advocate may also need to serve discovery on the mother to secure any information to which the father does not have direct access.

The father should keep these two sets of items in two different locations, preferably in the homes of trusted friends or family members. Having two full sets of these documents ensures that if one is not available, they will still have access to the other. A safe deposit box, or attorney's office, is not a good place to keep these items, as banks and law firms are not open after hours and on weekends.

In addition, if there is a chance that the child may be kidnapped to another country, a father should take the following extra precautions:

> If the child has dual citizenship, provide copies of the custody and time-share orders to the embassy of the country to which the child may be taken, and ask them not to issue a passport for the child. Place any passport the child already has in safekeeping, that is, in a secure place which is outside of the father's home. Call the United States State Department Passport Office, at 202-326-6168, to ask that the child's name be placed on a lookout list and that the father be notified if any attempt to apply for a passport for his child is made. If the child already has a passport, which the father has in his possession, request that the father be notified of any attempt to apply for a duplicate passport.

Should a Kidnapping Occur

Despite all precautions and best efforts, a father may find himself in the situation in which his child has in fact been taken, inappropriately, by the mother. By having taken the above precautions, he will be ready, and well-prepared to deal with this situation in a timely manner.

If a child is missing, the father should immediately take the following steps:

- Call the police and file a missing person report
- Have the police department enter the missing parties' name, description, Social Security numbers and driver's license information with the National Crime Information Center ("NCIC") to be listed in their computer (criminal charges do not need to be filed to take advantage of this)
- Call Child Quest International (1-800-248-8020)
- Call the National Center for Missing and Exploited Children (1-800-THE LOST)
- Call Vanished Children's Alliance Services (1-800-VANISHED)

- Check the local post office regularly to see if the other parent has put in a change of address form, indicating their new address
- Immediately upon determining where the child is, contact an attorney in that area, and have him or her prepare a complaint seeking a Writ of Habeas Corpus, giving the authorities in that state the right to take possession of the child and bring the child to the court

In addition, if the child has been kidnapped abroad, the father should:

- Call the Office of Citizens' Consular Services at 202-736-7000 and request that a "welfare and whereabouts search" be conducted for the child
- If the country to which the child has been taken is signatory to the Hague Convention, notify the State Department and request assistance in obtaining an "Order of Return" under the convention

EVALUATION OF FATHER ADVOCACY

There can be little doubt that keeping fathers involved in the lives of their children brings real, tangible benefits to the entire family unit, including not just the father and his children, but the children's mother as well. In addition to reducing the risk of youth crime, drug use, teen pregnancy, and truancy and providing moral and emotional support, the Census Bureau reports that fathers who have frequent and ongoing contact with their children comply fully with child support orders as much as 90 percent of the time.

From an individual perspective, it is important that the father's advocate be familiar not only with local laws and legal custom, but that they have a working understanding of the unique dynamics that come to play in the disunited family. Although there is currently no mechanism available for peer review of the father's advocate, both state and local bar associations and fathers' and childrens' rights organizations do track performance, and such information is readily available for the asking. The Fathers' Rights & Equality Exchange is one such organization that tracks performance of father's advocates across the country.

CONCLUSION

Single fathers are one of the most overlooked and undersupported groups in America today. Yet for every single father out there, there is at least one child who needs that father in his or her life. And while we decry the high rate of father absenteeism, our courts provide little relief or assistance for those fathers who are trying to stay involved in their children's lives. It is the role of the father's advocate to help these fathers navigate the family law system, and to find their way back home to their children. And, once there, to help keep them there.

REFERENCES

Blankenhorn, D. (1995). *Fatherless America: Confronting our most urgent social problems*. NY: Basic Books.

Federal Bureau of Census (1995, September). "1992 Child Support Supplement to the Federal Current Population Survey." Washington, DC: Government Printing Office.

Garfinkel, I. and McLanahan, S. (1986). *Single mothers and their children: A new American dilemma*. Washington, DC: Urban Institute Press.

Maccoby, E. E. and Mnookin, R. H. (1992). *Dividing the child: Social and legal dilemmas of custody*. Boston, MA: Harvard Press.

Saluter, A. F. and Lugaila, T. A. (1998). Marital status and living arrangements: March, 1996. *Current Population Reports*. Available online: <http://www.census.gov/prod/3/98pubs/p20-496.pdf>.

Chapter 10

English-Speaking Caribbean Immigrant Fathers: The Task of Unpacking the Cultural Pathways to Intervention

Jaipaul L. Roopnarine
Meera Shin
Tracey Y. Lewis

For decades, men of color have been broadly stereotyped in the United States as uninvolved and distant from the early caregiving and socialization of their children (see Moynihan, 1965). Now, however, there is a push within academic and policy circles to examine issues tied to fathering and fatherhood in diverse cultural groups from a resilient-adaptive framework (see Ahmeduzzaman and Roopnarine, 1992; Franklin and Davis, 2001; Gadsden, Pitt, and Tift, 2001; McAdoo and McAdoo, 1985; Roopnarine, 1997). That is, there is increasing recognition that men of color contribute in meaningful and varying ways to the social, economic, and intellectual well-being of their families. This approach engenders a more constructive platform for the examination of fatherhood in general because it focuses on family strengths. It concentrates on what men actually do within their families and avoids casting all men of color, regardless of educational and economic attainment or level of commitment to the family, as irresponsible. This approach is consistent with the generative fathering perspective that is woven throughout this book (Dollahite, Hawkins, and Brotherson, 1997; Hawkins and Dollahite, 1997).

No doubt, this shift in thinking has been aided, in part, by the rich and compelling work of psychocultural researchers and theorists (e.g., Harkness and Super, 1996; Levine et al., 1994; Ogbu, 1981; Weisner, 1998; Whiting and Whiting, 1975). They have long stressed the importance of understanding human development within the context of the social and physical environment. They provide ethnotheories regarding child-rearing customs, and explore the impact of different parental practices on the development of individuals. At the same time, clinicians and intervention strategists have taken notice of the change in intellectual climate too. Today, there is increasing recognition of the need to devise culturally-sensitive assessment tools and therapeutic approaches to improve the personal well-being of families in an increasingly complex and demanding world (see Baptiste, Hardy, and Lewis, 1997; Lonner, 1990; Triandis, 1990).

Understanding cultural pathways of development—customs, beliefs, and practices that guide child rearing—are major prerequisites to designing intervention strategies for working with diverse groups of families (Weisner, 1998). Researchers help to identify the outcomes of specific cultural practices, and to recognize the strengths and limitations of resources available to families.

Against this backdrop, this chapter recommends some strategies for working with Caribbean immigrant men residing in North America. In keeping with the tenets of the ecocultural theoretical framework (Weisner, 1998), before presenting strategies for working with Caribbean immigrant fathers, it is first necessary to provide some sociodemographic information and discuss factors that may affect Caribbean men's adjustment and integration into their new communities. It is also necessary to present the sociohistorical and cultural context for fathering and the cultural beliefs and practices that guide child care in different Caribbean ethnic communities. This chapter focuses on immigrant men who migrated from the English-speaking countries of the Caribbean (e.g., mainly Guyana, Trinidad and Tobago, Jamaica, Barbados, Antigua, and Grenada), and who are from different ethnic backgrounds (e.g., Indo-Caribbean, Chinese Caribbean, African Caribbean, Black Caribs, Amerindians, and Portuguese Caribbean, among others). Insofar as it is possible, an attempt will be made to avoid a unimodal treatment of the diverse groups of men and their different levels of involvement in fathering. In the past, there has been a tendency to characterize Caribbean men as "drunken," "lazy," "irresponsible," and "violent." As is the case with any other cultural group, Caribbean men display a wide array of paternal behaviors that range from a high degree of responsibility in family life to outright abandonment of paternal and familial responsibility. The suggestions for intervention are largely meant for those who are closer to the latter group. However, Caribbean men in general may find support for parenting and a forum for discussing the stresses and challenges of parenthood in a new society very beneficial.

CARIBBEAN MIGRATION

Within the Caribbean, there are diverse groups of people who speak different languages (e.g., English, French, Spanish, Hindi, Patois), and who live in countries that stretch from Guyana in South America to Cuba just below Florida. The diversity in the over 30 million people who inhabit the Caribbean may be attributed to Dutch, Spanish, English, and French colonization, intermarriages, and migration. After attempts to convert and enslave the native people (Arawaks and Caribs), and the subsequent decimation following Columbus's arrival to the "New World," the various European powers brought large numbers of African slaves to the region. After slavery was finally abolished in the early nineteenth century, East Indians were brought in as indentured servants to work as contract laborers in the very plantations where their African brethren were subjected to gross inhumanity. Smaller numbers of European, Chinese, and people of Middle-Eastern origins also settled in the area.

Population movement within and external to the Caribbean is not a new phenomenon and dates back to the early postemancipation period (1830s). There are several accounts of population movements from the Caribbean to different parts of Central, South, and North America between the 1830s and the time of World War II (see Grosfoguel, 1997; Marshall, 1982). However, we focus on English-speaking Caribbean immigrants who migrated to the United States following the Immigration Act of 1965. It is estimated that between 1965 and 1987 about 2.4 million people migrated from the Caribbean to the United States (U.S. Department of Justice, 1990) and this figure does not include illegal immigrants. Most Caribbean immigrants are employed in low-paying jobs (secondary job market), but a small and growing number are joining the professional ranks (see Grasmuck and Grosfoguel, 1997; Grosfoguel, 1997, for a discussion of these issues).

PSYCHOLOGICAL, SOCIAL, AND ECONOMIC ISSUES FACED BY CARIBBEAN IMMIGRANT FATHERS

Integration and Acculturation

Unlike their predecessors, Caribbean immigrants in North America are under less pressure to renounce their cultural practices and way of life in favor of the "Anglo-American" ideal. The once-dominant conception of immigration that emphasizes assimilation has been assailed as nearsighted. The term "transmigrants" has been used to describe people who move freely between the borders of several cultures, who retain multiple cultural identities, and who participate in economic, social, and educational institutions in several countries (Schiller, Basch, and Blanc, 1995). Racism and discrimination in North America and the constantly changing world business climate have persuaded transmigrants to distribute their political and economic loyalties to more than one nation state (Schiller, Basch, and Blanc, 1995). Indeed, the latter describes the social, economic, and political behaviors of some Caribbean immigrants in North America.

Because Caribbean immigrants live in homogeneous ethnic enclaves in metropolitan areas in North America, travel regularly to and from the Caribbean, provide economic support and maintain strong social ties to relatives in the Caribbean, assist fellow immigrants to find jobs and housing during the initial phases of immigration, and have some prior knowledge of life and customs in the United States, transitional and postimmigration stress may be lessened. We do not accept the sweeping proposal that all families experience extreme social and economic difficulties during and subsequent to immigration. Nor do all families engage in a swift process of acculturation. It is often difficult to determine the eventual acculturation of immigrants. We posit that the modern migratory process affects new immigrants from the Caribbean differently. Some flourish economically soon after immigration, others struggle to make a living and become fully participating members of their new communities.

Research on the adjustment patterns and child rearing strategies of immigrant families from around the world have pointed to the challenges parents face in a new society (see Horowitz, 1981; Szapocznik and Kurtines, 1993; Strier, 1996). Potential sources of stress among parents from the English-speaking Caribbean may include racism and discrimination due to minority status, violation of expectations about life in North America, conflicts between indigenous child rearing practices and those of the new society, difficulties in reuniting with children after long periods of separation due to serial migration, and loss of parental authority (Arnold, 1997; Baptiste, Hardy, and Lewis, 1997; daCosta, 1985).

The Family Context for Rearing Children

In our consideration of the family context for mating and rearing/minding children, we call attention to four factors: diverse family structural organization; parental beliefs about child rearing; parental child rearing practices; and conceptions of "manhood" and "fatherhood." Each of these has been discussed relative to Caribbean men's involvement with young children. For example, visiting and common-law unions have been examined with respect to childshifting practices (moving children to other households to be raised by kinship and nonkinship members), nonnormative child development outcomes, and limited social contacts with children (Crawford-Brown, 1997; Sharpe, 1997); and conceptions of manhood and fatherhood, the differential treatment of children and levels of paternal involvement, and husband-wife relationships (Brown, Anderson, and Chevannes, 1993; Brown et al., 1997). Based on work conducted in North America (see Millette, 1998; Roopnarine, 1999), the family social organization patterns and cultural scripts for child rearing in the following outline apply to families in the Caribbean and to Caribbean immigrants who have moved to North America within the past three decades.

Family Structural Organization

Among African-Caribbean families, progressive mating in nonlegal unions is a common practice and has been in existence for over

150 years. Some family scholars argue that African-Caribbean family/ mating patterns move from the structurally unstable to the structurally stable (Chevannes, 1993). Others, however, cite economic and educational status as possibly being responsible for the continued predominance of nonlegal unions as a context for bearing and rearing children (Brown, Anderson, and Chevannes 1993). Whatever the underlying causes, four predominant family structures have been identified within the Caribbean: visiting relationships, common-law unions, marital unions, and single-parent household families (see Millette, 1998). Little is known about the long-term effects of being raised in nonlegal unions, and what data do exist are at best confusing. We examine the characteristics of each of these family/mating forms in more detail.

Visiting/Friending Relationships. For most low-income African-Caribbean families, sexual relationships and childbearing commence in visiting unions. Men and women do not share a residence but meet at prearranged venues for sexual and social relationships. The roles of men in these relationships and their financial obligations to the visiting partner and biological offspring are nebulous at best, and women often see the union as transitory (Powell, 1986; Senior, 1991). Visiting unions are more prevalent in African-Caribbean than in Indo-Caribbean or Chinese-Caribbean families (see Smith, 1996). Visiting relationships constitute about 25 percent of mating relationships in the Caribbean (Roopnarine, 1997; Senior, 1991).

Common-Law Unions. After bearing children in visiting unions, men and women move into common-law unions with other partners, in which they share a residence and resources, and where there is the semblance of a traditional husband-wife relationship. Women assume responsibility for domestic tasks and men are expected to be the breadwinners. Although men may provide support for their own and/or partner's biological children, relationships between men and nonbiological children are often antagonistic (Flinn, 1992). Women and children in common-law unions are only narrowly protected by the law in a few Caribbean countries (e.g., Barbados). Roughly one-fifth of the unions in the Caribbean are common-law. As with visiting unions, common-law arrangements are far lower in Indo-Caribbean, Chinese-Caribbean, and Amerindians than in African-Caribbean families (see Smith, 1996).

Married Couples. After progressive mating, several offspring from different partners, and in some cases better economic stability, African-Caribbean men are more likely to settle into legal unions (Powell, 1986). This obviously occurs much later in a man's life; of men under thirty, only 9.35 percent were married compared to 54.3 percent for those over fifty years of age (Brown, Anderson, and Chevannes, 1993). Although couples view marriage positively, they do not see it as a prerequisite to personal happiness and there is a proclivity toward "partnerships." By contrast, marriage generally occurs much earlier and at higher rates among Indo-Caribbean and Chinese-Caribbean couples (88.4 percent among East Indians in Guyana) (Smith, 1996).

Single-Parent Households. Within Caribbean families, the term "single parent" refers to union rather than conjugal status. The proportion of Caribbean women as the de facto head of households is well documented. Estimates range from 22.4 percent in Guyana to 45.3 percent in Grenada (Massiah, 1982; Powell, 1986). Of these, about 50 percent have never been married and they tend to have low educational achievement and face extreme economic hardships. Indo-Caribbean women who head households are more often widows (Powell, 1986).

The prevalence of each of these family types among Caribbean immigrants in North America is undetermined. Large-scale surveys (Millette, 1998) and detailed ethnographic work (Roopnarine, 1999) suggest a wide range of family compositions in both African-Caribbean and Indo-Caribbean immigrants in the United States. Furthermore, because of the recency of arrival, serial migration, return migration, and movement to and from the Caribbean and the industrialized countries to the north, we suspect that the family patterns described above are represented in North America (e.g., the percentage of female-headed households in five counties in New York City and in Jamaica were quite comparable—33 percent and 34 percent respectively [Grasmuck and Grosfoguel, 1997]). We use these figures as a basis for recommending interventions for fathers.

Beliefs and Practices Regarding Child Rearing

Parental ethnotheories about child care and education represent a major component of early childhood socialization (Goodnow and Collins, 1990; Harkness and Super, 1996; Sigel, 1985). These cultural scripts drive the daily routines that parents utilize in child rearing and assist them in organizing children's cognitive and social environments. Understanding these cultural scripts provides greater hope for working with immigrant men from diverse cultural groups. Following are some of the main cultural beliefs about childhood socialization among Caribbean families:

1. Beliefs about parental control and guidance vary by socioeconomic status and ethnicity. Parents in low-income households prefer an authoritarian and restrictive approach to child rearing with a high degree of compliance on the part of children. Families in higher income groups appear to be more permissive. Indo-Caribbean mothers engage in prolonged, indulgent caregiving during the early childhood years (Roopnarine, 1999). Overall though, parents believe in authoritarian/punitive control combined with indulgence and protectiveness, especially with daughters (Leo-Rhynie, 1997). These trends have been observed in the United States and Britain (Arnold, 1997; Deyoung and Zigler, 1994; Roopnarine, 1999).

2. Tied to these beliefs is the belief that children should be obedient, compliant, and show respect to older members of society. These expectations are demonstrated in studies conducted across the Caribbean (Grant, Leo-Rhynie, and Alexander, 1983) and in Caribbean immigrants in the United States (Roopnarine, 1999).

3. Whether in the Caribbean or North America, parents believe in harsh discipline. Strict discipline in the form of spanking, demanding that children listen and not talk back to adults, and beliefs in the religious dictum "spare the rod, spoil the child" are all strongly endorsed by parents (Roopnarine, 1999).

4. Irrespective of ethnic group, parents believe that children should care for their aging parents. Recent data on Caribbean immigrant families in the United States bear this out (Roopnarine, 1999). However, in practice, this is changing among better-educated first generation children of immigrants.

5. Indo-Caribbean and African-Caribbean communities exhibit deep-seated religious beliefs (e.g., Hinduism, Christianity, Rastafarianism, and Mohammedanism). Ethnic indoctrination is also a central component of child rearing. There are impressive Caribbean-built

religious centers of worship in several urban areas (e.g., New York City, Toronto) that provide access to religious training for young children. There are celebrations (e.g., Phagwah in Queens) and festivals (Caribana in Toronto) that bring entire immigrant communities together.

6. Generally, Caribbean men believe that women are better prepared to be nurturers, and men providers (Brown et al., 1997). A mixed pattern of beliefs regarding husband-wife roles was documented among Caribbean immigrant men in the United States, though a majority subscribed to the view that women should be nurturers (Roopnarine, 1999).

Parental Practices and Styles

The aforementioned cultural beliefs serve as a map to the daily routines that parents employ in caring for and in nurturing their children. In other words, parental practices define the cultural pathways to desired child development outcomes in a given culture. The processes embedded in these cultural pathways are carefully orchestrated to assist children to develop social and technological skills commensurate with parental goals (see Weisner, 1998). Herein are some parental practices that Caribbean parents utilize:

1. Regardless of whether they reside in the Caribbean or North America, most parents do not depend on child development experts or community agencies for child rearing information. They draw upon parental folk theories and practices that have been passed down to them through generations (see Roopnarine and Brown, 1997).

2. Multiple caregiving is a common feature of parenting in the Caribbean (Flinn, 1992), and remains a deeply entrenched practice among Caribbean immigrants in the United States (Roopnarine, 1999). Simply put, children of Caribbean immigrants may be cared for by as many as six different individuals in a given week. In one study conducted in the New York City area, mothers, on average, provided 41 percent, fathers 32 percent, and others (aunts, uncles, grandparents, etc.) provided about 27 percent of the care preschool-aged children received during a typical weekday (Roopnarine, 1999). Almost identical estimates have been obtained for mother care versus other care in families residing in Trinidad (Flinn, 1992).

3. In both African-Caribbean and Indo-Caribbean families, discipline techniques are often harsh, involving the use of physical punishment and denigration. This is particularly so for families in the Caribbean (see Arnold, 1997). However, with increasing educational attainment of parents, there is the greater use of explanations and the withdrawal of privileges among immigrant families (Roopnarine, 1999).

4. Parents in general have limited knowledge about child development and, thus, some demand social and cognitive skills that often exceed children's age-appropriate developmental acumen.

Conceptions of Manhood and Fatherhood: A Very Traditional View

Attitudes toward virility, dominance over women, the man as the authority figure, double standards about extramarital affairs, and the traditional division of household labor run deep among men in the Caribbean (see Roopnarine and Brown, 1997), and among Caribbean immigrant men in the United States (Millette, 1998). One of the most penetrating accounts of "manhood" as seen through the eyes of Caribbean men was provided by Brown and her colleagues (Brown et al., 1997). In discussing manhood, Caribbean men focused primarily on three issues that fall into a life-cycle pattern: sexuality/sexual identity; the provider and protector role; and scriptural authority for family headship. Foremost, manhood is measured and affirmed through sexual prowess, number of sexual partners, and the number of offspring a man produces. But this evidence is not sufficient, as men must also demonstrate that they can provide for their families as well as protect them. Caribbean men believe these practices may ultimately confer the status of head of household upon them.

Parallel findings have been reported on Caribbean families in the United States. In classifying families as "maintainers," "social isolates," and "strivers," Millette (1998) found that maintainers and strivers tenaciously held on to the traditional belief that the man should be dominant and tough, and that wives should be obedient, loyal, and faithful. Among the social isolates, men were also viewed as the head of the household, but in this group there was more shared decision making. Despite these views, there was the feeling that the cultural scripts concerning manhood were starting to disintegrate a bit (Millette, 1998), but conceptions of manhood prevailing in the Caribbean still resonate quite clearly among Caribbean immigrant men.

Not surprisingly, the previously mentioned conceptions of manhood help shape conceptions of fatherhood. Because of the practice of mate-shifting and the acceptance of out-of-marriage births, the meaning of the social, intellectual, and economic responsibilities of fathers toward children is somewhat obscure. In a study of eighty-eight low-income households in Jamaica, no mother or father mentioned that men should be primary caregivers (Roopnarine et al., 1995). Men seem to place a great deal of emphasis on biological fatherhood, so much so that stigmas are attached to those men who cannot father children and to those who unknowingly raise "someone else's child" (Brown et al., 1997). Thus, most Caribbean men see fatherhood as a route to personal maturity, frequently noting that living under one roof with one's family is the ideal, but hardly essential for being a competent father (Brown, Anderson, and Chevannes, 1993). Quite the opposite is true for Indo-Caribbean men, who are far more likely to be fathers within a marital union. Nonetheless, fatherhood for them may be limited to provisioning for and offering guidance to children when deemed necessary (Roopnarine et al., 1997).

Although studies on the meaning of fatherhood among Caribbean immigrant men are now emerging (see Roopnarine, 1999), it may be fair to say that for a majority of these men, caring for young children in a cognitively and socially responsive manner is still difficult. Early child care remains the sacred domain of women. There are signs, however, that with higher levels of education, some Caribbean immigrant men may be deconstructing their traditional view of fatherhood (Roopnarine, 1999).

Understanding Levels of Paternal Involvement

Bearing in mind that Caribbean men historically have been presented in such a poor light, a short summary of their levels of involvement with young children is necessary. As with other cultural groups, levels of paternal responsibility among Caribbean men vary a good deal (Pleck, 1997). Because work on paternal involvement among Caribbean immigrant men is sparse, for the most part, we rely on data gathered in the Caribbean. Of the handful of studies published on Caribbean fathers (see Roopnarine, 1997), most suggest that low-income men are involved in caring for their children and are involved in their educational activities (Brown, Anderson, and Chevannes, 1993; Stycos and Back, 1964), and when they reside with their children rates of involvement fall well within those observed for North American men (Roopnarine et al., 1995). With education and better economic resources, paternal involvement appears more stable (Brown et al., 1997).

Data on Caribbean men from diverse economic backgrounds in two-parent families residing in the New York City area revealed that men spent, on average, about 4.4 hours on a typical weekday and 14.4 hours on the weekend caring for and being around their pre-kindergarten and kindergarten-age children. Furthermore, they spent, on average, about 7.8 hours per week in educational activities with their children. Again, levels of paternal involvement were linked to socioeconomic status (Roopnarine, 1999). As has been reported for other cultural groups (Jain, Belsky, and Crnic, 1996), men with more traditional, patriarchal values were less involved with their children.

But these rates of involvement neither speak to the quality of interactions between fathers and children nor men's competence in child rearing. And because men are not uniformly involved in their children's lives we may need to focus attention on types and levels, rather than mean rates of father involvement (see Jain, Belsky, and Crnic, 1996). Approaching paternal involvement from this angle may eventually permit us to identify specific behavioral traits and the factors that discourage men from becoming involved in their young children's lives (see Jain, Belsky, and Crnic, 1996). It is our belief that rates of paternal involvement among Caribbean men, especially low-income men, are still rather low. Caribbean immigrant men need to be more involved with their children.

PRACTICE STRATEGIES FOR WORKING WITH CARIBBEAN IMMIGRANT FATHERS

Having provided some necessary background information on Caribbean families and Caribbean immigrant men in the United States, we now turn to the task of recommending strategies for increasing paternal involvement with young children. As noted in the first chapter, culturally sensitive instruments and tools for assessing the well-being and mental performance of diverse groups of individuals and providing social and mental health services for them have been discussed at length in other publications (see Baptiste, Hardy, and Lewis, 1997; Gopaul-McNicol, 1993; Mirkin, 1990; Sue and Sue, 1990). Several issues have been discussed in this regard and include:

- the underutilization of social service programs because of their lack of sensitivity to cultural diversity, and also the lack of trust by some ethnic groups in going outside of the family for support and counseling
- the lack of appropriate training of social service professionals pursuant to the needs of diverse cultural groups
- pathology and diverse family functioning; barriers to effective counseling; communication styles and service delivery
- racial and cultural identity development
- cultural scripts or world views about child rearing and development
- marginality and minority status; acculturation and adaptation
- racism and discrimination; and therapeutic approaches for working with families (Baptiste, Hardy, and Lewis, 1997; Brislin, 1990; Gopaul-McNicol, 1993; Keats, 1997; Pederson and Pederson, 1989; Sue and Sue, 1990; Taylor, 1998).

Although we recognize the importance of each of these issues in working with diverse groups of families, it would be impossible to cover all of them in this chapter. Consequently, we highlight a few of them that appear most relevant for designing intervention strategies geared to improving father-child relationships during the preschool years.

Acknowledging that Caribbean immigrant families in the United States are not a homogeneous group, and that Caribbean immigrant fathers might see their level of involvement as quite acceptable in their communities, the following should be considered when designing interventions to increase paternal involvement. Caribbean immigrant fathers in general would profit from parenting programs that focus on child development; appropriate ways to work with, guide, and discipline young children at home; providing support and reinforcement in the parenting role; and reinforcing and respecting indigenous cultural practices. Programs that serve Caribbean immigrant men may be most effective if they pay attention to the following:

1. Programs must consider the legal status of immigrant fathers (U.S. citizen, resident alien, illegal alien, student, guest worker), and the stage of the immigration process in which they find themselves. It is important to realize, for instance, that men who are illegally residing in the United States may choose to remain out of the public light. Caribbean families may immigrate in different patterns (serial, family group) and over extended periods. Recent arrivals may be more susceptible to transitory stress (Baptiste, Hardy, and Lewis, 1997). Remember, though, some families move freely between countries, blurring the very notion of sending and host cultures. These families may experience less stress, suggesting that length of time in the United States is not a good barometer for measuring postimmigration problems. Not all families experience acculturation stress or accept the dominant cultural values and practices. Some families choose disenfranchisement and insulate themselves in ethnic enclaves, while others work on blending native Caribbean and dominant cultural values.

2. Programs must be respectful of family cultural practices/world views, and linguistic and communication preferences. They must embrace the notion that regardless of prior history of involvement in family life, Caribbean men are resilient and adaptable. Flexibility in program goals and approaches, trust between fatherhood agency/staff and fathers, and the belief that family needs could necessitate changes in program strategies are the hallmarks of any good intervention program (see Goupal-McNicol, 1993; Schorr, 1988). Simply put, staff members need to listen and to learn from the feedback they receive from fathers (Baptiste, Hardy, and Lewis, 1997).

3. Caribbean immigrant fathers and children are nested in extensive caregiving networks (Roopnarine, 1999). Success in involving fathers in interventions may depend on support from these other caregivers at various stages in the process. As stated earlier, Caribbean immigrant families depend on relatives and friends for child rearing information and to provide support for child care. Encouragement from extended kinship and nonkinship networks may be critical in sustaining intervention efforts.

4. Because of their ethnic heterogeneity, different family structures, and divergent religious beliefs, diverse approaches are sug-

gested in counseling and working with Caribbean immigrant fathers. For example, Indo-Caribbean men may be more willing to participate in a parenting program or support group if a Hindu priest recommends the program to them and it is housed within their temple. Similarly, among African-Caribbean men, recommendation to join a program from a friend or religious/community leader might be more successful in soliciting participation. Further, some men may need assistance in working through gender mistrust; others may need help in sharpening parenting skills.

5. Extend the intervention goals beyond father involvement and parenting skills. The objective should be to strengthen men's participation with children within the family and larger community (e.g., Caribbean clubs, educational institutions, religious organizations). Immigrant men may also need room to voice their feelings about living in North America, economic woes, and rejection/acceptance within their respective communities.

6. Finally, program objectives should be couched within a lifelong learner perspective. Men may need help with fathering and father involvement at different stages in the life cycle given mating patterns and cultural beliefs about when children should leave home.

AN APPROACH TO WORKING WITH FATHERS

Programs geared to increase paternal involvement with children utilize diverse approaches. Prior attempts to address paternal involvement have focused on: job training so that men can support their children; paternity leave and flexible work hours for fathers; new laws to establish paternity and punish "deadbeat dads"; fatherhood development curriculum; education for men that provides hands-on experience in caregiving and supplies child development and parenting information; aid from social and health service agencies to indigent fathers; and gender mistrust (Engle, 1993). A few of these programs have been hailed as very effective in increasing paternal involvement and responsibility. Regrettably, some programs are broad in scope and do not take into account the diversity in caregiving patterns of fathers. Jain, Belsky, and Crnic (1996) have grouped fathers into different categories based on their type and level of involvement with children: disciplinarians, disengaged, caretaker, and playmate/teacher. The following program was designed for work with low-income men in nonlegal unions in Kingston, Jamaica (disciplinarians and disengaged fathers), and could be implemented for work with Caribbean immigrant fathers in cities in the United States.

Fathers Incorporated: A Community-Based Program for Low-Income Men

Fathers Incorporated, established in 1991 in Kingston, Jamaica, has its roots in a parenting workshop designed for men only. Dr. Barry Chevannes, a professor at The University of the West Indies, organized and headed the workshop. Originally, the workshop focused on providing mutual support and explored definitions of fatherhood. In the initial session, the men felt so positively about such a forum for the expression of their concerns about fathers and fatherhood that they decided to meet on a regular basis. The working-class men who form the nucleus of the group (about ten to fifteen) meet regularly with a wider membership of about sixty men (Brown et al., 1997). The program holds discussions on being a father, men in society, family(ies) of origin, peer counselor training, and service activities for children. The men invite guest speakers regularly. A few years ago, the group received its first grant and hired a part-time staff person to be the coordinator. The group meets in the community.

Follow-up qualitative assessments of men who had been in the program for at least two years revealed several things: they uniformly stated that they now have a more complete understanding of fatherhood and carried more of the parenting responsibilities with their partners; they felt empowered talking about family issues with other men; they related the need to develop a strong bond with their partners; and despite economic hardship they are committed to the role of parent and partner. On the negative side, they spoke of the ridicule directed at men in Jamaican society who cannot provide for their children economically (Brown et al., 1997).

Relatedly, staff members at the Caribbean Child Development Centre (CCDC) at The University of the West Indies have created booklets, trained animators, and held focus groups for Caribbean fathers. The goal is to challenge men to examine their ethnotheories of "masculinity," "manhood," and "fatherhood," and their relationships or lack of relationships with their own father(s). By engaging in different exercises in the booklets, and through discussions in focus groups, men examine common stereotypes about manhood and fatherhood, gender mistrust, and what it means to be a responsible father. For convenience, the booklets produced by CCDC contain several skits presented in a step-by-step format. As of now no systematic data are available on the efficacy of these programs.

CONCLUSION

Using the basic background information provided in this chapter, we hope that social service professionals and child and family development experts will consider the worldviews, family structures, and child rearing practices in designing interventions that are culturally responsive to the needs of Caribbean immigrant fathers. Noteworthy are the beliefs about "manhood" and "fatherhood," the heterogeneity in family structures and parenting beliefs and practices, and the varied adjustment patterns of families following immigration. Attention to these issues should invite thinking along the lines of divergent intervention goals and objectives that address Caribbean immigrant men's different levels of involvement and stages in their marital "careers." There is also a clear need for better evaluation of such efforts.

REFERENCES

Ahmeduzzaman, M. and Roopnarine, J. L. (1992). Sociodemographic factors, functioning style, social support, and fathers' involvement with preschoolers in African-American families. *Journal of Marriage and the Family, 54*(3), 699-707.

Arnold, E. (1997). Issues in re-unification of migrant West Indian children in the United Kingdom. In J. L. Roopnarine and J. Brown (Eds.), *Caribbean families: Diversity among ethnic groups* (pp. 243-258). Norwood, NJ: Ablex.

Baptiste, D. A., Hardy, K. V., and Lewis, L. (1997). Clinical practice with Caribbean immigrant families in the United States: The intersection of emigration, immigration, culture, and race. In J. L. Roopnarine and J. Brown (Eds.), *Caribbean families: Diversity among ethnic groups* (pp. 275-303). Norwood, NJ: Ablex.

Brislin, R. W. (1990). *Applied cross-cultural psychology* (Volume 14). Beverly Hills, CA: Sage Publications.

Brown, J., Anderson, P., and Chevannes, B. (1993). *The contribution of Caribbean men to the family.* Report for the International Development Centre, Canada, Caribbean Child Development Centre, Mona, Jamaica: University of the West Indies.

Brown, J., Newland, A., Anderson, P., and Chevannes, B. (1997). Caribbean fatherhood: Underresearched, misunderstood. In J. L. Roopnarine and J. Brown (Eds.), *Caribbean families: Diversity among ethnic groups* (pp. 85-113). Norwood, NJ: Ablex.

Chevannes, B. (1993). "Stresses and strains: Situation analysis of the Caribbean family." Regional meeting prepatory to International Year of the Family, United Nations Economic Commission for Latin America and the Caribbean, Cartagena, Colombia.

Crawford-Brown, C. (1997). The impact of parent-child socialization on the development of conduct disorder in Jamaican male adolescents. In J. L. Roopnarine and J. Brown (Eds.), *Caribbean families: Diversity among ethnic groups* (pp. 205-222). Norwood, NJ: Ablex.

daCosta, E. (1985). *Reunion after long-term disruption of the parent-child bond in older children: Clinical features and psychodynamic issues.* Toronto: Clark Institute of Psychiatry.

Deyoung, Y. and Zigler, E. F. (1994). Machismo in two cultures: Relation to punitive child-rearing practices. *American Journal of Orthopsychiatry, 64*(3), 386-395.

Dollahite, D. C., Hawkins, A. J., and Brotherson, S. E. (1997). Fatherhood: A conceptual ethic of fathering as generative work. In A. J. Hawkins and D. C. Dollahite (Eds.), *Generative fathering: Beyond deficit perspectives* (pp. 17-35). Thousand Oaks, CA: Sage Publications.

Engle, P. (1993). "Is there a father instinct? Fathers' responsibility for children." Paper prepared for the Population Council, New York.

Flinn, M. (1992). Paternal care in a Caribbean village. In B. Hewlett (Ed.), *Father-child relations: Cultural and biosocial contexts* (pp. 57-84). New York: Aldine de Gruyter.

Franklin, A. J. and Davis, T. III (2001). Therapeutic support groups as a primary intervention for issues of fatherhood with African-American men. In J. Fagan and A. J. Hawkins (Eds.), *Clinical and educational interventions with fathers* (pp. 45-66). Binghamton, NY: The Haworth Press.

Gadsden, V. L., Pitt, E. W., and Tift, N. (2001). Research and practice on fathers in high-risk families: Exploring the need and potential areas for collaboration. In J. Fagan and A. J. Hawkins (Eds.), *Clinical and educational interventions with fathers* (pp. 257-283). Binghamton, NY: The Haworth Press.

Goodnow, J. and Collins, W. A. (1990). *Development according to parents.* Hove, Australia: Erlbaum.

Gopaul-McNicol, S. (1993). *Working with West Indian families.* New York: Guilford.

Grant, D. B. R., Leo-Rhynie, E., and Alexander, G. (1983). *Life style study: Children of the lesser world in the English speaking Caribbean: Volume 5, household structures and settings.* Kingston, Jamaica: Bernard Van Leer Foundation-Centre for Early Childhood Education.

Grasmuck, S. and Grosfoguel, R. (1997). Geopolitics, economic niches, and gendered social capital among recent Caribbean immigrants in New York City. *Sociological Perspectives, 40,* 339-363.

Grosfoguel, R. (1997). Colonial Caribbean migrations to France, the Netherlands, Great Britain and the United States. *Ethnic and Racial Studies, 20*(3), 594-612.

Harkness, S. and Super, S. (Eds.) (1996). *Parental cultural belief systems: Their origins, expressions, and consequences.* New York: Guilford.

Hawkins, A. J. and Dollahite, D. C. (Eds.) (1997). *Generative fathering: Beyond deficit perspectives.* Thousand Oaks, CA: Sage Publications.

Horowitz, R. T. (1981). The two worlds of childhood in Israel and USSR: The Soviet child in a state of dissonance. *Crossroads, 5,* 169-181.

Jain, A., Belsky, J., and Crnic, K. (1996). Beyond fathering behaviors: Types of dads. *Journal of Family Psychology, 4*(10), 431-442.

Keats, D. (1997). *Culture and the child: A guide for professionals in child care and development.* Chichester, Australia: Wiley.

Leo-Rhynie, E. (1997). Class, race, and gender issues in child rearing in the Caribbean. In J. L. Roopnarine and J. Brown (Eds.), *Caribbean families: Diversity among ethnic groups* (pp. 25-55). Norwood, NJ: Ablex.

Levine, R. A., Dixon, S., Levine, S., Richman, A., Leiderman, H., Keefer, C., and Brazelton, B. (1994). *Child care and culture.* New York: Cambridge University Press.

Lonner, W. (1990). An overview of cross-cultural testing and assessment. In R. W. Brislin (Ed.), *Applied cross-cultural psychology* (Volume 14, pp. 56-76). Beverly Hills, CA: Sage Publications.

Marshall, D. I. (1982). Migration as an agent of change in Caribbean Island ecosystem. *International Social Science Journal, 34*(3), 451-467.

Massiah, J. (1982). *Women who head households,* WICP. Institute of Social Research, Barbados: University of West Indies.

McAdoo, H. R. and McAdoo, J. L. (1985). *Black children: Social, educational, and parental environments.* Beverly Hills, CA: Sage Publications.

Millette, R. (1998). West Indian families in the United States. In R. Taylor (Ed.), *Minority families in the United States: A multicultural perspective* (Second edition, pp. 46-59). Upper Saddle River, NJ: Prentice Hall.

Mirkin, M., P. (1990). *The social and political contexts of family therapy.* Needham Heights, MA: Allyn & Bacon.

Moynihan, D. P. (1965). *The Negro family: A case for action.* Washington, DC: Office of Policy Planning and Research, U.S. Department of Labor.

Ogbu, J. (1981). Origins of human competence: A cultural-ecological perspective. *Child Development, 52,* 413-429.

Pederson, P. and Pederson, A. (1989). The cultural grid: A framework for multicultural counseling. *International Journal for the Advancement of Counseling, 12,* 299-307.

Pleck, J. (1997). Paternal involvement: Levels, sources, and consequences. In M. E. Lamb (Ed.), *The role of the father in child development* (Third edition, pp. 66-103). New York: Wiley.

Powell, D. (1986). Caribbean women and their responses to familial experience. *Social and Economic Studies, 35*(2), 83-130.

Roopnarine, J. L. (1997). Fathers in the English-speaking Caribbean: Not so marginal. *World Psychology, 3*(1), 191-210.

Roopnarine, J. L. (1999, April). "Father involvement and parental styles in Caribbean immigrant families." Paper presented at the American Educational Research Association Conference, Montreal, Canada.

Roopnarine, J. L. and Brown, J. (Eds.) (1997). *Caribbean families: Diversity among ethnic groups.* Norwood, NJ: Ablex.

Roopnarine, J. L., Brown, J., Snell-White, P., Riegraf, N. B., Crossley, D., Hossain, Z., and Webb, W. (1995). Father involvement in child care and household work in common-law dual-earner and single-earner families. *Journal of Applied Developmental Psychology, 16,* 35-52.

Roopnarine, J., Snell-White, P., Riegraf, N., Wolfsenberger, J., Hossain, Z., and Mathur, S. (1997). Family socialization in an East Indian village in Guyana: A focus on fathers. In J. L. Roopnarine and J. Brown (Eds.), *Caribbean families: Diversity among ethnic groups* (pp. 57-83). Norwood, NJ: Ablex.

Schiller, N. G., Basch, L., and Blanc, C. S. (1995). From immigrant to transmigrant: Theorizing transnational migration. *Anthropological Quarterly, 68*(1), 48-63.

Schorr, L. B. (1988). *Within our reach: Breaking the cycle of disadvantage.* New York: Anchor Press.

Senior, O. (1991). *Working miracles: Women's lives in the English-speaking Caribbean.* ISER, UWI, Barbados. London, James Curry, and Bloomington: Indiana University Press.

Sharpe, J. (1997). Mental-health issues and family socialization in the Caribbean. In J. L. Roopnarine and J. Brown (Eds.), *Caribbean families: Diversity among ethnic groups* (pp. 259-273). Norwood, NJ: Ablex.

Sigel, I. (1985). A conceptual analysis of beliefs. In I. Sigel, A. McGillicuddy-DeLisi, and J. Goodnow (Eds.), *Parental belief systems: The psychological consequences for children* (Second edition, pp. 345-371). Hillsdale, NJ: Erlbaum.

Smith, R. T. (1996). *The matrifocal family: Power, pluralism, and politics.* London: Routledge.

Strier, D. R. (1996). Coping strategies of immigrant parents: Directions for family therapy. *Family Process, 35*(3), 363-373.

Stycos, J. M. and Back, K. W. (1964). *The control of human fertility in Jamaica.* Ithaca, NY: Cornell University Press.

Sue, D. W. and Sue, D. (1990). *Counseling the culturally different* (Second edition). New York: Wiley.

Szapocznik, J. and Kurtines, W. (1993). Family psychology and cultural diversity: Opportunities for theory, research, and application. *American Psychologist, 48*(4), 400-407.

Taylor, R. (Ed.) (1998). *Minority families in the United States: A multicultural perspective* (Second edition). Upper Saddle River, NJ: Prentice Hall.

Triandis, H. (1990). Theoretical concepts that are applicable to the analysis of ethnocentrism. In R. W. Brislin (Ed.), *Applied cross-cultural psychology* (Volume 14, pp. 34-55). Beverly Hills, CA: Sage Publications.

U.S. Department of Justice, Immigration and Naturalization Service (1990). *Statistical Yearbook of the Immigration and Naturalization Service.* Washington, DC: U.S. Government Printing Office.

Weisner, T. (1998). Human development, child well-being, and the cultural project of development. In D. Sharma and K. Fischer (Eds.), *Socioemotional development across cultures. New Directions in Child Development, 81* (pp. 69-85). San Francisco, CA: Jossey-Bass.

Whiting, B. B. and Whiting, J. W. M. (1975). *Children of six cultures: A psychocultural analysis*. Cambridge, MA: Harvard University Press.

Chapter 11

Research and Practice on Fathers in High-Risk Families: Exploring the Need and Potential Areas for Collaboration

Vivian L. Gadsden
Edward W. Pitt
Neil Tift

Research and practice on father involvement and family support share a common and complex history spanning almost thirty years. Nested within this history are layers of research questions about the problems facing young fathers and families, particularly those experiencing economic hardship. Important questions of practice exist regarding the needs of programs and the practitioners who work in them, and there are equally important matters of policy concerning ways to ensure the well-being of children. These three domains—research, practice, and policy—are often linked in written and oral discussions, as though the connections among them occur in the natural course of work. However, in discussions on fathers and families, these domains do not always work together, despite growing efforts and frequent references to the importance of building good connections. Yet they have the potential to intersect in ways that promote efforts in the field, construct a critical knowledge base, and sustain collaboration. Therefore, in this chapter, we focus on the need for greater collaboration among researchers, practitioners, and policymakers in order to help the process along.[1]

This chapter is divided into five broad sections. We begin with a historical overview of the ways in which policymakers and researchers have approached efforts to support responsible fathering and families. Second, we focus on the lack of systematic data from practitioners about the issues and problems they face and the nature of support they need from researchers and policymakers to strengthen their work. Third, we discuss the use of focus groups to examine practitioners' perceptions of the critical issues faced by fathers and their families, as well as the issues that practitioners encounter in working with those fathers. Fourth, we present selected findings from focus groups and interviews conducted with practitioners about what might be gained from their collaborating with researchers and policymakers. Fifth, we conclude with a summary of emerging possibilities in which the domains of research, practice, and policy may be linked and the ways in which they could work together and begin to deepen mutual relationships of support and respect.

HISTORICAL OVERVIEW OF POLICY AND RESEARCH

As has been suggested by other authors throughout this volume, no single impetus exists for the current interest in fathers and families. Smith (1998) suggests that the apparent surge of effort to improve father involvement can be traced to an intertwining of concerns about father absence, family formation, the decline of marriage/increase in divorce, and the decay of communities. One such concern centered mostly on divorce and the consequences for children when fathers physically left the home. A second addressed father absence as an indicator of larger cultural problems and the decline of Western tradition. Declines in the quality of life of children and families were attributed primarily, if not solely, to the increased absence of fathers. A third concern was the growing problem of child poverty and child well-being and reflected three primary issues: (1) specific relationships between father absence and child and family poverty (e.g., the problems faced by poor mothers and children resulting from the loss of income); (2) poor fathers, often never married, for whom the problems and barriers presented by race, unemployment, and intergenerational hardship served as obstacles to supporting their children; and (3) child support enforcement.

Policy Context

Many of the issues that contributed to these three concerns were highlighted in the 1988 Family Support Act. In addition to casting the issue of father absence into the public discourse, the act set the stage for (re)new(ed) attention by researchers, practitioners, and policymakers to the needs of children and families. By 1988, several studies had begun to explore the impact of mother-headed households, changing patterns of family formation, and structural barriers to two-parent families. The divorce rate had increased substantially, as had the numbers of births to unmarried parents. Growing numbers of children were becoming vulnerable to hardship and intergenerational poverty in many pockets of urban and rural settings. Against this backdrop of change and the persistence of old and seemingly intractable problems, policy research and policy discussions were focused on child-centered programs. However, neither policy research nor new policy formulations seemed to grasp fully the impact of changing family constellations on children, nor had they seriously considered the role of fathers in children's well-being or family stability. The Family Support Act, some argue, represented a significant turning point, addressing for the first time major issues associated with financial child support, father absence, and the relationship of these issues to child welfare and family efficacy. It created a series of sanctions and incentives at both the federal and state levels by rewarding states that did a good job of collecting child support (and penalizing those that did not achieve basic standards).

The Family Support Act focused primarily on divorced fathers who had failed to honor child support orders. It was, perhaps, this relative inattention to other nonresidential, noncustodial fathers that initiated discussions about low-income, unmarried, noncustodial, nonresidential fathers who did not have the financial capacity to pay child support and, in a large number of cases, had not established paternity. The act also began to change the direction and goal of attention to poor children and mother-headed households while helping to set the policy and political stage for discussions about welfare reform. As one unexpected result, it helped to broaden once narrow perspectives about low-income fathers and families and thrust into discussions about these fathers the role of education and training, employment, legal paternity establishment, and alternative forms of child support.

The passage of the Family Support Act led to the establishment of two major research/practice demonstration projects designed for low-income fathers. The first, the Young Unwed Fathers Project, was coordinated by Public/Private Ventures and funded by a collection of six foundations along with the U.S. Department of Labor and the U.S. Department of Agriculture's Food and Nutrition Services. Conducted roughly from 1991 to 1993 in six cities (Annapolis, Maryland; Cleveland, Ohio; Fresno, California; Philadelphia, Pennsylvania; Racine, Wisconsin; and St. Petersburg, Florida), the project focused on young fathers between the ages of sixteen and twenty-five, providing them with educational assistance, employment and training, fatherhood development activities, and case management. The report from the demonstration (Achatz and MacAllum, 1994) explored how programs could improve the ability of young men to care for their children, both as financial providers and as nurturing parents.

The second project, the Parents' Fair Share Demonstration, was intended to increase the income potential of welfare families by increasing the earnings of the noncustodial parent and ensuring that these earnings were used for regular child support payments. Support for the study, conducted by the Manpower Demonstration Research Corporation, was provided by private foundations, the U.S. Department of Health and Human Services, and the U.S. Department of Labor. The project, which continued for almost ten years as an intervention and research study, began with eleven sites throughout the country. Each site focused on enhanced child support enforcement, employment and training, peer support and instruction in parenting skills, and mediation services.[2]

The two programs differed from most previous efforts in their target group (e.g., low-income fathers); funding streams (e.g., combination of public and private sources); and focus (e.g., capacity-building to engage fathers in supporting their children). However, they were not the first to address male responsibility or father involvement among low-income men. Between the 1960s and 1980s, a series of public- and private-funded male involvement programs emerged, typically located in low-income, African-American communities. The profile of these programs falls within three categories. One combined federal and community interests and was based largely on research from the 1960s on family life within African-American communities. Activities were designed to strengthen adolescent and young adult male involvement within families, father involvement within communities, and pregnancy prevention. A second category focused on cultural and political empowerment, rites of passage, and related activities and has continued to be a viable effort within African-American and more recently Latino communities and schools. A third category, which includes the current focus on fathering, connects the earlier interests of government agencies, researchers, practitioners, and communities to examine dimensions of father involvement, male fertility, and male reproductive health.

By the early 1990s, male involvement and early father-focused programs had raised public consciousness on issues related to men and fathers in low-income communities. The establishment of these early programs made more visible the impact of inequities in social access, education, and employment that militated against strong communities and family life. However, the Young Fathers and Parents' Fair Share Projects were successful in translating the sense of urgency that the early programs created into more systematic study and interventions to support low-income fathers. They focused on specific ways to increase children's financial support. Although both of the programs began with a relatively narrow focus on financial support, they brought to the forefront of policy research and public recognition the importance of a broader definition of father involvement. This includes the fact that children's well-being requires more than financial support. It draws attention to the need to recognize other aspects of child support that often are taken for granted (e.g., fathers' roles in child care, nurturing, and contributing to children's cognitive and psychosocial development). The project also found that issues such as unemployment, parenting, and intergenerational father absence need to be examined. However, what these demonstration projects did not address, was why fathers who were financially able to support their children often did not do so. They did not determine how to engage fathers positively in their children's lives, or how to determine what makes a responsible father. Different strands of research had investigated some of these issues, and new strands also were being developed in which related issues and nuanced problems were being identified and examined.

Strands of Inquiry in Research

Research on fathers reflects many of the social changes that occurred between the 1970s and 1990s. The country wrestled with issues related to race and discrimination, culture, and gender and the structural barriers they created for poor and ethnic minorities. Most notably, traditional roles assigned to men and women had become less defensible. Discussions about the importance of fathers being more integrally involved in children's development were taking shape, not simply as a response to the changing role of women but also as an overdue response to the needs of children to have multiple, deeply involved, caring adults available to them within and outside the home.

Three prominent strands of study connected the changes within the public sphere and research and created a context for the field. One strand focused on the impact of father presence/absence on children's schooling and general well-being. These studies linked father absence or lack of involvement with children to poor performance in school, poor quality of school experience, and higher drop-out rates (Dawson, 1991; Nord, 1998; Zill, 1976).

A second strand of studies, beginning in the1980s, pointed to the effects of divorce and includes basic and policy studies. Some of these studies examined the decline in family income and the increase in child poverty resulting from divorce and father absence, and found that divorce almost always meant a decline in living standards for women and children, with children of never-married mothers faring the worst (Garfinkel and McLanahan, 1986). Moreover, 75 percent of American children living in single-parent families were found to experience poverty before they turn eleven years old, compared to only 20 percent of children in two-parent families (National Commission on Children, 1993). Within this second strand, other studies focused on the quality of the interactions between children and fathers and between fathers and mothers after divorce or separation (Maccoby, Depner, and Mnookin, 1990). Common findings were that many children in father-absent homes had little or no contact with their fathers over time and that fathers were less likely to provide their children with parental guidance (Furstenberg and Cherlin, 1991).

A third strand of research in the 1980s and 1990s began to focus on a wider range of fathering behaviors, different contexts, and ethnically and culturally diverse father and family populations. Most of the work in this area examined African-American fathers. Some researchers, such as Philip Bowman (1988, 1989, 1990) examined the special challenges of fatherhood for African-American fathers and other fathers of color. Bowman found that certain cultural coping resources can buffer provider role strain, such as especially strong kinship bonds and religious beliefs. Other researchers sought to dispel the myth that black fathers are uninterested, unwilling parents. Harriet McAdoo (1981) and John McAdoo (1986) found that black fathers value their child-rearing role, are equally involved with their wives in decision-making, and adopt less authoritarian parenting styles than predicted by the literature. John McAdoo (1986) also found that when black families are more economically secure, fathers are more likely to be actively involved.

By the 1990s, it had become clear that much had been learned, but that the field had glaring weaknesses and imbalances. Referring to fatherhood over the past century, Ross Parke stated: "Today, and probably in earlier eras as well, there is no single type of father. Some fathers remain uninvolved; others are active participants, and some fathers are even raising children by themselves" (1996, p. 8). Gadsden and Hall (1996) point out that research studies historically focused on a select subset of fathers, mostly middle-class, white fathers, although programs typically serve low-income fathers and low-income fathers of color. Throughout the early to mid-1990s, most research continued to focus on children of divorce, although a few were beginning to examine fathers who were unmarried, adoptive fathers, step-fathers, or social fathers. In short, research did not represent the diversity of fathers, class, cultural and racial issues, or circumstances that encourage or thwart father involvement.

Summary

Attention at the policy level had expanded its focus to nonresidential, noncustodial fathers typically not identifiable or accessible through traditional venues such as legal marriage, paternity establishment, or court-imposed sanctions of responsibility. The landscape has changed over the past ten years, particularly in reference to poor families and as a result of welfare reform legislation. However, policy continues to focus disproportionately on paternity establishment and financial child support. Considerably less attention is paid to the factors that reduce the likelihood or the ability of many poor fathers to contribute to their children's financial support or engage in nurturing behavior with their children. Policy-focused research projects such as the Young Fathers Project and Parents Fair Share helped to identify the high level of risk experienced by poor fathers while also denoting the significant and possible ways that programs can provide interventions and support to men.

On the research side, studies conducted from the 1970s to the present have offered important frameworks to consider in developing the field. The data from these studies suggest that children in homes where fathers are present are at less risk for a range of negative outcomes, from performing poorly in school to engaging in criminal acts. Although the focus of studies is beginning to shift, with increasing numbers of studies examining low-income fathers and low-income fathers of color, several problems persist. The focus of research studies needs to be sharpened, and the content of research needs to be rethought to elevate issues such as the diversity in the types of fathers studied, the cultural and contextual factors that affect the impact of father involvement, and the appropriateness of the questions asked about urgent and perennial social problems.

By the early 1990s, salient weaknesses were becoming evident: the lack of realistic insights and data about the needs of fathers; the issues faced by special populations of fathers (e.g., those who were poor, chronically unemployed, unengaged with their children, young, or never-married); or sound approaches to connecting these fathers with their children and families in positive and nonconfrontational ways. Although child- and family-focused programs have existed for decades, these tend to attract and provide support to mothers who are typically the identified or assumed caregiver, the primary caregiver, or the sole caregiver. The challenge to the emerging field of fathers and families has been how to develop an area of work that broadens the notion of family to focus more intensively on fathers; how to ensure that the development of this work enhances rather than reduces support for children and mothers who continue to be children's primary caregivers; and how to increase positive outcomes for children. In this next section, we focus on one relatively unexplored resource for meeting the challenge—a more collaborative relationship between practitioners and researchers.

THE ARGUMENT
FOR PRACTICE-DERIVED RESEARCH

The critical examinations of the field during the 1980s and 1990s made more visible the relative absence of a reciprocal and respectful relationship between research, practice, and policy, particularly poignant in a field dominated by programs and practitioners. How could research be translated for use by practitioners? What were the best ways to identify and use knowledge from practice and programs serving diverse communities? What did researchers and policymakers need to know to learn from, inform, and include practitioners and vice versa? How could the variability and inconclusiveness of research studies, such as those cited in the previous section, be minimized and reports crafted differently so that practice-related issues would be addressed and findings and implications of interest to practitioners would be highlighted? A significant number of practitioners had emerged by the 1990s, working in schools and churches and with divorce courts and correctional institutions. Some of these practitioners were in support programs for middle-class fathers, but most worked with low-income, minority communities, often with unmarried fathers or fathers of color.

The significance of practice-informed research is neither new nor novel in strong research communities. It has been a part of social science agendas and organizations such as the National Council on Family Relations and the Society for Research in Child Development for several decades. However, in a field such as fathers and families— where charismatic movements and advocacy are as likely to dominate the public image as sound studies, effective though struggling programs, or appropriate social policies—the issues facing researchers and practitioners provide a particularly good backdrop for considering future work that can make a difference to children and families. Beginning in 1994, the National Center on Fathers and Families (NCOFF), began to focus on the challenge that practice-informed work presented. NCOFF conducted field studies, using interviews and focus groups, to explore and understand practitioners' perspectives and their experiences in programs. NCOFF continues to focus on creating useful frameworks that develop practice-derived and practice-informed research, in other words, identifying: (1) strands of knowledge from research that could be useful in supporting fathers and families and in designing and evaluating programs and their effects, and (2) knowledge from practice that could deepen the research questions and agendas developed by researchers and policymakers. One result of the work has been the creation of the Fathers and Families Core Learnings, a framework for studying father involvement and family well-being (see Table 11.1). Another result of this work has been the identification of barriers to father involvement with children.

The Core Learnings consist of seven hypotheses that focus on the developmental effects of fathering for children, families, and fathers themselves. These seven hypotheses are tested regularly through the ongoing practice and research of specialists who are implementing innovative work with fathers and families and are examining the impact of father involvement on children, mothers, and families in general. To formulate the Core Learnings, NCOFF, between 1994 and 1997, interviewed more than 100 practitioners in focus groups, conducted face-to-face individual interviews, and completed telephone surveys. In this section, we report the findings of these meetings at two points: the first (T1) occurred in 1994, shortly after NCOFF's establishment and at the first formal meeting of what subsequently became the National Practitioners Network for Fathers and Families; the second (T2) occurred in 1996-1997 during an expanded follow-up analysis of activities in the field.

Table 11.1. The Core Learnings and Related Research Questions

---

1. Fathers care (even if that caring is not always shown in conventional ways).

What are the personal, familial, and social complexities to fathers caring? To what degree do these complexities revolve around social and developmental needs of young fathers or the problems encountered in making role transitions? How can fathers be supported to be involved more deeply with their children? What are the cultural practices that may be used as indicators of father caring?

2. Father presence matters (in terms of economic well-being, social support, and development).

What does it matter that a father is in the home—to a child's emotional, social, and cognitive development? From the child's point of view, what difference does it make to live with or have access to one parent only? What is the impact of fathers who are physically present but emotionally absent in children's lives? How does father absence affect family well-being? For example, how does father absence contribute to poverty in families?

3. Joblessness is a major impediment to family formation and father involvement.

What is the relationship between father involvement and joblessness, particularly among African-American fathers and other fathers of color? How does joblessness and limited access to well-paying employment affect family formation choices and patterns, parenting activities, and decisions to marry? What is the relationship between unemployment and involvement in illegal economies? What changes in behavior and support occur as a result of gainful employment?

4. Existing approaches to public benefits, child support enforcement, and paternity establishment operate to provide obstacles and disincentives to father involvement. Moreover, the disincentives are sufficiently compelling as to have prompted the emergence of a phenomenon dubbed "underground fathers"—men who acknowledge paternity and are involved in the lives of their children but who refuse to participate as fathers in the formal systems.

How do current initiatives, e.g., welfare reform, affect father involvement and support? How complex are the systemic barriers to father involvement, e.g., at local and state levels? What are the specific policy changes necessary to ensure father engagement and to support young parents' commitment to the welfare of their children? What is the nature of systemic barriers encountered by programs and fathers in providing support to their children, and what approaches do they use to override or minimize the impact of the barriers? To what degree does race, culture, ethnicity, and gender exacerbate problems of access to the system?

5. A growing number of young fathers and mothers need additional support to develop the skills they will need to share the responsibility for parenting.

How do some fragile families "make it" and why do others not, i.e., what strengths characterize these families and what social supports are available to them? What hardships work against their resiliency? What are the effective models of program support, including innovative approaches, practices, techniques, and strategies, and what are the outcomes of program participation for parents and children? What techniques used to promote coparenting services among divorced and separating couples can be applied successfully to fragile families? How do the approaches used in coparenting programs cohere with those in father, mother, and family-focused programs?

6. The transition from biological father to committed parent has significant developmental implications for young fathers.

What is the impact of young fatherhood on the behaviors and attitudes of young fathers, e.g., the need to complete high school, improve literacy, and obtain employment? That is, how does the presence of a baby and family change or affect the behaviors of young fathers? What is the nature of support to young men and women making the transition to parenthood? What are the inherent difficulties in making the transition?

7. The behaviors of young parents, both fathers and mothers, are influenced significantly by intergenerational beliefs and practices within families of origin.

What is the quantity and quality of social support available within families of origin and how do these families influence the parenting behaviors of young fathers and their participation in coparenting efforts? What are the beliefs and practices that exist within families, and how are these beliefs, practices, and the values associated with them transmitted? What are the intricacies within young fathers' and mothers' personal stories and intergenerational legacies that predispose them to succumb to problems or to rise above hardships, i.e., what personal and familial factors contribute to the ability of individual parents or fragile families to chart a future for themselves and their children? How do they redirect their energies to "make it" or concede to what they think are their failures?

Source: NCOFF Mission Statement (1994). Philadelphia, PA: National Center on Fathers and Families, Graduate School of Education. University of Pennsylvania.

FOCUS GROUP PARTICIPANTS
AND PROCEDURES

Focus group participants in T1 were thirty frontline practitioners and program administrators invited to attend a roundtable, sponsored by the Philadelphia Children's Network (PCN) and NCOFF and held as a preconference to the Family Reunion III: The Role of Men in Children's Lives Conference in Nashville.[3] All participants were selected from among individual practitioners and agencies recommended by family specialists, demonstration sites such as Parents Fair Share and Public/Private Ventures, and emerging networks of practitioners that had been identified and compiled by PCN, a policy and practice-focused agency that housed the Responsive Fathers Program.[4] NCOFF built upon data collected through individual interviews and focus groups conducted several months earlier by PCN.

Of the thirty practitioners, six were women, and twenty-four were men. Most served low-skilled fathers and young mothers and families; however, the focus of their work cut across a range of issues such as father-child (re)engagement, workforce development and employment, entrepreneurship, cooperative parenting, and reimmersion within communities (after absences due to drug dependency, incarceration, etc.). Approximately ten practitioners represented early childhood programs (two federally funded programs: Head Start and Healthy Start), and privately funded early learning programs. Eighteen practitioners were identified as working in responsible fatherhood programs or paternal involvement programs, including seven which were or had been with the Parents Fair Share or Public/Private Ventures Programs, and two serving fathers across income levels and family relationships. One was involved in a family court effort, and two focused on fathers in the workplace. Practitioners represented states in the South, Midwest, West, and Northeast. In addition, eight family researchers and evaluators who had been involved in father-related research and evaluation projects such as Parents Fair Share and Public/Private Ventures Programs also attended.

Three focus group meetings were held with the full group. Then follow-up individual, face-to-face, and telephone interviews were held with ten of the original group. Focus group participants were given two primary tasks. First, they were asked to share their observations and to identify main themes about responsible fathering and father engagement that had emerged from their work with children, parents, and families. Second, they were given a list of "learnings" identified by other practitioners and by researchers in meetings and conferences and through telephone interviews conducted by PCN and NCOFF. The focus group participants were asked to respond to five questions that focused on:

1. Whether (and the degree to which) the learnings listed were consistent with, differed from, or were contradicted by their experience
2. Additional learnings and/or questions that would inform their work
3. Reforms they would be prepared to support
4. Additional policy changes for which they would advocate
5. Learning(s) from their program that holds the most far-reaching implications for changing practice, improving the work of practitioners, and informing research and policy

In T2, NCOFF revisited the issues that had surfaced in the field between the 1994 focus groups and 1996 by conducting a second series of focus groups in six cities (Atlanta, Georgia; Austin, Texas; Baltimore, Maryland; Los Angeles, California; Minneapolis, Minnesota; Philadelphia, Pennsylvania, which included participants from New York City). Approximately seventy people participated, twelve from the T1 group. Follow-up individual telephone interviews were conducted with twelve practitioners. T2 focus group participants were primarily identified through three approaches: (1) contacting previous participants from the T1 focus group, (2) seeking nominations from T1 participants, and (3) selecting from programs listed in NCOFF's program database.[5] The focus groups and the follow-up interviews with selected practitioners were intended to explore how practice and programs had changed since the original formulation of the Core Learnings, what practitioners had learned from their work that cohered with or differed from previous learnings and experiences with fathers and families, and how research and policy could support the development of effective approaches for the field.

Approximately 60 percent of the participants in T2 (both focus groups and interviews) were male and represented a wide range of experiences and roles within their organizations. They served as directors, associate directors, program coordinators, social workers, and counselors. Most were active practitioners who worked directly with clients on a regular basis; other participants supported programs in different capacities, from providing direct assistance such as mentoring to serving as advocates.

Most programs were father-focused and were established specifically to enhance father involvement in families or to provide support and resources to fathers and other men in general. Programs not catering specifically to fathers typically fell into one of three categories: (1) they offered general parent education services, (2) they were geared toward assisting mothers but included father groups, or (3) they concentrated on giving guidance to parents and children encountering difficult circumstances. Most programs were funded through public funds, and 50 percent received only public funding. Others were funded through private sources or a combination of private and public support.

The populations served by programs that identified as father-focused also varied. Programs reportedly served a wide range of fathers, including noncustodial, unemployed, low-income, middle-income, single, never-married, and divorced fathers, white fathers, and fathers of color. Many clients who were served by the programs enrolled voluntarily; however, a small number of programs served only fathers who were mandated by the courts to attend.

Although a great variety of ideas and opinions were presented by focus group participants, some of the most compelling issues seemed to be commonly known realities of service provision to fathers and families. The practitioners' comments offered insights into the original Core Learnings and suggested that additional themes addressing specific vulnerabilities faced by fathers and families be integrated. These focused on fathers' lack of educational preparation, isolation, and limited intergenerational support systems. In the next section, we provide a synthesis of the practitioners' perspectives by first providing a summary statement of the issues and then highlighting major questions raised. The questions located at the end of the summary statements in the text reflect the suggestions of practitioners about ways in which researchers could be helpful and work more collaboratively with them.

LEARNINGS FROM FATHER-FOCUSED PRACTICE AND PROGRAMS

Fathers Care and Father Presence Matters

The first two Core Learnings encompass a range of issues that combine the nurturing, educational, and financial roles that fathers play in children's cognitive development, physical health, and social well-being. "Fathers Care" focuses on whether and how fathers demonstrate concern through diverse behaviors and practices; "Father Presence Matters" focuses on the continuum of involvement by fathers within children's lives and the ways in which the physical and/or emotional presence of a father influences children's development and shapes their experiences, interactions, and relationships within and outside the family. Practitioners suggested that the salient theme centers on how to define a "good father,"'. stating that "not all fathers care" and that "*good* fathers matter."

Primary Questions for Core Learnings 1 and 2

- Are there generic, child-motivated ways of caring?
- What is fathering?
- What kind of involvement makes a difference?

Employment and Joblessness

The major thrust of Core Learning 3, "Employment and Joblessness," is that joblessness and problems of employment and employability serve as impediments to family formation and family involvement. It addresses the ways in which a father's ability to obtain and sustain employment influences father engagement, particularly within many minority communities, such as African-American and Latino communities. Practitioners noted that education plays a major role in fathers' joblessness as do fathers' attitude toward, experience with, and exposure to work and work settings.

Primary Questions for Core Learning 3

- How does having or not having a job interfere with fathering?
- How do education and schooling contribute to increased employment options and to sustained father involvement?

Systemic Barriers

Both divorced and never-married fathers reportedly refer to the "system" as counterproductive in their efforts to be "good" fathers. One might imagine that the bureaucratic nature of government systems could create obstacles. However, if the concept of barriers were broadened to include personal and community barriers, several other obstacles might well be identified, including lack of income, chronic unemployment, and the lack of jobs with adequate pay. Moreover, fathers often live in communities that lack appropriate resources to prepare young men for today's job market.

Primary Questions for Core Learning 4

- What specifically about the system serves as a barrier, could be eliminated as a barrier, or could serve as an incentive for father engagement?
- What is the range and scope of interaction between the system and fathers, not limited to noncustodial, nonresidential fathers; issues of child support and paternity establishment; or child custody?
- How can fathers earn credit for in-kind support?

Cooperative/Collaborative Parenting (Coparenting)

Although most research and practice on cooperative parenting has focused on parents separated by divorce, Core Learning 5 addresses the range of cooperative relationships that exist between cohabitating parents, parents separated by divorce, and never-married, nonresidential parents. Practitioners highlighted the significance of cooperative parenting for parents of all ages, not simply for young parents. However, at the center of a discussion about coparenting, they suggest, should be a focus on parenting and diversity of parenting styles affected by culture and by the historical and changing roles of women and men. Thus, questions about cooperative parenting by necessity should address negotiations around the role of fathers and mothers. Recent concepts such as "team parenting," emerging from the fragile families initiatives, represent specific subsets of interests and focus on hard-to-reach and, typically, never-married parents. The larger question that begs for a response from the field is how to deepen our knowledge of parenting and coparenting for diverse populations of families.

Primary Questions for Core Learning 5

- What are the inherent risks and possibilities for parents and children when parents do not sufficiently work with each other?
- How do existing social and familial systems encourage or discourage parents assuming and sharing responsibilities for children?

Role Transitions

Core Learning 6, "Role Transitions," focuses on how the transition to parenthood affects the life course of fathers and mothers and how life transitions affect parenting choices, behaviors, and practices. Practitioners noted that such transitions require changes in attitudes and that maturity and age play a role in how successfully a parent will make the transition to parenthood. This, they suggested, raises questions about what role age and maturity play in the transition to committed fatherhood, motherhood, and parenthood, and whether and how the transition can be built upon as points of entry for teaching and learning.

Primary Questions for Core Learning 6

- What role does the age of a father play in the transition to committed fatherhood?
- What approaches are necessary to increase adolescent males' knowledge of the expectations regarding fathering and enhance their ability to make the transition at points when they are financially and emotionally prepared and capable of responsible fathering?

Intergenerational Learning

The Core Learning on "Intergenerational Learning" assumes that families of origin play a critical role in defining and shaping the practices, choices, and behaviors of parents—that is, that the behaviors of parents are influenced significantly by the beliefs and practices of earlier generations or within family cultures, and that the behaviors and attitudes of parents in the current generation will affect subsequent generations. Practitioners indicated that this learning is the foundation for all the others.

Primary Questions for Core Learning 7

- If we accept that models of parenting are transmitted from one generation to another, what are appropriate examples of parenting models and who decides whether and how these models are implemented and assessed?
- What are different cultural models of parenting?
- What are their strengths?
- How do programs identify and utilize intergenerational knowledge?
- What is the impact of families of origin?

Barriers to Positive Father Involvement

Practitioners identified and named six barriers that may interfere with positive father involvement. These barriers are embedded in but less explicitly stated in the Core Learnings.

1. *Poor schooling and lack of access to educational opportunities, which limit employment options of fathers.* Poor schooling, the participants suggested, affects more than a father's or mother's ability to get a job and provide financial support for children. It also influences how parents interact with schools and teachers; the degree to which they believe they can contribute to their children's education; and how they work with vested individuals within families, communities, and schools to ensure the well-being of children.

2. *Increased vulnerability for many fathers and families, including conditions associated with poverty, drug use, incarceration, and family violence.* Problems of poverty, drug use, and incarceration are obstacles to father involvement and often reduce fathers' engagement and the quality of that engagement. These and related problems often lead to other problems of unhealthy and violent family interactions, the practitioners suggested. Many fathers find themselves grappling with issues of power, personal defeat, and the role of men and fathers in communities and families.

3. *Intergenerational isolation and the development of personal meaning and responsibility*. Practitioners noted that many young, low-income fathers have lived in communities separated from the larger society and are victimized by entrenched poverty over several generations as well as considerable breakdown of their community. As a result of having grown up in these neighborhoods, many of the fathers experience a sense of isolation and hopelessness about their future. They also lack knowledge about how to plan for the future and how to respond to the expectations of society regarding responsible fatherhood. The birth of a child is a difficult transition for many fathers, but this event is also seen as an opportunity to develop a sense of personal responsibility and meaning in one's life. This search for meaning often has a spiritual dimension or may lead to greater participation in traditional religious institutions.

4. *Lack of early preparation for the responsibilities of parenthood and family life*. Practitioners argued that the first order of business should be to educate children about the realities of parenthood from a very young age. They suggested two reasons for early preparation. First, getting young people to understand the day-to-day difficulties of parenthood and the sacrifices that have to be made on a regular basis can have a significant impact on teen pregnancy and unwanted pregnancy in general. Second, children need to be educated about parenting and the responsibility associated with it. Such education would focus on teaching skills to young people so they become healthy, well-adjusted adults and parents.

5. *Different beliefs about manhood and womanhood*. Practitioners have discovered that many masculine ideals devalue the qualities that are necessary for active fatherhood. They stressed that the male ideals of control and suppression of emotions interfere with creating a healthy family life and a nurturing environment for children. Societal messages that promote control as a male virtue combined with messages that the home is the woman's domain deter men from playing an active role in family life and increase the lure of the streets. Furthermore, "sexist" thinking and the automatic association of women with child care have led to the assumption that "parenting is innate and not real work because women do it." As a result of failing to appreciate how much work is entailed in

parenting, the public (as an entity and as individual parents) does not view it as a skill that must be developed and does not support sufficient societal investment in child rearing.

6. *Erosion of community cohesiveness and power to set standards.* Practitioners stated that at one time family, school, and community worked together and presented a unified front against behavior that was considered undesirable. Now, practitioners argued, parents must be ever vigilant to protect their children from the threats of the community, whether those threats are drug dealers on street corners or media messages that advocate wanton consumerism and meaningless sex. For most practitioners interviewed, the disintegration of the local community is one of the most immediate threats to children's well-being.

Enlisting Community Support in (Re)Connecting Fathers and Families

One issue that came out strongly in the practitioners' commentaries was the need to engage communities in programmatic efforts that address father-related matters and help to influence social systems concerned with families (NCOFF, 1998). Reinforced in reviews from the field (e.g., Kane, Gadsden, and Armorer, 1997; Levine and Pitt, 1995; Levine, Murphy, and Wilson, 1993), this theme suggests that systematic analysis of programs for fathers will help identify which elements of a program are essential for reconnecting fathers to families. This analysis needs to recognize, utilize, and carefully examine the role of communities in creating the culture (within and outside the cultural traditions of an ethnic group or social class) of families or contributing to the cultures that families develop themselves (Gadsden, 1998). This involves developing expectations of fathers and mothers as parents, as part of extended families, and of the community itself. It entails promoting opportunities that increase the involvement of fathers and help to mitigate difficult life circumstances that interfere with child welfare and family stability. And finally, it involves building upon community strengths to enhance the lives of families and children.

Creative approaches are needed to engage communities in efforts to support fathers and families; there are no foolproof approaches to enlisting this support. However, from our work in the field, we have identified at least four broad ways to expand community interest and demonstrate programmatic and research investment. These include:

1. Exploring the community through visits and informal discussions that help to gauge the presence of and potential for community supports and learning about the culture(s) of the community and its families
2. Following up with a more formal survey of potential support sources (e.g., surveying the community and identifying stakeholders through interviews with community leaders who have achieved local visibility; community members, both the most prominent and the hardest to reach; and community institutions, such as churches, recreation centers, and social service agencies)
3. Sharing information and creating a reciprocal relationship of respect and cooperation through explicit activities that can support fathers and shaping a collaboration which builds on mutual understandings of need, potential, and community and program responsibility
4. Establishing a clear understanding of the goals of different stakeholders, maintaining at the center the role that positive father involvement plays in supporting families, contributing to community development, and increasing pathways of opportunity for future generations of children

Communities differ in the scope of their resources and the drain on these resources. However, without formal training, programs typically are not able to assess these resources; investigate the beliefs, practices, and experiences of those in communities; monitor the impact of a program on a community; or study the nature of relationships that can lead to positive father involvement. With this knowledge, researchers and policymakers can build on efforts that are already working within communities. We suggest that this knowledge needs to be expanded with research that informs us not only about whether efforts are working but also about *how* efforts are working, what the nuanced issues and problems are, and what approaches are most useful to invite and sustain father involvement in the lives of families and community.

CREATING A CONTEXT FOR COLLABORATION

Based upon a review of policy and research discussions and interviews with practitioners, we suggest an agenda that integrates the historical issues and reduces the significance of false dichotomies of father presence versus father absence. Also needed is expansive work within ethnically, culturally, and financially diverse communities; greater familiarity by researchers and practitioners with one another's work; and more attention to the nature of practice itself and the work of practitioners. Increased involvement by each of the three—researchers, practitioners, and policymakers—in the conceptualization of research activities and other efforts is also suggested.

Although family specialists grapple with the concept of "fatherhood" as an issue, it is perhaps most immediately an issue for practitioners who serve fathers and families on a daily basis. Although many practitioners agree that the definition of fatherhood should extend beyond the emphasis on financial provision, they are sometimes unsure of what the new criteria for being a good father should be. After all, being a good father once meant living with the family and providing for its material needs, seemingly both too much and too little to ask of fathers.

Practitioners are intimately aware of the extraordinary responsibilities of guiding clients in their family roles. They look to research to provide an informed, "third-party" perspective that might alleviate some of the pressure they feel. The discussions during the focus group meetings were infused with practitioners' own experiences, suggesting that their personal backgrounds play a major role in guiding their interactions with the fathers in their programs. Practitioners who work with young fathers were sensitive to the fact that they are taking the place of parents in the young men's lives and were aware that, like the young men's own parents, they bring a great deal of "baggage" to this relationship. They often admitted that in teaching parenting they are forced to take a stand on issues that they may not have resolved for themselves. On the one hand, practitioners need to be able to relate in a personal way to fathers' experiences; on the other hand, these personal experiences are not supposed to influence the practitioner-father relationship negatively. Practitioners indicated that outcome-based research would be an important alternative resource that would guide them toward helping fathers and families make positive changes.

In situations in which their own experience seemed inadequate, most of the practitioners whom we interviewed or to whom we have spoken in other settings envisioned research as a neutral place (with respect to their particular circumstance) to turn for information about issues that concern practitioners themselves, such as negotiating practitioners' authority with clients, reducing the disconnection between "the rhetoric of programs" and the lifestyles of the practitioners, or addressing important issues with the few programs available. For instance, several practitioners asked how to provide a supportive atmosphere for fathers without encouraging them to become dependent on practitioners.

Both within the field studies and in the commentaries of researchers, there is an interest, a need, and an urgency for increased collaborations. Research, practitioners noted, can help them by presenting a macrolevel analysis of the outcomes of interventions. Practitioners around the country struggle with the same issues in a variety of programs, and research can enable the individual practitioner to benefit from the experience of others on a much larger scale than is possible from working in one community. Like the proverbial blind men trying to identify an elephant, with each man groping at a foot or an ear or a trunk, practitioners working intensively in local communities are often prevented from seeing the overall picture. Research can enable them to examine issues from a variety of angles and can add new perspectives to existing approaches to promoting father involvement.

The divide between researchers, practitioners, and policymakers has been widest in defining and determining fathers' contributions. Policymakers, for example, have been concerned with the financial provision part of child support while researchers and practitioners have been equally concerned, if not more concerned, with fathers' emotional and physical presence as a form of child support. Whether and how men contribute to their children's lives is influenced by cultural, class, and social factors that have fallen typically outside traditional policy analyses.

The divide between these groups is narrowing, as each seeks ways to ensure that fathers make contributions in both financial and emotional domains. There are multiple areas in which researcher and practitioner interests intersect. One such area of collaboration is in program evaluations and assessments of program participant progress. Collaborations among researchers, practitioners, and policymakers can assist in the development of appropriate measures and indicators to help programs monitor change in fathers and outcomes for children and families.[6] The record detailing the measurement of programs or activities is limited, and research on the effectiveness of these programs has been anecdotal at best. The studies that do exist focus either on what fathers from two-parent families contribute to children's well-being or what the links are between father absence and a variety of negative outcomes for children and society. At the same time, the determination of indicators of effectiveness is driving government services and is quickly becoming a prerequisite for funding from private sources such as foundations. Emerging government policies and legislation such as the Fathers Count Act have identified specific outcomes for interventions. Researchers, practitioners, and policy analysts share a common goal, namely the strengthening of father involvement in children's lives; and they possess expertise that can benefit one another's work. However, they may not share a common language or way of conceptualizing responsible fathering, which may act as barriers to shared work (Kane, Gadsden, and Armorer, 1997).

A second area for collaboration concerns gaining access to understudied populations of fathers (such as low-income Puerto Rican fathers). Practitioners who work in communities and with families may have access to particular populations of fathers that would be of interest to researchers. Practitioners may be more aware of the complexity of fathers' lives, particularly poor fathers and fathers of color. Also, they may serve as sources of information regarding fathers' developmental issues—especially for young inner-city men—and how these issues may influence their fathering. Their perception of fathers may incorporate a greater understanding and sensitivity to the barriers (e.g., racism in employment) experienced by poor fathers who do care about their children but are invested in material provision as an important component of their own identity as fathers. Researchers need to understand and appreciate the rich and textured perspective that many practitioners can offer to them regarding father caregiving and father-child-family relationships.

At this early stage, it is possible to link the independent and overlapping areas of father involvement, family support, and child well-being by seeking approaches, measures, and data that assist different types of organizations. What works for practitioners *can* work for researchers and policymakers as well. However, the ability to recognize the cross-cutting interests—and possibilities—will depend on the willingness of all constituencies to pursue an understanding of the needs of a range of families. At the same time, they all must increase their commitment to improving the lives of children and families who are experiencing hardship. They must respond to the problems faced by programs and practitioners who serve fathers and families and must address the cultural, ethnic, and racial histories of families. Systemic and structural barriers that reduce, rather than enhance, positive child and family outcomes must be eliminated.

NOTES

1. Portions of this chapter have been drawn from National Center on Fathers and Families activities funded by the Annie E. Casey Foundation, including the *Fathers and Families Core Learnings: An Update from the Field* (1997), with contributions by Danielle Kane and Keisha Armorer, and Eric Brenner.

2. Recent data on Parents Fair Share Programs can be found in reports from the Manpower Demonstration and Research Corporation, New York, NY (see Bloom and Sherwood, 1994; Doolittle and Lynn, 1998; and Doolittle et al., 1998).

3. The Family Reunion Conferences are policy-focused conferences held annually in Nashville and hosted by Vice President Al Gore and Tipper Gore.

4. The Philadelphia Children's Network is a child and family advocacy think tank focused on creating positive options for children and families and effective policy development. It is the predecessor to NCOFF.

5. The names of programs were identified from NCOFF advertisements in a range of publications and contributions from the The Fatherhood Program of the Families and Work Institute, the National Fatherhood Initiative, the Coalition for Community Foundations, and the National Practitioners Network for Fathers and Families.

6. See Gadsden et al. (2000).

BIBLIOGRAPHY

Achatz, M. and MacAllum, C. A. (1994). *Young unwed fathers: Report from the field.* Philadelphia, PA: Public/Private Ventures.

Bloom, D. and Sherwood, K. (1994). *Matching opportunities to obligations: Lessons for child support reform from the Parents' Fair Share Pilot Phase.* New York: Manpower Demonstration Research Corporation.

Bowman, P. J. (1988). Postindustrial displacement and family-role strains: Challenges to the black family. In P. Voydanhoff and L. Majka (Eds.), *Families and economic distress: Coping strategies and social policy. New perspectives on family* (pp. 75-96). Newbury Park, CA: Sage.

Bowman, P. J. (1989). Research perspectives on black men: Role strain and adaptation across the adult life cycle. In R.L. Jones (Ed.), *Black adult development and aging* (pp. 117-150). Berkeley, CA: Cobb and Henry.

Bowman, P. J. (1990). Coping with provider-role strain: Adaptive cultural resources among black husband-fathers. *Journal of Black Psychology, 16*(2), 1-21.

Dawson, D. A. (1991). Family structure and children's health and well-being: Data from the 1988 National Health Interview Survey on Child Health. *Journal of Marriage and the Family, 53,* 573-584.

Doolittle, F. and Lynn, S. (1998, May). *Working with low-income cases: Lessons for the Child Support Enforcement System from Parents' Fair Share.* New York: Manpower Demonstration Research Corporation.

Doolittle, F., Knox, V., Miller, C., and Rowser, S. (1998, September). *Building opportunities, enforcing obligations: Implementation and interim impact of Parents' Fair Share.* New York: Manpower Demonstration Research Corporation.

Furstenberg, F. F. Jr. and Cherlin, A. J. (1991). *Divided families: What happens to children when parents part.* Cambridge, MA: Harvard University Press.

Gadsden, V. L. (1998). Family cultures and literacy learning. In J. Osborn and F. Lehr (Eds.), *Literacy for all: Issues in teaching and learning* (pp. 32-50). New York: The Guilford Press.

Gadsden, V. L., Fagan, J., Ray, A., and Davis J. E. (Eds.) (2000). *The fathering indicators framework.* Philadelphia, PA: National Center on Fathers and Families, University of Pennsylvania.

Gadsden, V. L. and Hall, M. (1996, January). *Intergenerational learning: A review of the literature* [LR-CP-96-07]. Philadelphia, PA: National Center on Fathers and Families, University of Pennsylvania.

Garfinkel, I. and McLanahan, S. (1986). *Single mothers and their children: A new American dilemma.* Washington, DC: Urban Institute Press.

Hosley, C. A. and R. Montemayor (1997). Fathers and adolescents. In M. Lamb (Ed.), *The role of the father in child development* (pp. 162-178). New York: Wiley.

Hossain, Z. and Roopnarine, J. L. (1993). Division of household labor and childcare in dual-earner African-American families with infants. *Sex Roles, 29,* 571-583.

Hossain, Z. and Roopnarine, J. L. (1994). African-American fathers' involvement with infants: Relationship to their functioning style, support, education, and income. *Infant Behavior & Development, 17*(2), 175-184.

Kane, D., Gadsden, V. L., and Armorer, K. (1997). *The fathers and families core learnings: An update from the field.* Philadelphia, PA: National Center on Fathers and Families, University of Pennsylvania.

Levine, J. A., Murphy, D., and Wilson, S. (1993). *Getting men involved: Strategies for early-childhood programs.* New York: Scholastic.

Levine, J. A. and Pitt, E. (1995). *New expectations: Community strategies for responsible fatherhood.* New York: Families and Work Institute.

Maccoby, E. E., Buchanan, C. M., Mnookin, R. H., and Dornbusch, S.M. (1993). Postdivorce roles of mothers and fathers in the lives of their children. *Journal of Family Psychology, 7,* 24-38.

Maccoby, E. E., Depner, C. E., and Mnookin, R. H. (1990). Coparenting in the second year after divorce. *Journal of Marriage and the Family, 52,* 141-155.

McAdoo, H. P. (1981). *Black families.* Newbury Park, CA: Sage.

McAdoo, J. L. (1986). A black perspective on the father's role in child development. *Marriage and Family Review, 9*(3-4), 117-133.

National Center on Fathers and Families (1998). *Fathers and families practitioner researcher summit.* Philadelphia, PA: National Center on Fathers and Families, University of Pennsylvania.

National Commission on Children (1993). *Just the facts: A summary of recent information on America's children and their families.* Washington, DC: National Commission on Children.

Nord, C. W. (1998, June). *Nonresident fathers can make a difference in children's school performance.* Washington, DC: National Center for Education Statistics, U.S. Department of Education, Office of Educational Research and Improvement.

Parke, R. D. (1996). Fatherhood: Myths and realities. In R. D. Parke (Ed.), *Fatherhood* (pp. 1-16). Cambridge, MA: Harvard University Press.

Pruett, K. D. (1989). The nurturing male: A longitudinal study of primary nurturing fathers. In S. H. Cath, A. Gurwitt, and L. Gunsberg (Eds.), *Fathers and their families* (pp. 389-405). Hillsdale, NJ: Analytic Press.

Pruett, K. D. (1995). The paternal presence. In J. L. Shapiro, M. J. Diamond, and M. Greenberg (Eds.), *Becoming a father: Contemporary, social, developmental, and clinical perspectives* (pp. 36-42). New York: Springer.

Smith, R. (1998). Interview for State of the Field Report. Summer 1998. Annie E. Casey Foundation, Baltimore, MD.

Zill, N. (1976). Family change and student achievement: What have we learned, what it means for schools. In A. Booth and J. F. Dunn (Eds.), *Family-school links: How do they affect educational outcomes?* (pp. 139-174). Mahwah, NJ: Lawrence Erlbaum Associates.

Chapter 12

Clinical and Educational Interventions with Fathers: A Synthesis

Alan J. Hawkins
Jay Fagan

The wide range of clinical and educational interventions for fathers presented in this volume calls for a synthesis to conclude the book. Although much of the value of this book for clinicians and educators undoubtedly will be found in individual chapters focused on specific interventions for particular populations of fathers, valuable ideas may be gleaned by thinking about the chapters as a whole that will increase our abilities to move scholarship and practice forward in the field of fathering interventions.

In this concluding chapter, we attempt a brief synthesis that focuses on four specific issues. First, we note the considerable need for better evaluations of interventions for fathers. Second, we comment positively on the value of a generative fathering conceptual framework for approaching intervention work with fathers, but note the need to attend to institutional barriers faced by fathers. Third, we highlight the value and necessity of creative, nontraditional intervention approaches to supporting fathers, and call for greater sensitivity to the ways men experience the world, as well as the important systemic nature of fathering specifically involving the critical mother-father relationship. Finally, we note what is missing in this volume and where greater attention is needed from researchers and practitioners.

THE NEED FOR EVALUATION

The first point of synthesis that comes from a review of the intervention programs described in this volume is the need for more and better evaluation. The lack of rigorous evaluation research in parenting education programs has been an ongoing problem (Darling, 1987; Small, 1990). Although there is a stronger tradition of clinical program evaluation, outcome studies, to date, of clinical programs for fathers are rare. The chapters in this volume contain much wisdom—or best practices—from practitioners who are involved in cutting-edge intervention work with fathers in various challenging circumstances. What is generally missing, however, is rigorous, ongoing assessment of attitudinal and behavioral change on the part of fathers. Granted, the field of fathering intervention is young, and programs for fathers are usually initiated at the grass-roots level in response to a serious need with resources inadequate to a comprehensive evaluation study. Still, the need for better evaluation studies to test the benefits of specific interventions for fathers is clear; empirical data is needed to buttress best-practices wisdom.

This need to know if behavioral change follows from educational and clinical intervention and if certain inputs actually produce certain outputs is scientific and technological. Just as important, a need exists for good evaluation studies due to a broader context of some scholarly doubt that parenting, in general, and fathering, in particular, matter much to children's development (Harris, 1998; Silverstein and Auerbach, 1999). In addition, evaluation studies are needed to determine if programs for fathers are cost effective; several researchers have suggested that although such programs may be effective, the small number of fathers who become involved has policy implications regarding the best use of resources (Fagan and Iglesias, 1999).

Better evaluation studies will include assessing attitudinal and behavioral outcomes for fathers in a wide range of circumstances and family structures, as well as ethnic and cultural groups. In addition, long-term follow-up evaluations will be needed to determine if program outcomes survive. Furthermore, outcome assessments must include children's well-being and development to determine if the hypothesized benefits of greater father involvement for children are achieved. Also needed are studies that compare the effect of different interventions and various practices on a set of desired outcomes, as well as comparative studies of the cost-effectiveness of such interventions. If fatherhood legislation recently introduced into the U.S. Congress eventually becomes law, funds for supporting fathering programs will increase, but they will go to programs that show evidence of their effectiveness. And some of this increase in funds should be reinvested in rigorous, ongoing, evaluation research.

THE VALUE OF A GENERATIVE
FATHERING FRAMEWORK

Our second point of synthesis is an encouraging note on the organizing conceptual framework of this volume. Intervention work and intervention studies are usually pragmatic and avoid explicit connections to conceptual frameworks. Yet this volume has demonstrated the value of organizing fathering interventions under a generative fathering framework (Dollahite and Hawkins, 1998; Dollahite, Hawkins, and Brotherson, 1997). As noted in the introduction, this framework: (1) recognizes that fathers have a social-psychological need to respond to the needs of the next generation; (2) de-emphasizes thinking about fathers as deficient, and emphasizes fathers' strengths and potentials for growth (Hawkins and Dollahite, 1997); (3) respects the diversity of parenting styles among fathers from various ethnic, racial, and class backgrounds; and (4) avoids setting a minimum standard that excludes fathers who may be struggling but striving to become responsible fathers. The authors in this volume note that fathers—even those disconnected from their children by very challenging circumstances— have a strong, internal desire to be involved with their children (Chapters 3, 5, and 9). Moreover, the authors of these chapters consistently note the strengths that men bring to this endeavor, even those with little direct experience (e.g., Chapter 5). Also, the potential for positive change and growth is evident throughout the book in the various interventions, as is a sensitivity to working with fathers within their unique cultures and circumstances (Chapters 2, 4, and 10).

Although we are encouraged that the generative fathering framework provides a solid conceptual foundation for approaching interventions with fathers, we note the need to attend to the substantial institutional barriers fathers face that can inhibit their developmental efforts to be generative fathers. Most authors in this volume outline the need to intervene with institutions as well as with individuals if they are to achieve their aims of helping fathers (Chapters 5, 7, and 11). We believe that working with fathers, even at the micro-intervention level, should be viewed as social change practice as well as clinical or educational practice.

There are a number of different ways in which interventions for fathers can be viewed as social change practice. Several contributors to this book have noted that even well-intentioned organizations often are not prepared for the ramifications of working with fathers. For example, some female staff members may be ambivalent about working with fathers and consequently they may interfere with such initiatives (Chapter 7). Many agencies use assessment tools that are not sensitive to the variety of family structures in which fathers are involved. Agencies may need to develop and implement new procedures for inquiring about fathers and other family members. These are just a few examples of the many ways in which practitioners may need to affect change within their organizations in an attempt to serve fathers and ultimately to conduct family-centered practice.

Working with fathers also can be understood as social change practice from the standpoint that such interventions may have an impact on more than just the man and his family. Fathers who have had positive experiences participating in educational or clinical interventions may become ambassadors of responsible fatherhood to other men and boys. This may occur as these fathers model responsible behavior and attitudes or directly prepare other men to participate in a fathering intervention (Chapter 1). As more men participate in interventions for fathers, the culture of fatherhood that traditionally has eschewed involvement in social services is also likely to change. Each man who participates in an intervention paves the way for another man, who otherwise would avoid fathering programs, to take advantage of those services. Men will not only find it easier to participate in such programs, but they will also have to respond to higher levels of expectation for their involvement.

THE NEED FOR CREATIVE, NONTRADITIONAL INTERVENTION APPROACHES

A third point of synthesis is the observation that practitioners seeking to intervene to help fathers will need to look beyond traditional social services, clinical practices, and educational approaches. Merely extending to fathers the traditional services and programs that have helped mothers (e.g., parenting education) likely will not work well. At the foundation of this observation is the evidence presented throughout this volume that men's help-seeking behavior is different in important ways from that of women (Chapters 1, 2, and 6). Fathers appear to be more difficult to reach, more cautious about the values and goals of intervention programs, more private in their personal change efforts, and have fewer supports systems for positive change. For instance, fathers may be more open and responsive to large religious gatherings that urge commitment to responsible fathering than to small-group therapies that explore the emotional innerworlds of fathering (Chapter 8). Similarly, many fathers may respond better to Web-based information and programs than to traditional, classroom-based family life education (Chapter 6). These are hypotheses that require empirical confirmation, but the initial evidence presented in this volume suggests that practitioners may need to break some molds of traditional approaches if they are to succeed in their efforts to help fathers.

Closely connected to this point is the need for practitioners to understand men's lives, male development, and masculinity. Effective intervention for fathers begins with good understanding of and respect for fathers' unique experiences as men, and the ways they perceive their special work to care for the next generation (Chapter 1).

Furthermore, one critical difference to working effectively with fathers that becomes clear in this volume is the need to be sensitive to the role mothers play in men's fathering endeavors (Chapters 2 and 7). As other scholars have consistently suggested (Belsky et al., 1991; Cummings and O'Reilly, 1997; Doherty, Kouneski, and Erickson, 1998; Lamb, 1997; Parke, 1996; Pleck, 1997), fathering is a systemic phenomenon: mothers mediate men's involvement in their children's lives in important ways, whether or not they are married. The challenge for practitioners working with fathers, then, is not only to understand men better, but also to understand the important ways in which mothers are involved in promoting and inhibiting fathers' involvement with their children in many different contexts.

THE NEED TO FIND WHAT IS MISSING

A final point of synthesis derives not from what is presented in the book but from what is missing. Undoubtedly, there are other interventions for fathers that received little or no attention in this volume. We focus, however, on what we believe to be the most crucial and easily overlooked areas for intervention. Doherty, Kouneski, and Erickson, drawing on the work of Levine and Pitt (1995), outlined four elements of responsible fathering. A man behaves responsibly when:

1. He waits to make a baby until he is prepared emotionally and financially to support his child.
2. He establishes his legal paternity if and when he does make a baby.
3. He actively shares with the child's mother in the continuing emotional and physical care of their child, from pregnancy onwards.
4. He shares with the child's mother in the continuing financial support of their child, from pregnancy onwards (1998, p. 279).

Although the interventions described in this volume certainly address ways of promoting the third and fourth points, they do not well address the first two points. Any overall strategy to increase responsible fathering in our society must include a substantial effort to reduce the proportion of births to fathers who are not ready to accept the responsibilities accompanying that transition. Programs attempting to prevent premature fathering are not chronicled in this volume. It is our impression that pregnancy-prevention programs are directed mostly at teenage girls; young men are conspicuously absent as a primary target audience for pregnancy prevention (Gallagher, 1999). Young men have much to gain by postponing fatherhood, as well. Also missing in this volume is a chapter dealing with the success of some states to establish legal paternity of all children and whether it helps encourage more responsible fathering behavior in the long run. Nor are programs to help young men establish stronger desires to be good fathers described in this volume. We urge both practitioners and scholars to give more attention to these fundamental aspects of responsible fathering.

Furthermore, little attention is paid to marriage promotion and enhancement as a basis for good fathering in this volume. Citing the empirical work that consistently links marital status and marital quality to responsible fathering, numerous scholars and policymakers have called for greater attention to establishing and maintaining good marriages as a critical way to strengthen fathering in the United States (Blankenhorn, 1995; Doherty, Kouneski, and Erickson, 1998; Horn and Bush, 1997; Horn, 1998/1999; Moorehouse Research Institute, 1999; Nock, 1998; Ooms, 1998; Popenoe, 1996). Although this issue is controversial and important debates on how to do this will continue, little doubt exists that helping mothers and fathers establish good marriages and providing them with the relationship tools to keep marriages strong will increase the quantity and quality of fathering in the United States. Even in communities in which the economic and social realities of life make formal marriage difficult, promoting marriage or marriageability can help promote stronger connections between fathers and children (Moorehouse Research Institute, 1999). This book has not illuminated this issue. But we urge fathering practitioners and researchers not to ignore this fundamental and potentially significant way to help fathers in their generative desires to be involved with their children.

CONCLUSION

Scott Coltrane, a prominent researcher on fathering, argues that various trends are coming together to help more fathers become responsible family men (Coltrane, 1996). If his optimism is to be validated, we believe practitioners, researchers, and policymakers will need to play a role. Our hope is that this collection of chapters on intervention programs for fathers and the commentary that surrounds it will promote more and better work by clinicians, family-life educators, researchers, and policymakers who desire to promote generative fathering in our society.

REFERENCES

Belsky, J., Youngblade, L., Rovine, M., and Volling, B. (1991). Patterns of marital change and parent-child interaction. *Journal of Marriage and the Family, 53*, 487-498.

Blankenhorn, D. (1995). *Fatherless America: Confronting our most urgent social problem.* New York: Basic Books.

Coltrane, S. (1996). *Family man: Fatherhood, housework, and gender equity.* New York: Oxford University Press.

Cummings, E. M. and O'Reilly, A. W. (1997). Fathers in family context: Effects of marital quality on child adjustment. In M. E. Lamb (Ed.), *The role of the father in child development* (Volume 3, pp. 49-65). New York: John Wiley & Sons.

Darling, C. A. (1987). Family life education. In M. B. Sussman and S. K. Steinmetz (Eds.), *Handbook of marriage and the family* (pp. 815-833). New York: Plenum.

Doherty, W. J., Kouneski, E. F., and Erickson, M. F. (1998). Responsible fathering: An overview and conceptual framework. *Journal of Marriage and the Family, 60,* 277-292.

Dollahite, D. C. and Hawkins, A. J. (1998). A conceptual ethic of generative fathering. *Journal of Men's Studies, 7*(1), 109-132.

Dollahite, D. C., Hawkins, A. J., and Brotherson, S. E. (1997). Fatherwork: A conceptual ethic of fathering as generative work. In A. J. Hawkins and D. C. Dollahite (Eds.), *Generative fathering: Beyond deficit perspectives* (pp. 17-35). Thousand Oaks, CA: Sage.

Fagan, J. and Iglesias, A. (1999). Father involvement program effects on fathers, father figures, and their Head Start children. *Early Childhood Research Quarterly, 14*(2), 243-269.

Gallagher, M. (1999). *The age of unwed mothers: Is teen pregnancy the problem?* New York: Institute for American Values.

Harris, J. R. (1998). *The nurture assumption: Why children turn out the way they do.* New York: Free Press.

Hawkins, A. J. and Dollahite, D. C. (Eds.) (1997). *Generative fathering: Beyond deficit perspectives.* Thousand Oaks, CA: Sage.

Horn, W. F. (1998/1999). Fatherhood programs: Improving their effectiveness. *Fatherhood Today, 3*(3), 3.

Horn, W. F. and Bush, A. (1997). *Fathers, marriage, and welfare reform.* Indianapolis, IN: Hudson Institute.

Lamb, M. E. (1997). Fathers and child development: An introductory overview. In M. E. Lamb (Ed.), *The role of the father in child development* (Third edition, pp. 1-18). New York: John Wiley & Sons.

Levine, J. A. and Pitt, E. W. (1995). *New expectations: Community strategies for responsible fatherhood.* New York: Families and Work Institute.

Moorehouse Research Institute and the Institute for American Values (1999). *Turning the corner on father absence in black America.* Atlanta and New York: Moorehouse Research Institute and the Institute for American Values.

Nock, S. L. (1998). *Marriage in men's lives.* New York: Oxford University.

Ooms, T. (1998). *Toward more perfect unions.* Washington, DC: Family Impact Seminar.

Parke, R. D. (1996). *Fatherhood.* Cambridge, MA: Harvard University.

Pleck, J. H. (1997). Paternal involvement: Levels, sources, and consequences. In M. E. Lamb (Ed.), *The role of the father in child development* (Third edition, pp. 66-103). New York: John Wiley & Sons.

Popenoe, D. (1996). *Life without father.* New York: Free Press.

Silverstein, L. B. and Auerbach, C. F. (1999). Deconstructing the essential father. *American Psychologist, 54,* 397-407.

Small, S. A. (1990). Some issues regarding the evaluation of family life education programs. *Family Relations, 39,* 132-135.

Index